QUICK REFERENCE TABLES

BEVERLY S. VANCE
Southwest Tennessee Community College

BUSINESS MATH

ELEVENTH EDITION

Cheryl Cleaves
Southwest Tennessee Community College, Emerita

Margie Hobbs
Southwest Tennessee Community College, Emerita

Jeffrey Noble
Madison College

Pearson

The author and publisher of this book have used their best efforts in preparing this book. These efforts include the development, research, and testing of the theories and programs to determine their effectiveness. The author and publisher make no warranty of any kind, expressed or implied, with regard to these programs or the documentation contained in this book. The author and publisher shall not be liable in any event for incidental or consequential damages in connection with, or arising out of, the furnishing, performance, or use of these programs.

Reproduced by Pearson from electronic files supplied by the author.

Publishing as Pearson, 330 Hudson Street, NY NY 10013

9 18

Pearson

ISBN-13: 978-0-13-457024-2
ISBN-10: 0-13-457024-3

CONTENTS

Wage Bracket Method Tables for Income Tax Withholding

MARRIED Persons—**WEEKLY** Payroll Period

(For Wages Paid through December 31, 2015)

And the wages are–		And the number of withholding allowances claimed is—										
At least	But less than	0	1	2	3	4	5	6	7	8	9	10
		The amount of income tax to be withheld is—										
$ 0	$170	$0	$0	$0	$0	$0	$0	$0	$0	$0	$0	$0
170	175	1	0	0	0	0	0	0	0	0	0	0
175	180	1	0	0	0	0	0	0	0	0	0	0
180	185	2	0	0	0	0	0	0	0	0	0	0
185	190	2	0	0	0	0	0	0	0	0	0	0
190	195	3	0	0	0	0	0	0	0	0	0	0
195	200	3	0	0	0	0	0	0	0	0	0	0
200	210	4	0	0	0	0	0	0	0	0	0	0
210	220	5	0	0	0	0	0	0	0	0	0	0
220	230	6	0	0	0	0	0	0	0	0	0	0
230	240	7	0	0	0	0	0	0	0	0	0	0
240	250	8	0	0	0	0	0	0	0	0	0	0
250	260	9	1	0	0	0	0	0	0	0	0	0
260	270	10	2	0	0	0	0	0	0	0	0	0
270	280	11	3	0	0	0	0	0	0	0	0	0
280	290	12	4	0	0	0	0	0	0	0	0	0
290	300	13	5	0	0	0	0	0	0	0	0	0
300	310	14	6	0	0	0	0	0	0	0	0	0
310	320	15	7	0	0	0	0	0	0	0	0	0
320	330	16	8	1	0	0	0	0	0	0	0	0
330	340	17	9	2	0	0	0	0	0	0	0	0
340	350	18	10	3	0	0	0	0	0	0	0	0
350	360	19	11	4	0	0	0	0	0	0	0	0
360	370	20	12	5	0	0	0	0	0	0	0	0
370	380	21	13	6	0	0	0	0	0	0	0	0
380	390	22	14	7	0	0	0	0	0	0	0	0
390	400	23	15	8	0	0	0	0	0	0	0	0
400	410	24	16	9	1	0	0	0	0	0	0	0
410	420	25	17	10	2	0	0	0	0	0	0	0
420	430	26	18	11	3	0	0	0	0	0	0	0
430	440	27	19	12	4	0	0	0	0	0	0	0
440	450	28	20	13	5	0	0	0	0	0	0	0
450	460	29	21	14	6	0	0	0	0	0	0	0
460	470	30	22	15	7	0	0	0	0	0	0	0
470	480	31	23	16	8	0	0	0	0	0	0	0
480	490	32	24	17	9	1	0	0	0	0	0	0
490	500	33	25	18	10	2	0	0	0	0	0	0
500	510	34	26	19	11	3	0	0	0	0	0	0
510	520	35	27	20	12	4	0	0	0	0	0	0
520	530	36	28	21	13	5	0	0	0	0	0	0
530	540	38	29	22	14	6	0	0	0	0	0	0
540	550	39	30	23	15	7	0	0	0	0	0	0
550	560	41	31	24	16	8	1	0	0	0	0	0
560	570	42	32	25	17	9	2	0	0	0	0	0
570	580	44	33	26	18	10	3	0	0	0	0	0
580	590	45	34	27	19	11	4	0	0	0	0	0
590	600	47	35	28	20	12	5	0	0	0	0	0
600	610	48	37	29	21	13	6	0	0	0	0	0
610	620	50	38	30	22	14	7	0	0	0	0	0
620	630	51	40	31	23	15	8	0	0	0	0	0
630	640	53	41	32	24	16	9	1	0	0	0	0
640	650	54	43	33	25	17	10	2	0	0	0	0
650	660	56	44	34	26	18	11	3	0	0	0	0
660	670	57	46	35	27	19	12	4	0	0	0	0
670	680	59	47	36	28	20	13	5	0	0	0	0
680	690	60	49	37	29	21	14	6	0	0	0	0
690	700	62	50	39	30	22	15	7	0	0	0	0
700	710	63	52	40	31	23	16	8	0	0	0	0
710	720	65	53	42	32	24	17	9	1	0	0	0
720	730	66	55	43	33	25	18	10	2	0	0	0
730	740	68	56	45	34	26	19	11	3	0	0	0
740	750	69	58	46	35	27	20	12	4	0	0	0
750	760	71	59	48	36	28	21	13	5	0	0	0
760	770	72	61	49	38	29	22	14	6	0	0	0
770	780	74	62	51	39	30	23	15	7	0	0	0
780	790	75	64	52	41	31	24	16	8	0	0	0
790	800	77	65	54	42	32	25	17	9	1	0	0

Publication 15 (2015)

Wage Bracket Method Tables for Income Tax Withholding

MARRIED Persons—**WEEKLY** Payroll Period

(For Wages Paid through December 31, 2015)

And the wages are–		And the number of withholding allowances claimed is—										
At least	But less than	0	1	2	3	4	5	6	7	8	9	10
		The amount of income tax to be withheld is—										
$800	**$810**	$78	$67	$55	$44	$33	$26	$18	$10	$2	$0	$0
810	**820**	80	68	57	45	34	27	19	11	3	0	0
820	**830**	81	70	58	47	35	28	20	12	4	0	0
830	**840**	83	71	60	48	37	29	21	13	5	0	0
840	**850**	84	73	61	50	38	30	22	14	6	0	0
850	**860**	86	74	63	51	40	31	23	15	7	0	0
860	**870**	87	76	64	53	41	32	24	16	8	1	0
870	**880**	89	77	66	54	43	33	25	17	9	2	0
880	**890**	90	79	67	56	44	34	26	18	10	3	0
890	**900**	92	80	69	57	46	35	27	19	11	4	0
900	**910**	93	82	70	59	47	36	28	20	12	5	0
910	**920**	95	83	72	60	49	37	29	21	13	6	0
920	**930**	96	85	73	62	50	39	30	22	14	7	0
930	**940**	98	86	75	63	52	40	31	23	15	8	0
940	**950**	99	88	76	65	53	42	32	24	16	9	1
950	**960**	101	89	78	66	55	43	33	25	17	10	2
960	**970**	102	91	79	68	56	45	34	26	18	11	3
970	**980**	104	92	81	69	58	46	35	27	19	12	4
980	**990**	105	94	82	71	59	48	36	28	20	13	5
990	**1,000**	107	95	84	72	61	49	37	29	21	14	6
1,000	**1,010**	108	97	85	74	62	51	39	30	22	15	7
1,010	**1,020**	110	98	87	75	64	52	40	31	23	16	8
1,020	**1,030**	111	100	88	77	65	54	42	32	24	17	9
1,030	**1,040**	113	101	90	78	67	55	43	33	25	18	10
1,040	**1,050**	114	103	91	80	68	57	45	34	26	19	11
1,050	**1,060**	116	104	93	81	70	58	46	35	27	20	12
1,060	**1,070**	117	106	94	83	71	60	48	36	28	21	13
1,070	**1,080**	119	107	96	84	73	61	49	38	29	22	14
1,080	**1,090**	120	109	97	86	74	63	51	39	30	23	15
1,090	**1,100**	122	110	99	87	76	64	52	41	31	24	16
1,100	**1,110**	123	112	100	89	77	66	54	42	32	25	17
1,110	**1,120**	125	113	102	90	79	67	55	44	33	26	18
1,120	**1,130**	126	115	103	92	80	69	57	45	34	27	19
1,130	**1,140**	128	116	105	93	82	70	58	47	35	28	20
1,140	**1,150**	129	118	106	95	83	72	60	48	37	29	21
1,150	**1,160**	131	119	108	96	85	73	61	50	38	30	22
1,160	**1,170**	132	121	109	98	86	75	63	51	40	31	23
1,170	**1,180**	134	122	111	99	88	76	64	53	41	32	24
1,180	**1,190**	135	124	112	101	89	78	66	54	43	33	25
1,190	**1,200**	137	125	114	102	91	79	67	56	44	34	26
1,200	**1,210**	138	127	115	104	92	81	69	57	46	35	27
1,210	**1,220**	140	128	117	105	94	82	70	59	47	36	28
1,220	**1,230**	141	130	118	107	95	84	72	60	49	37	29
1,230	**1,240**	143	131	120	108	97	85	73	62	50	39	30
1,240	**1,250**	144	133	121	110	98	87	75	63	52	40	31
1,250	**1,260**	146	134	123	111	100	88	76	65	53	42	32
1,260	**1,270**	147	136	124	113	101	90	78	66	55	43	33
1,270	**1,280**	149	137	126	114	103	91	79	68	56	45	34
1,280	**1,290**	150	139	127	116	104	93	81	69	58	46	35
1,290	**1,300**	152	140	129	117	106	94	82	71	59	48	36
1,300	**1,310**	153	142	130	119	107	96	84	72	61	49	38
1,310	**1,320**	155	143	132	120	109	97	85	74	62	51	39
1,320	**1,330**	156	145	133	122	110	99	87	75	64	52	41
1,330	**1,340**	158	146	135	123	112	100	88	77	65	54	42
1,340	**1,350**	159	148	136	125	113	102	90	78	67	55	44
1,350	**1,360**	161	149	138	126	115	103	91	80	68	57	45
1,360	**1,370**	162	151	139	128	116	105	93	81	70	58	47
1,370	**1,380**	164	152	141	129	118	106	94	83	71	60	48
1,380	**1,390**	165	154	142	131	119	108	96	84	73	61	50
1,390	**1,400**	167	155	144	132	121	109	97	86	74	63	51
1,400	**1,410**	168	157	145	134	122	111	99	87	76	64	53
1,410	**1,420**	170	158	147	135	124	112	100	89	77	66	54
1,420	**1,430**	171	160	148	137	125	114	102	90	79	67	56
1,430	**1,440**	173	161	150	138	127	115	103	92	80	69	57
1,440	**1,450**	174	163	151	140	128	117	105	93	82	70	59
1,450	**1,460**	176	164	153	141	130	118	106	95	83	72	60
1,460	**1,470**	177	166	154	143	131	120	108	96	85	73	62
1,470	**1,480**	179	167	156	144	133	121	109	98	86	75	63
1,480	**1,490**	180	169	157	146	134	123	111	99	88	76	65

$1,490 and over — Use Table 1(b) for a **MARRIED person** on page 45. Also see the instructions on page 43.

Publication 15 (2015)

Wage Bracket Method Tables for Income Tax Withholding

SINGLE Persons—**BIWEEKLY** Payroll Period

(For Wages Paid through December 31, 2015)

And the wages are–		And the number of withholding allowances claimed is—										
At least	But less than	0	1	2	3	4	5	6	7	8	9	10
		The amount of income tax to be withheld is—										
$ 0	$105	$0	$0	$0	$0	$0	$0	$0	$0	$0	$0	$0
105	110	2	0	0	0	0	0	0	0	0	0	0
110	115	2	0	0	0	0	0	0	0	0	0	0
115	120	3	0	0	0	0	0	0	0	0	0	0
120	125	3	0	0	0	0	0	0	0	0	0	0
125	130	4	0	0	0	0	0	0	0	0	0	0
130	135	4	0	0	0	0	0	0	0	0	0	0
135	140	5	0	0	0	0	0	0	0	0	0	0
140	145	5	0	0	0	0	0	0	0	0	0	0
145	150	6	0	0	0	0	0	0	0	0	0	0
150	155	6	0	0	0	0	0	0	0	0	0	0
155	160	7	0	0	0	0	0	0	0	0	0	0
160	165	7	0	0	0	0	0	0	0	0	0	0
165	170	8	0	0	0	0	0	0	0	0	0	0
170	175	8	0	0	0	0	0	0	0	0	0	0
175	180	9	0	0	0	0	0	0	0	0	0	0
180	185	9	0	0	0	0	0	0	0	0	0	0
185	190	10	0	0	0	0	0	0	0	0	0	0
190	195	10	0	0	0	0	0	0	0	0	0	0
195	200	11	0	0	0	0	0	0	0	0	0	0
200	205	11	0	0	0	0	0	0	0	0	0	0
205	210	12	0	0	0	0	0	0	0	0	0	0
210	215	12	0	0	0	0	0	0	0	0	0	0
215	220	13	0	0	0	0	0	0	0	0	0	0
220	225	13	0	0	0	0	0	0	0	0	0	0
225	230	14	0	0	0	0	0	0	0	0	0	0
230	235	14	0	0	0	0	0	0	0	0	0	0
235	240	15	0	0	0	0	0	0	0	0	0	0
240	245	15	0	0	0	0	0	0	0	0	0	0
245	250	16	1	0	0	0	0	0	0	0	0	0
250	260	17	1	0	0	0	0	0	0	0	0	0
260	270	18	2	0	0	0	0	0	0	0	0	0
270	280	19	3	0	0	0	0	0	0	0	0	0
280	290	20	4	0	0	0	0	0	0	0	0	0
290	300	21	5	0	0	0	0	0	0	0	0	0
300	310	22	6	0	0	0	0	0	0	0	0	0
310	320	23	7	0	0	0	0	0	0	0	0	0
320	330	24	8	0	0	0	0	0	0	0	0	0
330	340	25	9	0	0	0	0	0	0	0	0	0
340	350	26	10	0	0	0	0	0	0	0	0	0
350	360	27	11	0	0	0	0	0	0	0	0	0
360	370	28	12	0	0	0	0	0	0	0	0	0
370	380	29	13	0	0	0	0	0	0	0	0	0
380	390	30	14	0	0	0	0	0	0	0	0	0
390	400	31	15	0	0	0	0	0	0	0	0	0
400	410	32	16	1	0	0	0	0	0	0	0	0
410	420	33	17	2	0	0	0	0	0	0	0	0
420	430	34	18	3	0	0	0	0	0	0	0	0
430	440	35	19	4	0	0	0	0	0	0	0	0
440	450	36	20	5	0	0	0	0	0	0	0	0
450	460	37	21	6	0	0	0	0	0	0	0	0
460	470	39	22	7	0	0	0	0	0	0	0	0
470	480	40	23	8	0	0	0	0	0	0	0	0
480	490	42	24	9	0	0	0	0	0	0	0	0
490	500	43	25	10	0	0	0	0	0	0	0	0
500	520	45	27	11	0	0	0	0	0	0	0	0
520	540	48	29	13	0	0	0	0	0	0	0	0
540	560	51	31	15	0	0	0	0	0	0	0	0
560	580	54	33	17	2	0	0	0	0	0	0	0
580	600	57	35	19	4	0	0	0	0	0	0	0
600	620	60	37	21	6	0	0	0	0	0	0	0
620	640	63	40	23	8	0	0	0	0	0	0	0
640	660	66	43	25	10	0	0	0	0	0	0	0
660	680	69	46	27	12	0	0	0	0	0	0	0
680	700	72	49	29	14	0	0	0	0	0	0	0
700	720	75	52	31	16	1	0	0	0	0	0	0
720	740	78	55	33	18	3	0	0	0	0	0	0
740	760	81	58	35	20	5	0	0	0	0	0	0
760	780	84	61	38	22	7	0	0	0	0	0	0
780	800	87	64	41	24	9	0	0	0	0	0	0

Publication 15 (2015)

Wage Bracket Method Tables for Income Tax Withholding

SINGLE Persons—**BIWEEKLY** Payroll Period

(For Wages Paid through December 31, 2015)

And the wages are–		And the number of withholding allowances claimed is—										
At least	But less than	0	1	2	3	4	5	6	7	8	9	10
		The amount of income tax to be withheld is—										
$800	**$820**	$90	$67	$44	$26	$11	$0	$0	$0	$0	$0	$0
820	**840**	93	70	47	28	13	0	0	0	0	0	0
840	**860**	96	73	50	30	15	0	0	0	0	0	0
860	**880**	99	76	53	32	17	1	0	0	0	0	0
880	**900**	102	79	56	34	19	3	0	0	0	0	0
900	**920**	105	82	59	36	21	5	0	0	0	0	0
920	**940**	108	85	62	39	23	7	0	0	0	0	0
940	**960**	111	88	65	42	25	9	0	0	0	0	0
960	**980**	114	91	68	45	27	11	0	0	0	0	0
980	**1,000**	117	94	71	48	29	13	0	0	0	0	0
1,000	**1,020**	120	97	74	51	31	15	0	0	0	0	0
1,020	**1,040**	123	100	77	54	33	17	2	0	0	0	0
1,040	**1,060**	126	103	80	57	35	19	4	0	0	0	0
1,060	**1,080**	129	106	83	60	37	21	6	0	0	0	0
1,080	**1,100**	132	109	86	63	40	23	8	0	0	0	0
1,100	**1,120**	135	112	89	66	43	25	10	0	0	0	0
1,120	**1,140**	138	115	92	69	46	27	12	0	0	0	0
1,140	**1,160**	141	118	95	72	49	29	14	0	0	0	0
1,160	**1,180**	144	121	98	75	52	31	16	0	0	0	0
1,180	**1,200**	147	124	101	78	55	33	18	2	0	0	0
1,200	**1,220**	150	127	104	81	58	35	20	4	0	0	0
1,220	**1,240**	153	130	107	84	61	38	22	6	0	0	0
1,240	**1,260**	156	133	110	87	64	41	24	8	0	0	0
1,260	**1,280**	159	136	113	90	67	44	26	10	0	0	0
1,280	**1,300**	162	139	116	93	70	47	28	12	0	0	0
1,300	**1,320**	165	142	119	96	73	50	30	14	0	0	0
1,320	**1,340**	168	145	122	99	76	53	32	16	1	0	0
1,340	**1,360**	171	148	125	102	79	56	34	18	3	0	0
1,360	**1,380**	174	151	128	105	82	59	36	20	5	0	0
1,380	**1,400**	177	154	131	108	85	62	39	22	7	0	0
1,400	**1,420**	180	157	134	111	88	65	42	24	9	0	0
1,420	**1,440**	183	160	137	114	91	68	45	26	11	0	0
1,440	**1,460**	186	163	140	117	94	71	48	28	13	0	0
1,460	**1,480**	189	166	143	120	97	74	51	30	15	0	0
1,480	**1,500**	192	169	146	123	100	77	54	32	17	2	0
1,500	**1,520**	195	172	149	126	103	80	57	34	19	4	0
1,520	**1,540**	199	175	152	129	106	83	60	37	21	6	0
1,540	**1,560**	204	178	155	132	109	86	63	40	23	8	0
1,560	**1,580**	209	181	158	135	112	89	66	43	25	10	0
1,580	**1,600**	214	184	161	138	115	92	69	46	27	12	0
1,600	**1,620**	219	187	164	141	118	95	72	49	29	14	0
1,620	**1,640**	224	190	167	144	121	98	75	52	31	16	0
1,640	**1,660**	229	193	170	147	124	101	78	55	33	18	2
1,660	**1,680**	234	196	173	150	127	104	81	58	35	20	4
1,680	**1,700**	239	200	176	153	130	107	84	61	38	22	6
1,700	**1,720**	244	205	179	156	133	110	87	64	41	24	8
1,720	**1,740**	249	210	182	159	136	113	90	67	44	26	10
1,740	**1,760**	254	215	185	162	139	116	93	70	47	28	12
1,760	**1,780**	259	220	188	165	142	119	96	73	50	30	14
1,780	**1,800**	264	225	191	168	145	122	99	76	53	32	16
1,800	**1,820**	269	230	194	171	148	125	102	79	56	34	18
1,820	**1,840**	274	235	197	174	151	128	105	82	59	36	20
1,840	**1,860**	279	240	202	177	154	131	108	85	62	39	22
1,860	**1,880**	284	245	207	180	157	134	111	88	65	42	24
1,880	**1,900**	289	250	212	183	160	137	114	91	68	45	26
1,900	**1,920**	294	255	217	186	163	140	117	94	71	48	28
1,920	**1,940**	299	260	222	189	166	143	120	97	74	51	30
1,940	**1,960**	304	265	227	192	169	146	123	100	77	54	32
1,960	**1,980**	309	270	232	195	172	149	126	103	80	57	34
1,980	**2,000**	314	275	237	198	175	152	129	106	83	60	37
2,000	**2,020**	319	280	242	203	178	155	132	109	86	63	40
2,020	**2,040**	324	285	247	208	181	158	135	112	89	66	43
2,040	**2,060**	329	290	252	213	184	161	138	115	92	69	46
2,060	**2,080**	334	295	257	218	187	164	141	118	95	72	49
2,080	**2,100**	339	300	262	223	190	167	144	121	98	75	52

$2,100 and over Use Table 2(a) for a **SINGLE person** on page 45. Also see the instructions on page 43.

Wage Bracket Method Tables for Income Tax Withholding

MARRIED Persons—**BIWEEKLY** Payroll Period

(For Wages Paid through December 31, 2015)

And the wages are–		And the number of withholding allowances claimed is—										
At least	But less than	0	1	2	3	4	5	6	7	8	9	10
		The amount of income tax to be withheld is—										
$ 0	**$340**	$0	$0	$0	$0	$0	$0	$0	$0	$0	$0	$0
340	**350**	1	0	0	0	0	0	0	0	0	0	0
350	**360**	2	0	0	0	0	0	0	0	0	0	0
360	**370**	3	0	0	0	0	0	0	0	0	0	0
370	**380**	4	0	0	0	0	0	0	0	0	0	0
380	**390**	5	0	0	0	0	0	0	0	0	0	0
390	**400**	6	0	0	0	0	0	0	0	0	0	0
400	**410**	7	0	0	0	0	0	0	0	0	0	0
410	**420**	8	0	0	0	0	0	0	0	0	0	0
420	**430**	9	0	0	0	0	0	0	0	0	0	0
430	**440**	10	0	0	0	0	0	0	0	0	0	0
440	**450**	11	0	0	0	0	0	0	0	0	0	0
450	**460**	12	0	0	0	0	0	0	0	0	0	0
460	**470**	13	0	0	0	0	0	0	0	0	0	0
470	**480**	14	0	0	0	0	0	0	0	0	0	0
480	**490**	15	0	0	0	0	0	0	0	0	0	0
490	**500**	16	1	0	0	0	0	0	0	0	0	0
500	**520**	18	3	0	0	0	0	0	0	0	0	0
520	**540**	20	5	0	0	0	0	0	0	0	0	0
540	**560**	22	7	0	0	0	0	0	0	0	0	0
560	**580**	24	9	0	0	0	0	0	0	0	0	0
580	**600**	26	11	0	0	0	0	0	0	0	0	0
600	**620**	28	13	0	0	0	0	0	0	0	0	0
620	**640**	30	15	0	0	0	0	0	0	0	0	0
640	**660**	32	17	1	0	0	0	0	0	0	0	0
660	**680**	34	19	3	0	0	0	0	0	0	0	0
680	**700**	36	21	5	0	0	0	0	0	0	0	0
700	**720**	38	23	7	0	0	0	0	0	0	0	0
720	**740**	40	25	9	0	0	0	0	0	0	0	0
740	**760**	42	27	11	0	0	0	0	0	0	0	0
760	**780**	44	29	13	0	0	0	0	0	0	0	0
780	**800**	46	31	15	0	0	0	0	0	0	0	0
800	**820**	48	33	17	2	0	0	0	0	0	0	0
820	**840**	50	35	19	4	0	0	0	0	0	0	0
840	**860**	52	37	21	6	0	0	0	0	0	0	0
860	**880**	54	39	23	8	0	0	0	0	0	0	0
880	**900**	56	41	25	10	0	0	0	0	0	0	0
900	**920**	58	43	27	12	0	0	0	0	0	0	0
920	**940**	60	45	29	14	0	0	0	0	0	0	0
940	**960**	62	47	31	16	0	0	0	0	0	0	0
960	**980**	64	49	33	18	2	0	0	0	0	0	0
980	**1,000**	66	51	35	20	4	0	0	0	0	0	0
1,000	**1,020**	68	53	37	22	6	0	0	0	0	0	0
1,020	**1,040**	70	55	39	24	8	0	0	0	0	0	0
1,040	**1,060**	72	57	41	26	10	0	0	0	0	0	0
1,060	**1,080**	75	59	43	28	12	0	0	0	0	0	0
1,080	**1,100**	78	61	45	30	14	0	0	0	0	0	0
1,100	**1,120**	81	63	47	32	16	1	0	0	0	0	0
1,120	**1,140**	84	65	49	34	18	3	0	0	0	0	0
1,140	**1,160**	87	67	51	36	20	5	0	0	0	0	0
1,160	**1,180**	90	69	53	38	22	7	0	0	0	0	0
1,180	**1,200**	93	71	55	40	24	9	0	0	0	0	0
1,200	**1,220**	96	73	57	42	26	11	0	0	0	0	0
1,220	**1,240**	99	76	59	44	28	13	0	0	0	0	0
1,240	**1,260**	102	79	61	46	30	15	0	0	0	0	0
1,260	**1,280**	105	82	63	48	32	17	2	0	0	0	0
1,280	**1,300**	108	85	65	50	34	19	4	0	0	0	0
1,300	**1,320**	111	88	67	52	36	21	6	0	0	0	0
1,320	**1,340**	114	91	69	54	38	23	8	0	0	0	0
1,340	**1,360**	117	94	71	56	40	25	10	0	0	0	0
1,360	**1,380**	120	97	74	58	42	27	12	0	0	0	0
1,380	**1,400**	123	100	77	60	44	29	14	0	0	0	0
1,400	**1,420**	126	103	80	62	46	31	16	0	0	0	0
1,420	**1,440**	129	106	83	64	48	33	18	2	0	0	0
1,440	**1,460**	132	109	86	66	50	35	20	4	0	0	0
1,460	**1,480**	135	112	89	68	52	37	22	6	0	0	0
1,480	**1,500**	138	115	92	70	54	39	24	8	0	0	0

Publication 15 (2015)

Wage Bracket Method Tables for Income Tax Withholding

MARRIED Persons—**BIWEEKLY** Payroll Period

(For Wages Paid through December 31, 2015)

And the wages are–		And the number of withholding allowances claimed is—										
At least	But less than	0	1	2	3	4	5	6	7	8	9	10
		The amount of income tax to be withheld is—										
$1,500	$1,520	$141	$118	$95	$72	$56	$41	$26	$10	$0	$0	$0
1,520	1,540	144	121	98	75	58	43	28	12	0	0	0
1,540	1,560	147	124	101	78	60	45	30	14	0	0	0
1,560	1,580	150	127	104	81	62	47	32	16	1	0	0
1,580	1,600	153	130	107	84	64	49	34	18	3	0	0
1,600	1,620	156	133	110	87	66	51	36	20	5	0	0
1,620	1,640	159	136	113	90	68	53	38	22	7	0	0
1,640	1,660	162	139	116	93	70	55	40	24	9	0	0
1,660	1,680	165	142	119	96	73	57	42	26	11	0	0
1,680	1,700	168	145	122	99	76	59	44	28	13	0	0
1,700	1,720	171	148	125	102	79	61	46	30	15	0	0
1,720	1,740	174	151	128	105	82	63	48	32	17	1	0
1,740	1,760	177	154	131	108	85	65	50	34	19	3	0
1,760	1,780	180	157	134	111	88	67	52	36	21	5	0
1,780	1,800	183	160	137	114	91	69	54	38	23	7	0
1,800	1,820	186	163	140	117	94	71	56	40	25	9	0
1,820	1,840	189	166	143	120	97	74	58	42	27	11	0
1,840	1,860	192	169	146	123	100	77	60	44	29	13	0
1,860	1,880	195	172	149	126	103	80	62	46	31	15	0
1,880	1,900	198	175	152	129	106	83	64	48	33	17	2
1,900	1,920	201	178	155	132	109	86	66	50	35	19	4
1,920	1,940	204	181	158	135	112	89	68	52	37	21	6
1,940	1,960	207	184	161	138	115	92	70	54	39	23	8
1,960	1,980	210	187	164	141	118	95	72	56	41	25	10
1,980	2,000	213	190	167	144	121	98	75	58	43	27	12
2,000	2,020	216	193	170	147	124	101	78	60	45	29	14
2,020	2,040	219	196	173	150	127	104	81	62	47	31	16
2,040	2,060	222	199	176	153	130	107	84	64	49	33	18
2,060	2,080	225	202	179	156	133	110	87	66	51	35	20
2,080	2,100	228	205	182	159	136	113	90	68	53	37	22
2,100	2,120	231	208	185	162	139	116	93	70	55	39	24
2,120	2,140	234	211	188	165	142	119	96	73	57	41	26
2,140	2,160	237	214	191	168	145	122	99	76	59	43	28
2,160	2,180	240	217	194	171	148	125	102	79	61	45	30
2,180	2,200	243	220	197	174	151	128	105	82	63	47	32
2,200	2,220	246	223	200	177	154	131	108	85	65	49	34
2,220	2,240	249	226	203	180	157	134	111	88	67	51	36
2,240	2,260	252	229	206	183	160	137	114	91	69	53	38
2,260	2,280	255	232	209	186	163	140	117	94	71	55	40
2,280	2,300	258	235	212	189	166	143	120	97	74	57	42
2,300	2,320	261	238	215	192	169	146	123	100	77	59	44
2,320	2,340	264	241	218	195	172	149	126	103	80	61	46
2,340	2,360	267	244	221	198	175	152	129	106	83	63	48
2,360	2,380	270	247	224	201	178	155	132	109	86	65	50
2,380	2,400	273	250	227	204	181	158	135	112	89	67	52
2,400	2,420	276	253	230	207	184	161	138	115	92	69	54
2,420	2,440	279	256	233	210	187	164	141	118	95	72	56
2,440	2,460	282	259	236	213	190	167	144	121	98	75	58
2,460	2,480	285	262	239	216	193	170	147	124	101	78	60
2,480	2,500	288	265	242	219	196	173	150	127	104	81	62
2,500	2,520	291	268	245	222	199	176	153	130	107	84	64
2,520	2,540	294	271	248	225	202	179	156	133	110	87	66
2,540	2,560	297	274	251	228	205	182	159	136	113	90	68
2,560	2,580	300	277	254	231	208	185	162	139	116	93	70
2,580	2,600	303	280	257	234	211	188	165	142	119	96	73
2,600	2,620	306	283	260	237	214	191	168	145	122	99	76
2,620	2,640	309	286	263	240	217	194	171	148	125	102	79
2,640	2,660	312	289	266	243	220	197	174	151	128	105	82
2,660	2,680	315	292	269	246	223	200	177	154	131	108	85
2,680	2,700	318	295	272	249	226	203	180	157	134	111	88
2,700	2,720	321	298	275	252	229	206	183	160	137	114	91
2,720	2,740	324	301	278	255	232	209	186	163	140	117	94
2,740	2,760	327	304	281	258	235	212	189	166	143	120	97
2,760	2,780	330	307	284	261	238	215	192	169	146	123	100
2,780	2,800	333	310	287	264	241	218	195	172	149	126	103
2,800	2,820	336	313	290	267	244	221	198	175	152	129	106
2,820	2,840	339	316	293	270	247	224	201	178	155	132	109
2,840	2,860	342	319	296	273	250	227	204	181	158	135	112
2,860	2,880	345	322	299	276	253	230	207	184	161	138	115
$2,880 and over		Use Table 2(b) for a **MARRIED person** on page 45. Also see the instructions on page 43.										

Wage Bracket Method Tables for Income Tax Withholding

SINGLE Persons—**SEMIMONTHLY** Payroll Period

(For Wages Paid through December 31, 2015)

And the wages are–		And the number of withholding allowances claimed is—										
At least	But less than	0	1	2	3	4	5	6	7	8	9	10
		The amount of income tax to be withheld is—										
$ 0	$115	$0	$0	$0	$0	$0	$0	$0	$0	$0	$0	$0
115	120	2	0	0	0	0	0	0	0	0	0	0
120	125	3	0	0	0	0	0	0	0	0	0	0
125	130	3	0	0	0	0	0	0	0	0	0	0
130	135	4	0	0	0	0	0	0	0	0	0	0
135	140	4	0	0	0	0	0	0	0	0	0	0
140	145	5	0	0	0	0	0	0	0	0	0	0
145	150	5	0	0	0	0	0	0	0	0	0	0
150	155	6	0	0	0	0	0	0	0	0	0	0
155	160	6	0	0	0	0	0	0	0	0	0	0
160	165	7	0	0	0	0	0	0	0	0	0	0
165	170	7	0	0	0	0	0	0	0	0	0	0
170	175	8	0	0	0	0	0	0	0	0	0	0
175	180	8	0	0	0	0	0	0	0	0	0	0
180	185	9	0	0	0	0	0	0	0	0	0	0
185	190	9	0	0	0	0	0	0	0	0	0	0
190	195	10	0	0	0	0	0	0	0	0	0	0
195	200	10	0	0	0	0	0	0	0	0	0	0
200	205	11	0	0	0	0	0	0	0	0	0	0
205	210	11	0	0	0	0	0	0	0	0	0	0
210	215	12	0	0	0	0	0	0	0	0	0	0
215	220	12	0	0	0	0	0	0	0	0	0	0
220	225	13	0	0	0	0	0	0	0	0	0	0
225	230	13	0	0	0	0	0	0	0	0	0	0
230	235	14	0	0	0	0	0	0	0	0	0	0
235	240	14	0	0	0	0	0	0	0	0	0	0
240	245	15	0	0	0	0	0	0	0	0	0	0
245	250	15	0	0	0	0	0	0	0	0	0	0
250	260	16	0	0	0	0	0	0	0	0	0	0
260	270	17	0	0	0	0	0	0	0	0	0	0
270	280	18	1	0	0	0	0	0	0	0	0	0
280	290	19	2	0	0	0	0	0	0	0	0	0
290	300	20	3	0	0	0	0	0	0	0	0	0
300	310	21	4	0	0	0	0	0	0	0	0	0
310	320	22	5	0	0	0	0	0	0	0	0	0
320	330	23	6	0	0	0	0	0	0	0	0	0
330	340	24	7	0	0	0	0	0	0	0	0	0
340	350	25	8	0	0	0	0	0	0	0	0	0
350	360	26	9	0	0	0	0	0	0	0	0	0
360	370	27	10	0	0	0	0	0	0	0	0	0
370	380	28	11	0	0	0	0	0	0	0	0	0
380	390	29	12	0	0	0	0	0	0	0	0	0
390	400	30	13	0	0	0	0	0	0	0	0	0
400	410	31	14	0	0	0	0	0	0	0	0	0
410	420	32	15	0	0	0	0	0	0	0	0	0
420	430	33	16	0	0	0	0	0	0	0	0	0
430	440	34	17	1	0	0	0	0	0	0	0	0
440	450	35	18	2	0	0	0	0	0	0	0	0
450	460	36	19	3	0	0	0	0	0	0	0	0
460	470	37	20	4	0	0	0	0	0	0	0	0
470	480	38	21	5	0	0	0	0	0	0	0	0
480	490	39	22	6	0	0	0	0	0	0	0	0
490	500	41	23	7	0	0	0	0	0	0	0	0
500	520	43	25	8	0	0	0	0	0	0	0	0
520	540	46	27	10	0	0	0	0	0	0	0	0
540	560	49	29	12	0	0	0	0	0	0	0	0
560	580	52	31	14	0	0	0	0	0	0	0	0
580	600	55	33	16	0	0	0	0	0	0	0	0
600	620	58	35	18	1	0	0	0	0	0	0	0
620	640	61	37	20	3	0	0	0	0	0	0	0
640	660	64	39	22	5	0	0	0	0	0	0	0
660	680	67	42	24	7	0	0	0	0	0	0	0
680	700	70	45	26	9	0	0	0	0	0	0	0
700	720	73	48	28	11	0	0	0	0	0	0	0
720	740	76	51	30	13	0	0	0	0	0	0	0
740	760	79	54	32	15	0	0	0	0	0	0	0
760	780	82	57	34	17	1	0	0	0	0	0	0
780	800	85	60	36	19	3	0	0	0	0	0	0

Publication 15 (2015)

Wage Bracket Method Tables for Income Tax Withholding

SINGLE Persons—**SEMIMONTHLY** Payroll Period

(For Wages Paid through December 31, 2015)

And the wages are–		And the number of withholding allowances claimed is—										
At least	But less than	0	1	2	3	4	5	6	7	8	9	10
		The amount of income tax to be withheld is—										
$800	$820	$88	$63	$38	$21	$5	$0	$0	$0	$0	$0	$0
820	840	91	66	41	23	7	0	0	0	0	0	0
840	860	94	69	44	25	9	0	0	0	0	0	0
860	880	97	72	47	27	11	0	0	0	0	0	0
880	900	100	75	50	29	13	0	0	0	0	0	0
900	920	103	78	53	31	15	0	0	0	0	0	0
920	940	106	81	56	33	17	0	0	0	0	0	0
940	960	109	84	59	35	19	2	0	0	0	0	0
960	980	112	87	62	37	21	4	0	0	0	0	0
980	1,000	115	90	65	40	23	6	0	0	0	0	0
1,000	1,020	118	93	68	43	25	8	0	0	0	0	0
1,020	1,040	121	96	71	46	27	10	0	0	0	0	0
1,040	1,060	124	99	74	49	29	12	0	0	0	0	0
1,060	1,080	127	102	77	52	31	14	0	0	0	0	0
1,080	1,100	130	105	80	55	33	16	0	0	0	0	0
1,100	1,120	133	108	83	58	35	18	1	0	0	0	0
1,120	1,140	136	111	86	61	37	20	3	0	0	0	0
1,140	1,160	139	114	89	64	39	22	5	0	0	0	0
1,160	1,180	142	117	92	67	42	24	7	0	0	0	0
1,180	1,200	145	120	95	70	45	26	9	0	0	0	0
1,200	1,220	148	123	98	73	48	28	11	0	0	0	0
1,220	1,240	151	126	101	76	51	30	13	0	0	0	0
1,240	1,260	154	129	104	79	54	32	15	0	0	0	0
1,260	1,280	157	132	107	82	57	34	17	1	0	0	0
1,280	1,300	160	135	110	85	60	36	19	3	0	0	0
1,300	1,320	163	138	113	88	63	38	21	5	0	0	0
1,320	1,340	166	141	116	91	66	41	23	7	0	0	0
1,340	1,360	169	144	119	94	69	44	25	9	0	0	0
1,360	1,380	172	147	122	97	72	47	27	11	0	0	0
1,380	1,400	175	150	125	100	75	50	29	13	0	0	0
1,400	1,420	178	153	128	103	78	53	31	15	0	0	0
1,420	1,440	181	156	131	106	81	56	33	17	0	0	0
1,440	1,460	184	159	134	109	84	59	35	19	2	0	0
1,460	1,480	187	162	137	112	87	62	37	21	4	0	0
1,480	1,500	190	165	140	115	90	65	40	23	6	0	0
1,500	1,520	193	168	143	118	93	68	43	25	8	0	0
1,520	1,540	196	171	146	121	96	71	46	27	10	0	0
1,540	1,560	199	174	149	124	99	74	49	29	12	0	0
1,560	1,580	202	177	152	127	102	77	52	31	14	0	0
1,580	1,600	205	180	155	130	105	80	55	33	16	0	0
1,600	1,620	208	183	158	133	108	83	58	35	18	1	0
1,620	1,640	211	186	161	136	111	86	61	37	20	3	0
1,640	1,660	214	189	164	139	114	89	64	39	22	5	0
1,660	1,680	218	192	167	142	117	92	67	42	24	7	0
1,680	1,700	223	195	170	145	120	95	70	45	26	9	0
1,700	1,720	228	198	173	148	123	98	73	48	28	11	0
1,720	1,740	233	201	176	151	126	101	76	51	30	13	0
1,740	1,760	238	204	179	154	129	104	79	54	32	15	0
1,760	1,780	243	207	182	157	132	107	82	57	34	17	1
1,780	1,800	248	210	185	160	135	110	85	60	36	19	3
1,800	1,820	253	213	188	163	138	113	88	63	38	21	5
1,820	1,840	258	217	191	166	141	116	91	66	41	23	7
1,840	1,860	263	222	194	169	144	119	94	69	44	25	9
1,860	1,880	268	227	197	172	147	122	97	72	47	27	11
1,880	1,900	273	232	200	175	150	125	100	75	50	29	13
1,900	1,920	278	237	203	178	153	128	103	78	53	31	15
1,920	1,940	283	242	206	181	156	131	106	81	56	33	17
1,940	1,960	288	247	209	184	159	134	109	84	59	35	19
1,960	1,980	293	252	212	187	162	137	112	87	62	37	21
1,980	2,000	298	257	215	190	165	140	115	90	65	40	23
2,000	2,020	303	262	220	193	168	143	118	93	68	43	25
2,020	2,040	308	267	225	196	171	146	121	96	71	46	27
2,040	2,060	313	272	230	199	174	149	124	99	74	49	29
2,060	2,080	318	277	235	202	177	152	127	102	77	52	31
2,080	2,100	323	282	240	205	180	155	130	105	80	55	33
2,100	2,120	328	287	245	208	183	158	133	108	83	58	35
2,120	2,140	333	292	250	211	186	161	136	111	86	61	37

$2,140 and over Use Table 3(a) for a **SINGLE person** on page 45. Also see the instructions on page 43.

Wage Bracket Method Tables for Income Tax Withholding

MARRIED Persons—**SEMIMONTHLY** Payroll Period

(For Wages Paid through December 31, 2015)

And the wages are–		And the number of withholding allowances claimed is—										
At least	But less than	0	1	2	3	4	5	6	7	8	9	10
		The amount of income tax to be withheld is—										
$ 0	**$360**	$0	$0	$0	$0	$0	$0	$0	$0	$0	$0	$0
360	**370**	1	0	0	0	0	0	0	0	0	0	0
370	**380**	2	0	0	0	0	0	0	0	0	0	0
380	**390**	3	0	0	0	0	0	0	0	0	0	0
390	**400**	4	0	0	0	0	0	0	0	0	0	0
400	**410**	5	0	0	0	0	0	0	0	0	0	0
410	**420**	6	0	0	0	0	0	0	0	0	0	0
420	**430**	7	0	0	0	0	0	0	0	0	0	0
430	**440**	8	0	0	0	0	0	0	0	0	0	0
440	**450**	9	0	0	0	0	0	0	0	0	0	0
450	**460**	10	0	0	0	0	0	0	0	0	0	0
460	**470**	11	0	0	0	0	0	0	0	0	0	0
470	**480**	12	0	0	0	0	0	0	0	0	0	0
480	**490**	13	0	0	0	0	0	0	0	0	0	0
490	**500**	14	0	0	0	0	0	0	0	0	0	0
500	**520**	15	0	0	0	0	0	0	0	0	0	0
520	**540**	17	1	0	0	0	0	0	0	0	0	0
540	**560**	19	3	0	0	0	0	0	0	0	0	0
560	**580**	21	5	0	0	0	0	0	0	0	0	0
580	**600**	23	7	0	0	0	0	0	0	0	0	0
600	**620**	25	9	0	0	0	0	0	0	0	0	0
620	**640**	27	11	0	0	0	0	0	0	0	0	0
640	**660**	29	13	0	0	0	0	0	0	0	0	0
660	**680**	31	15	0	0	0	0	0	0	0	0	0
680	**700**	33	17	0	0	0	0	0	0	0	0	0
700	**720**	35	19	2	0	0	0	0	0	0	0	0
720	**740**	37	21	4	0	0	0	0	0	0	0	0
740	**760**	39	23	6	0	0	0	0	0	0	0	0
760	**780**	41	25	8	0	0	0	0	0	0	0	0
780	**800**	43	27	10	0	0	0	0	0	0	0	0
800	**820**	45	29	12	0	0	0	0	0	0	0	0
820	**840**	47	31	14	0	0	0	0	0	0	0	0
840	**860**	49	33	16	0	0	0	0	0	0	0	0
860	**880**	51	35	18	1	0	0	0	0	0	0	0
880	**900**	53	37	20	3	0	0	0	0	0	0	0
900	**920**	55	39	22	5	0	0	0	0	0	0	0
920	**940**	57	41	24	7	0	0	0	0	0	0	0
940	**960**	59	43	26	9	0	0	0	0	0	0	0
960	**980**	61	45	28	11	0	0	0	0	0	0	0
980	**1,000**	63	47	30	13	0	0	0	0	0	0	0
1,000	**1,020**	65	49	32	15	0	0	0	0	0	0	0
1,020	**1,040**	67	51	34	17	1	0	0	0	0	0	0
1,040	**1,060**	69	53	36	19	3	0	0	0	0	0	0
1,060	**1,080**	71	55	38	21	5	0	0	0	0	0	0
1,080	**1,100**	73	57	40	23	7	0	0	0	0	0	0
1,100	**1,120**	75	59	42	25	9	0	0	0	0	0	0
1,120	**1,140**	77	61	44	27	11	0	0	0	0	0	0
1,140	**1,160**	80	63	46	29	13	0	0	0	0	0	0
1,160	**1,180**	83	65	48	31	15	0	0	0	0	0	0
1,180	**1,200**	86	67	50	33	17	0	0	0	0	0	0
1,200	**1,220**	89	69	52	35	19	2	0	0	0	0	0
1,220	**1,240**	92	71	54	37	21	4	0	0	0	0	0
1,240	**1,260**	95	73	56	39	23	6	0	0	0	0	0
1,260	**1,280**	98	75	58	41	25	8	0	0	0	0	0
1,280	**1,300**	101	77	60	43	27	10	0	0	0	0	0
1,300	**1,320**	104	79	62	45	29	12	0	0	0	0	0
1,320	**1,340**	107	82	64	47	31	14	0	0	0	0	0
1,340	**1,360**	110	85	66	49	33	16	0	0	0	0	0
1,360	**1,380**	113	88	68	51	35	18	1	0	0	0	0
1,380	**1,400**	116	91	70	53	37	20	3	0	0	0	0
1,400	**1,420**	119	94	72	55	39	22	5	0	0	0	0
1,420	**1,440**	122	97	74	57	41	24	7	0	0	0	0
1,440	**1,460**	125	100	76	59	43	26	9	0	0	0	0
1,460	**1,480**	128	103	78	61	45	28	11	0	0	0	0
1,480	**1,500**	131	106	81	63	47	30	13	0	0	0	0
1,500	**1,520**	134	109	84	65	49	32	15	0	0	0	0
1,520	**1,540**	137	112	87	67	51	34	17	1	0	0	0
1,540	**1,560**	140	115	90	69	53	36	19	3	0	0	0
1,560	**1,580**	143	118	93	71	55	38	21	5	0	0	0
1,580	**1,600**	146	121	96	73	57	40	23	7	0	0	0

Publication 15 (2015)

Wage Bracket Method Tables for Income Tax Withholding

MARRIED Persons—**SEMIMONTHLY** Payroll Period

(For Wages Paid through December 31, 2015)

And the wages are–		And the number of withholding allowances claimed is—										
At least	But less than	0	1	2	3	4	5	6	7	8	9	10
		The amount of income tax to be withheld is—										
$1,600	$1,620	$149	$124	$99	$75	$59	$42	$25	$9	$0	$0	$0
1,620	1,640	152	127	102	77	61	44	27	11	0	0	0
1,640	1,660	155	130	105	80	63	46	29	13	0	0	0
1,660	1,680	158	133	108	83	65	48	31	15	0	0	0
1,680	1,700	161	136	111	86	67	50	33	17	0	0	0
1,700	1,720	164	139	114	89	69	52	35	19	2	0	0
1,720	1,740	167	142	117	92	71	54	37	21	4	0	0
1,740	1,760	170	145	120	95	73	56	39	23	6	0	0
1,760	1,780	173	148	123	98	75	58	41	25	8	0	0
1,780	1,800	176	151	126	101	77	60	43	27	10	0	0
1,800	1,820	179	154	129	104	79	62	45	29	12	0	0
1,820	1,840	182	157	132	107	82	64	47	31	14	0	0
1,840	1,860	185	160	135	110	85	66	49	33	16	0	0
1,860	1,880	188	163	138	113	88	68	51	35	18	1	0
1,880	1,900	191	166	141	116	91	70	53	37	20	3	0
1,900	1,920	194	169	144	119	94	72	55	39	22	5	0
1,920	1,940	197	172	147	122	97	74	57	41	24	7	0
1,940	1,960	200	175	150	125	100	76	59	43	26	9	0
1,960	1,980	203	178	153	128	103	78	61	45	28	11	0
1,980	2,000	206	181	156	131	106	81	63	47	30	13	0
2,000	2,020	209	184	159	134	109	84	65	49	32	15	0
2,020	2,040	212	187	162	137	112	87	67	51	34	17	1
2,040	2,060	215	190	165	140	115	90	69	53	36	19	3
2,060	2,080	218	193	168	143	118	93	71	55	38	21	5
2,080	2,100	221	196	171	146	121	96	73	57	40	23	7
2,100	2,120	224	199	174	149	124	99	75	59	42	25	9
2,120	2,140	227	202	177	152	127	102	77	61	44	27	11
2,140	2,160	230	205	180	155	130	105	80	63	46	29	13
2,160	2,180	233	208	183	158	133	108	83	65	48	31	15
2,180	2,200	236	211	186	161	136	111	86	67	50	33	17
2,200	2,220	239	214	189	164	139	114	89	69	52	35	19
2,220	2,240	242	217	192	167	142	117	92	71	54	37	21
2,240	2,260	245	220	195	170	145	120	95	73	56	39	23
2,260	2,280	248	223	198	173	148	123	98	75	58	41	25
2,280	2,300	251	226	201	176	151	126	101	77	60	43	27
2,300	2,320	254	229	204	179	154	129	104	79	62	45	29
2,320	2,340	257	232	207	182	157	132	107	82	64	47	31
2,340	2,360	260	235	210	185	160	135	110	85	66	49	33
2,360	2,380	263	238	213	188	163	138	113	88	68	51	35
2,380	2,400	266	241	216	191	166	141	116	91	70	53	37
2,400	2,420	269	244	219	194	169	144	119	94	72	55	39
2,420	2,440	272	247	222	197	172	147	122	97	74	57	41
2,440	2,460	275	250	225	200	175	150	125	100	76	59	43
2,460	2,480	278	253	228	203	178	153	128	103	78	61	45
2,480	2,500	281	256	231	206	181	156	131	106	81	63	47
2,500	2,520	284	259	234	209	184	159	134	109	84	65	49
2,520	2,540	287	262	237	212	187	162	137	112	87	67	51
2,540	2,560	290	265	240	215	190	165	140	115	90	69	53
2,560	2,580	293	268	243	218	193	168	143	118	93	71	55
2,580	2,600	296	271	246	221	196	171	146	121	96	73	57
2,600	2,620	299	274	249	224	199	174	149	124	99	75	59
2,620	2,640	302	277	252	227	202	177	152	127	102	77	61
2,640	2,660	305	280	255	230	205	180	155	130	105	80	63
2,660	2,680	308	283	258	233	208	183	158	133	108	83	65
2,680	2,700	311	286	261	236	211	186	161	136	111	86	67
2,700	2,720	314	289	264	239	214	189	164	139	114	89	69
2,720	2,740	317	292	267	242	217	192	167	142	117	92	71
2,740	2,760	320	295	270	245	220	195	170	145	120	95	73
2,760	2,780	323	298	273	248	223	198	173	148	123	98	75
2,780	2,800	326	301	276	251	226	201	176	151	126	101	77
2,800	2,820	329	304	279	254	229	204	179	154	129	104	79
2,820	2,840	332	307	282	257	232	207	182	157	132	107	82
2,840	2,860	335	310	285	260	235	210	185	160	135	110	85
2,860	2,880	338	313	288	263	238	213	188	163	138	113	88
2,880	2,900	341	316	291	266	241	216	191	166	141	116	91
2,900	2,920	344	319	294	269	244	219	194	169	144	119	94

$2,920 and over Use Table 3(b) for a **MARRIED person** on page 45. Also see the instructions on page 43.

Wage Bracket Method Tables for Income Tax Withholding

SINGLE Persons—**MONTHLY** Payroll Period

(For Wages Paid through December 31, 2015)

And the wages are–		And the number of withholding allowances claimed is—										
At least	But less than	0	1	2	3	4	5	6	7	8	9	10
		The amount of income tax to be withheld is—										
$ 0	**$220**	$0	$0	$0	$0	$0	$0	$0	$0	$0	$0	$0
220	**230**	3	0	0	0	0	0	0	0	0	0	0
230	**240**	4	0	0	0	0	0	0	0	0	0	0
240	**250**	5	0	0	0	0	0	0	0	0	0	0
250	**260**	6	0	0	0	0	0	0	0	0	0	0
260	**270**	7	0	0	0	0	0	0	0	0	0	0
270	**280**	8	0	0	0	0	0	0	0	0	0	0
280	**290**	9	0	0	0	0	0	0	0	0	0	0
290	**300**	10	0	0	0	0	0	0	0	0	0	0
300	**320**	12	0	0	0	0	0	0	0	0	0	0
320	**340**	14	0	0	0	0	0	0	0	0	0	0
340	**360**	16	0	0	0	0	0	0	0	0	0	0
360	**380**	18	0	0	0	0	0	0	0	0	0	0
380	**400**	20	0	0	0	0	0	0	0	0	0	0
400	**420**	22	0	0	0	0	0	0	0	0	0	0
420	**440**	24	0	0	0	0	0	0	0	0	0	0
440	**460**	26	0	0	0	0	0	0	0	0	0	0
460	**480**	28	0	0	0	0	0	0	0	0	0	0
480	**500**	30	0	0	0	0	0	0	0	0	0	0
500	**520**	32	0	0	0	0	0	0	0	0	0	0
520	**540**	34	1	0	0	0	0	0	0	0	0	0
540	**560**	36	3	0	0	0	0	0	0	0	0	0
560	**580**	38	5	0	0	0	0	0	0	0	0	0
580	**600**	40	7	0	0	0	0	0	0	0	0	0
600	**640**	43	10	0	0	0	0	0	0	0	0	0
640	**680**	47	14	0	0	0	0	0	0	0	0	0
680	**720**	51	18	0	0	0	0	0	0	0	0	0
720	**760**	55	22	0	0	0	0	0	0	0	0	0
760	**800**	59	26	0	0	0	0	0	0	0	0	0
800	**840**	63	30	0	0	0	0	0	0	0	0	0
840	**880**	67	34	0	0	0	0	0	0	0	0	0
880	**920**	71	38	4	0	0	0	0	0	0	0	0
920	**960**	75	42	8	0	0	0	0	0	0	0	0
960	**1,000**	80	46	12	0	0	0	0	0	0	0	0
1,000	**1,040**	86	50	16	0	0	0	0	0	0	0	0
1,040	**1,080**	92	54	20	0	0	0	0	0	0	0	0
1,080	**1,120**	98	58	24	0	0	0	0	0	0	0	0
1,120	**1,160**	104	62	28	0	0	0	0	0	0	0	0
1,160	**1,200**	110	66	32	0	0	0	0	0	0	0	0
1,200	**1,240**	116	70	36	3	0	0	0	0	0	0	0
1,240	**1,280**	122	74	40	7	0	0	0	0	0	0	0
1,280	**1,320**	128	78	44	11	0	0	0	0	0	0	0
1,320	**1,360**	134	84	48	15	0	0	0	0	0	0	0
1,360	**1,400**	140	90	52	19	0	0	0	0	0	0	0
1,400	**1,440**	146	96	56	23	0	0	0	0	0	0	0
1,440	**1,480**	152	102	60	27	0	0	0	0	0	0	0
1,480	**1,520**	158	108	64	31	0	0	0	0	0	0	0
1,520	**1,560**	164	114	68	35	2	0	0	0	0	0	0
1,560	**1,600**	170	120	72	39	6	0	0	0	0	0	0
1,600	**1,640**	176	126	76	43	10	0	0	0	0	0	0
1,640	**1,680**	182	132	82	47	14	0	0	0	0	0	0
1,680	**1,720**	188	138	88	51	18	0	0	0	0	0	0
1,720	**1,760**	194	144	94	55	22	0	0	0	0	0	0
1,760	**1,800**	200	150	100	59	26	0	0	0	0	0	0
1,800	**1,840**	206	156	106	63	30	0	0	0	0	0	0
1,840	**1,880**	212	162	112	67	34	0	0	0	0	0	0
1,880	**1,920**	218	168	118	71	38	4	0	0	0	0	0
1,920	**1,960**	224	174	124	75	42	8	0	0	0	0	0
1,960	**2,000**	230	180	130	80	46	12	0	0	0	0	0
2,000	**2,040**	236	186	136	86	50	16	0	0	0	0	0
2,040	**2,080**	242	192	142	92	54	20	0	0	0	0	0
2,080	**2,120**	248	198	148	98	58	24	0	0	0	0	0
2,120	**2,160**	254	204	154	104	62	28	0	0	0	0	0
2,160	**2,200**	260	210	160	110	66	32	0	0	0	0	0
2,200	**2,240**	266	216	166	116	70	36	3	0	0	0	0
2,240	**2,280**	272	222	172	122	74	40	7	0	0	0	0
2,280	**2,320**	278	228	178	128	78	44	11	0	0	0	0
2,320	**2,360**	284	234	184	134	84	48	15	0	0	0	0
2,360	**2,400**	290	240	190	140	90	52	19	0	0	0	0

Publication 15 (2015)

Wage Bracket Method Tables for Income Tax Withholding

SINGLE Persons—**MONTHLY** Payroll Period

(For Wages Paid through December 31, 2015)

And the wages are–		And the number of withholding allowances claimed is—										
At least	But less than	0	1	2	3	4	5	6	7	8	9	10
		The amount of income tax to be withheld is—										
$2,400	$2,440	$296	$246	$196	$146	$96	$56	$23	$0	$0	$0	$0
2,440	2,480	302	252	202	152	102	60	27	0	0	0	0
2,480	2,520	308	258	208	158	108	64	31	0	0	0	0
2,520	2,560	314	264	214	164	114	68	35	2	0	0	0
2,560	2,600	320	270	220	170	120	72	39	6	0	0	0
2,600	2,640	326	276	226	176	126	76	43	10	0	0	0
2,640	2,680	332	282	232	182	132	82	47	14	0	0	0
2,680	2,720	338	288	238	188	138	88	51	18	0	0	0
2,720	2,760	344	294	244	194	144	94	55	22	0	0	0
2,760	2,800	350	300	250	200	150	100	59	26	0	0	0
2,800	2,840	356	306	256	206	156	106	63	30	0	0	0
2,840	2,880	362	312	262	212	162	112	67	34	0	0	0
2,880	2,920	368	318	268	218	168	118	71	38	4	0	0
2,920	2,960	374	324	274	224	174	124	75	42	8	0	0
2,960	3,000	380	330	280	230	180	130	80	46	12	0	0
3,000	3,040	386	336	286	236	186	136	86	50	16	0	0
3,040	3,080	392	342	292	242	192	142	92	54	20	0	0
3,080	3,120	398	348	298	248	198	148	98	58	24	0	0
3,120	3,160	404	354	304	254	204	154	104	62	28	0	0
3,160	3,200	410	360	310	260	210	160	110	66	32	0	0
3,200	3,240	416	366	316	266	216	166	116	70	36	3	0
3,240	3,280	422	372	322	272	222	172	122	74	40	7	0
3,280	3,320	428	378	328	278	228	178	128	78	44	11	0
3,320	3,360	437	384	334	284	234	184	134	84	48	15	0
3,360	3,400	447	390	340	290	240	190	140	90	52	19	0
3,400	3,440	457	396	346	296	246	196	146	96	56	23	0
3,440	3,480	467	402	352	302	252	202	152	102	60	27	0
3,480	3,520	477	408	358	308	258	208	158	108	64	31	0
3,520	3,560	487	414	364	314	264	214	164	114	68	35	2
3,560	3,600	497	420	370	320	270	220	170	120	72	39	6
3,600	3,640	507	426	376	326	276	226	176	126	76	43	10
3,640	3,680	517	433	382	332	282	232	182	132	82	47	14
3,680	3,720	527	443	388	338	288	238	188	138	88	51	18
3,720	3,760	537	453	394	344	294	244	194	144	94	55	22
3,760	3,800	547	463	400	350	300	250	200	150	100	59	26
3,800	3,840	557	473	406	356	306	256	206	156	106	63	30
3,840	3,880	567	483	412	362	312	262	212	162	112	67	34
3,880	3,920	577	493	418	368	318	268	218	168	118	71	38
3,920	3,960	587	503	424	374	324	274	224	174	124	75	42
3,960	4,000	597	513	430	380	330	280	230	180	130	80	46
4,000	4,040	607	523	440	386	336	286	236	186	136	86	50
4,040	4,080	617	533	450	392	342	292	242	192	142	92	54
4,080	4,120	627	543	460	398	348	298	248	198	148	98	58
4,120	4,160	637	553	470	404	354	304	254	204	154	104	62
4,160	4,200	647	563	480	410	360	310	260	210	160	110	66
4,200	4,240	657	573	490	416	366	316	266	216	166	116	70
4,240	4,280	667	583	500	422	372	322	272	222	172	122	74
4,280	4,320	677	593	510	428	378	328	278	228	178	128	78
4,320	4,360	687	603	520	437	384	334	284	234	184	134	84
4,360	4,400	697	613	530	447	390	340	290	240	190	140	90
4,400	4,440	707	623	540	457	396	346	296	246	196	146	96
4,440	4,480	717	633	550	467	402	352	302	252	202	152	102
4,480	4,520	727	643	560	477	408	358	308	258	208	158	108
4,520	4,560	737	653	570	487	414	364	314	264	214	164	114
4,560	4,600	747	663	580	497	420	370	320	270	220	170	120
4,600	4,640	757	673	590	507	426	376	326	276	226	176	126
4,640	4,680	767	683	600	517	433	382	332	282	232	182	132
4,680	4,720	777	693	610	527	443	388	338	288	238	188	138
4,720	4,760	787	703	620	537	453	394	344	294	244	194	144
4,760	4,800	797	713	630	547	463	400	350	300	250	200	150
4,800	4,840	807	723	640	557	473	406	356	306	256	206	156
4,840	4,880	817	733	650	567	483	412	362	312	262	212	162
4,880	4,920	827	743	660	577	493	418	368	318	268	218	168
4,920	4,960	837	753	670	587	503	424	374	324	274	224	174
4,960	5,000	847	763	680	597	513	430	380	330	280	230	180
5,000	5,040	857	773	690	607	523	440	386	336	286	236	186
5,040	5,080	867	783	700	617	533	450	392	342	292	242	192

$5,080 and over — Use Table 4(a) for a **SINGLE person** on page 45. Also see the instructions on page 43.

Publication 15 (2015)

Wage Bracket Method Tables for Income Tax Withholding

MARRIED Persons—**MONTHLY** Payroll Period

(For Wages Paid through December 31, 2015)

And the wages are–		And the number of withholding allowances claimed is—										
At least	But less than	0	1	2	3	4	5	6	7	8	9	10
		The amount of income tax to be withheld is—										
$ 0	$720	$0	$0	$0	$0	$0	$0	$0	$0	$0	$0	$0
720	760	2	0	0	0	0	0	0	0	0	0	0
760	800	6	0	0	0	0	0	0	0	0	0	0
800	840	10	0	0	0	0	0	0	0	0	0	0
840	880	14	0	0	0	0	0	0	0	0	0	0
880	920	18	0	0	0	0	0	0	0	0	0	0
920	960	22	0	0	0	0	0	0	0	0	0	0
960	1,000	26	0	0	0	0	0	0	0	0	0	0
1,000	1,040	30	0	0	0	0	0	0	0	0	0	0
1,040	1,080	34	1	0	0	0	0	0	0	0	0	0
1,080	1,120	38	5	0	0	0	0	0	0	0	0	0
1,120	1,160	42	9	0	0	0	0	0	0	0	0	0
1,160	1,200	46	13	0	0	0	0	0	0	0	0	0
1,200	1,240	50	17	0	0	0	0	0	0	0	0	0
1,240	1,280	54	21	0	0	0	0	0	0	0	0	0
1,280	1,320	58	25	0	0	0	0	0	0	0	0	0
1,320	1,360	62	29	0	0	0	0	0	0	0	0	0
1,360	1,400	66	33	0	0	0	0	0	0	0	0	0
1,400	1,440	70	37	4	0	0	0	0	0	0	0	0
1,440	1,480	74	41	8	0	0	0	0	0	0	0	0
1,480	1,520	78	45	12	0	0	0	0	0	0	0	0
1,520	1,560	82	49	16	0	0	0	0	0	0	0	0
1,560	1,600	86	53	20	0	0	0	0	0	0	0	0
1,600	1,640	90	57	24	0	0	0	0	0	0	0	0
1,640	1,680	94	61	28	0	0	0	0	0	0	0	0
1,680	1,720	98	65	32	0	0	0	0	0	0	0	0
1,720	1,760	102	69	36	2	0	0	0	0	0	0	0
1,760	1,800	106	73	40	6	0	0	0	0	0	0	0
1,800	1,840	110	77	44	10	0	0	0	0	0	0	0
1,840	1,880	114	81	48	14	0	0	0	0	0	0	0
1,880	1,920	118	85	52	18	0	0	0	0	0	0	0
1,920	1,960	122	89	56	22	0	0	0	0	0	0	0
1,960	2,000	126	93	60	26	0	0	0	0	0	0	0
2,000	2,040	130	97	64	30	0	0	0	0	0	0	0
2,040	2,080	134	101	68	34	1	0	0	0	0	0	0
2,080	2,120	138	105	72	38	5	0	0	0	0	0	0
2,120	2,160	142	109	76	42	9	0	0	0	0	0	0
2,160	2,200	146	113	80	46	13	0	0	0	0	0	0
2,200	2,240	150	117	84	50	17	0	0	0	0	0	0
2,240	2,280	155	121	88	54	21	0	0	0	0	0	0
2,280	2,320	161	125	92	58	25	0	0	0	0	0	0
2,320	2,360	167	129	96	62	29	0	0	0	0	0	0
2,360	2,400	173	133	100	66	33	0	0	0	0	0	0
2,400	2,440	179	137	104	70	37	4	0	0	0	0	0
2,440	2,480	185	141	108	74	41	8	0	0	0	0	0
2,480	2,520	191	145	112	78	45	12	0	0	0	0	0
2,520	2,560	197	149	116	82	49	16	0	0	0	0	0
2,560	2,600	203	153	120	86	53	20	0	0	0	0	0
2,600	2,640	209	159	124	90	57	24	0	0	0	0	0
2,640	2,680	215	165	128	94	61	28	0	0	0	0	0
2,680	2,720	221	171	132	98	65	32	0	0	0	0	0
2,720	2,760	227	177	136	102	69	36	2	0	0	0	0
2,760	2,800	233	183	140	106	73	40	6	0	0	0	0
2,800	2,840	239	189	144	110	77	44	10	0	0	0	0
2,840	2,880	245	195	148	114	81	48	14	0	0	0	0
2,880	2,920	251	201	152	118	85	52	18	0	0	0	0
2,920	2,960	257	207	157	122	89	56	22	0	0	0	0
2,960	3,000	263	213	163	126	93	60	26	0	0	0	0
3,000	3,040	269	219	169	130	97	64	30	0	0	0	0
3,040	3,080	275	225	175	134	101	68	34	1	0	0	0
3,080	3,120	281	231	181	138	105	72	38	5	0	0	0
3,120	3,160	287	237	187	142	109	76	42	9	0	0	0
3,160	3,200	293	243	193	146	113	80	46	13	0	0	0
3,200	3,240	299	249	199	150	117	84	50	17	0	0	0
3,240	3,280	305	255	205	155	121	88	54	21	0	0	0
3,280	3,320	311	261	211	161	125	92	58	25	0	0	0
3,320	3,360	317	267	217	167	129	96	62	29	0	0	0
3,360	3,400	323	273	223	173	133	100	66	33	0	0	0

Wage Bracket Method Tables for Income Tax Withholding

MARRIED Persons—**MONTHLY** Payroll Period

(For Wages Paid through December 31, 2015)

And the wages are–		And the number of withholding allowances claimed is—										
At least	But less than	0	1	2	3	4	5	6	7	8	9	10
		The amount of income tax to be withheld is—										
$3,400	**$3,440**	$329	$279	$229	$179	$137	$104	$70	$37	$4	$0	$0
3,440	**3,480**	335	285	235	185	141	108	74	41	8	0	0
3,480	**3,520**	341	291	241	191	145	112	78	45	12	0	0
3,520	**3,560**	347	297	247	197	149	116	82	49	16	0	0
3,560	**3,600**	353	303	253	203	153	120	86	53	20	0	0
3,600	**3,640**	359	309	259	209	159	124	90	57	24	0	0
3,640	**3,680**	365	315	265	215	165	128	94	61	28	0	0
3,680	**3,720**	371	321	271	221	171	132	98	65	32	0	0
3,720	**3,760**	377	327	277	227	177	136	102	69	36	2	0
3,760	**3,800**	383	333	283	233	183	140	106	73	40	6	0
3,800	**3,840**	389	339	289	239	189	144	110	77	44	10	0
3,840	**3,880**	395	345	295	245	195	148	114	81	48	14	0
3,880	**3,920**	401	351	301	251	201	152	118	85	52	18	0
3,920	**3,960**	407	357	307	257	207	157	122	89	56	22	0
3,960	**4,000**	413	363	313	263	213	163	126	93	60	26	0
4,000	**4,040**	419	369	319	269	219	169	130	97	64	30	0
4,040	**4,080**	425	375	325	275	225	175	134	101	68	34	1
4,080	**4,120**	431	381	331	281	231	181	138	105	72	38	5
4,120	**4,160**	437	387	337	287	237	187	142	109	76	42	9
4,160	**4,200**	443	393	343	293	243	193	146	113	80	46	13
4,200	**4,240**	449	399	349	299	249	199	150	117	84	50	17
4,240	**4,280**	455	405	355	305	255	205	155	121	88	54	21
4,280	**4,320**	461	411	361	311	261	211	161	125	92	58	25
4,320	**4,360**	467	417	367	317	267	217	167	129	96	62	29
4,360	**4,400**	473	423	373	323	273	223	173	133	100	66	33
4,400	**4,440**	479	429	379	329	279	229	179	137	104	70	37
4,440	**4,480**	485	435	385	335	285	235	185	141	108	74	41
4,480	**4,520**	491	441	391	341	291	241	191	145	112	78	45
4,520	**4,560**	497	447	397	347	297	247	197	149	116	82	49
4,560	**4,600**	503	453	403	353	303	253	203	153	120	86	53
4,600	**4,640**	509	459	409	359	309	259	209	159	124	90	57
4,640	**4,680**	515	465	415	365	315	265	215	165	128	94	61
4,680	**4,720**	521	471	421	371	321	271	221	171	132	98	65
4,720	**4,760**	527	477	427	377	327	277	227	177	136	102	69
4,760	**4,800**	533	483	433	383	333	283	233	183	140	106	73
4,800	**4,840**	539	489	439	389	339	289	239	189	144	110	77
4,840	**4,880**	545	495	445	395	345	295	245	195	148	114	81
4,880	**4,920**	551	501	451	401	351	301	251	201	152	118	85
4,920	**4,960**	557	507	457	407	357	307	257	207	157	122	89
4,960	**5,000**	563	513	463	413	363	313	263	213	163	126	93
5,000	**5,040**	569	519	469	419	369	319	269	219	169	130	97
5,040	**5,080**	575	525	475	425	375	325	275	225	175	134	101
5,080	**5,120**	581	531	481	431	381	331	281	231	181	138	105
5,120	**5,160**	587	537	487	437	387	337	287	237	187	142	109
5,160	**5,200**	593	543	493	443	393	343	293	243	193	146	113
5,200	**5,240**	599	549	499	449	399	349	299	249	199	150	117
5,240	**5,280**	605	555	505	455	405	355	305	255	205	155	121
5,280	**5,320**	611	561	511	461	411	361	311	261	211	161	125
5,320	**5,360**	617	567	517	467	417	367	317	267	217	167	129
5,360	**5,400**	623	573	523	473	423	373	323	273	223	173	133
5,400	**5,440**	629	579	529	479	429	379	329	279	229	179	137
5,440	**5,480**	635	585	535	485	435	385	335	285	235	185	141
5,480	**5,520**	641	591	541	491	441	391	341	291	241	191	145
5,520	**5,560**	647	597	547	497	447	397	347	297	247	197	149
5,560	**5,600**	653	603	553	503	453	403	353	303	253	203	153
5,600	**5,640**	659	609	559	509	459	409	359	309	259	209	159
5,640	**5,680**	665	615	565	515	465	415	365	315	265	215	165
5,680	**5,720**	671	621	571	521	471	421	371	321	271	221	171
5,720	**5,760**	677	627	577	527	477	427	377	327	277	227	177
5,760	**5,800**	683	633	583	533	483	433	383	333	283	233	183
5,800	**5,840**	689	639	589	539	489	439	389	339	289	239	189
5,840	**5,880**	695	645	595	545	495	445	395	345	295	245	195
5,880	**5,920**	701	651	601	551	501	451	401	351	301	251	201
5,920	**5,960**	707	657	607	557	507	457	407	357	307	257	207
5,960	**6,000**	713	663	613	563	513	463	413	363	313	263	213
6,000	**6,040**	719	669	619	569	519	469	419	369	319	269	219
6,040	**6,080**	725	675	625	575	525	475	425	375	325	275	225
6,080	**6,120**	731	681	631	581	531	481	431	381	331	281	231

$6,120 and over Use Table 4(b) for a **MARRIED person** on page 45. Also see the instructions on page 43.

Wage Bracket Method Tables for Income Tax Withholding

SINGLE Persons—**DAILY** Payroll Period

(For Wages Paid through December 31, 2015)

And the wages are–		And the number of withholding allowances claimed is—										
At least	But less than	0	1	2	3	4	5	6	7	8	9	10
		The amount of income tax to be withheld is—										
$0	$15	$0	$0	$0	$0	$0	$0	$0	$0	$0	$0	$0
15	18	1	0	0	0	0	0	0	0	0	0	0
18	21	1	0	0	0	0	0	0	0	0	0	0
21	24	1	0	0	0	0	0	0	0	0	0	0
24	27	2	0	0	0	0	0	0	0	0	0	0
27	30	2	0	0	0	0	0	0	0	0	0	0
30	33	2	1	0	0	0	0	0	0	0	0	0
33	36	3	1	0	0	0	0	0	0	0	0	0
36	39	3	1	0	0	0	0	0	0	0	0	0
39	42	3	2	0	0	0	0	0	0	0	0	0
42	45	3	2	0	0	0	0	0	0	0	0	0
45	48	4	2	1	0	0	0	0	0	0	0	0
48	51	4	3	1	0	0	0	0	0	0	0	0
51	54	5	3	1	0	0	0	0	0	0	0	0
54	57	5	3	2	0	0	0	0	0	0	0	0
57	60	6	3	2	0	0	0	0	0	0	0	0
60	63	6	4	2	1	0	0	0	0	0	0	0
63	66	7	4	2	1	0	0	0	0	0	0	0
66	69	7	5	3	1	0	0	0	0	0	0	0
69	72	7	5	3	2	0	0	0	0	0	0	0
72	75	8	6	3	2	0	0	0	0	0	0	0
75	78	8	6	4	2	1	0	0	0	0	0	0
78	81	9	7	4	2	1	0	0	0	0	0	0
81	84	9	7	5	3	1	0	0	0	0	0	0
84	87	10	7	5	3	2	0	0	0	0	0	0
87	90	10	8	6	3	2	0	0	0	0	0	0
90	93	11	8	6	4	2	1	0	0	0	0	0
93	96	11	9	6	4	2	1	0	0	0	0	0
96	99	12	9	7	5	3	1	0	0	0	0	0
99	102	12	10	7	5	3	1	0	0	0	0	0
102	105	12	10	8	6	3	2	0	0	0	0	0
105	108	13	11	8	6	4	2	1	0	0	0	0
108	111	13	11	9	6	4	2	1	0	0	0	0
111	114	14	11	9	7	5	3	1	0	0	0	0
114	117	14	12	10	7	5	3	1	0	0	0	0
117	120	15	12	10	8	5	3	2	0	0	0	0
120	123	15	13	11	8	6	4	2	0	0	0	0
123	126	16	13	11	9	6	4	2	1	0	0	0
126	129	16	14	11	9	7	4	3	1	0	0	0
129	132	16	14	12	10	7	5	3	1	0	0	0
132	135	17	15	12	10	8	5	3	2	0	0	0
135	138	17	15	13	10	8	6	4	2	0	0	0
138	141	18	16	13	11	9	6	4	2	1	0	0
141	144	18	16	14	11	9	7	4	3	1	0	0
144	147	19	16	14	12	9	7	5	3	1	0	0
147	150	19	17	15	12	10	8	5	3	2	0	0
150	153	20	17	15	13	10	8	6	3	2	0	0
153	156	20	18	15	13	11	9	6	4	2	1	0
156	159	21	18	16	14	11	9	7	4	3	1	0
159	162	22	19	16	14	12	9	7	5	3	1	0
162	165	22	19	17	15	12	10	8	5	3	2	0
165	168	23	20	17	15	13	10	8	6	3	2	0
168	171	24	20	18	15	13	11	8	6	4	2	1
171	174	25	21	18	16	14	11	9	7	4	3	1
174	177	25	22	19	16	14	12	9	7	5	3	1
177	180	26	22	19	17	14	12	10	8	5	3	2
180	183	27	23	20	17	15	13	10	8	6	3	2
183	186	28	24	20	18	15	13	11	8	6	4	2
186	189	28	25	21	18	16	13	11	9	7	4	2
189	192	29	25	22	19	16	14	12	9	7	5	3
192	195	30	26	22	19	17	14	12	10	7	5	3
195	198	31	27	23	19	17	15	13	10	8	6	3
198	201	31	28	24	20	18	15	13	11	8	6	4
201	204	32	28	25	21	18	16	13	11	9	7	4
204	207	33	29	25	21	18	16	14	12	9	7	5
207	210	34	30	26	22	19	17	14	12	10	7	5
210	213	34	31	27	23	19	17	15	12	10	8	6
213	216	35	31	28	24	20	18	15	13	11	8	6
216	219	36	32	28	24	21	18	16	13	11	9	6
219	222	37	33	29	25	21	18	16	14	12	9	7
222	225	37	34	30	26	22	19	17	14	12	10	7

Publication 15 (2015)

Wage Bracket Method Tables for Income Tax Withholding

SINGLE Persons—**DAILY** Payroll Period

(For Wages Paid through December 31, 2015)

And the wages are–		And the number of withholding allowances claimed is—										
At least	But less than	0	1	2	3	4	5	6	7	8	9	10
		The amount of income tax to be withheld is—										
$225	**$228**	$38	$34	$31	$27	$23	$19	$17	$15	$12	$10	$8
228	**231**	39	35	31	27	24	20	17	15	13	11	8
231	**234**	40	36	32	28	24	21	18	16	13	11	9
234	**237**	40	37	33	29	25	21	18	16	14	11	9
237	**240**	41	37	34	30	26	22	19	17	14	12	10
240	**243**	42	38	34	30	27	23	19	17	15	12	10
243	**246**	43	39	35	31	27	24	20	17	15	13	10
246	**249**	43	40	36	32	28	24	20	18	16	13	11
249	**252**	44	40	37	33	29	25	21	18	16	14	11
252	**255**	45	41	37	33	30	26	22	19	16	14	12
255	**258**	46	42	38	34	30	27	23	19	17	15	12
258	**261**	46	43	39	35	31	27	23	20	17	15	13
261	**264**	47	43	40	36	32	28	24	20	18	16	13
264	**267**	48	44	40	36	33	29	25	21	18	16	14
267	**270**	49	45	41	37	33	30	26	22	19	16	14
270	**273**	49	46	42	38	34	30	26	23	19	17	15
273	**276**	50	46	43	39	35	31	27	23	20	17	15
276	**279**	51	47	43	39	36	32	28	24	20	18	15
279	**282**	52	48	44	40	36	33	29	25	21	18	16
282	**285**	52	49	45	41	37	33	29	26	22	19	16
285	**288**	53	49	46	42	38	34	30	26	22	19	17
288	**291**	54	50	46	42	39	35	31	27	23	20	17
291	**294**	55	51	47	43	39	36	32	28	24	20	18
294	**297**	55	52	48	44	40	36	32	29	25	21	18
297	**300**	56	52	49	45	41	37	33	29	25	22	19
300	**303**	57	53	49	45	42	38	34	30	26	22	19
303	**306**	58	54	50	46	42	39	35	31	27	23	19
306	**309**	58	55	51	47	43	39	35	32	28	24	20
309	**312**	59	55	52	48	44	40	36	32	28	25	21
312	**315**	60	56	52	48	45	41	37	33	29	25	22
315	**318**	61	57	53	49	45	42	38	34	30	26	22
318	**321**	61	58	54	50	46	42	38	35	31	27	23
321	**324**	62	58	55	51	47	43	39	35	31	28	24
324	**327**	63	59	55	51	48	44	40	36	32	28	25
327	**330**	64	60	56	52	48	45	41	37	33	29	25
330	**333**	64	61	57	53	49	45	41	38	34	30	26
333	**336**	65	61	58	54	50	46	42	38	34	31	27
336	**339**	66	62	58	54	51	47	43	39	35	31	28
339	**341**	67	63	59	55	51	47	44	40	36	32	28
341	**343**	67	63	59	56	52	48	44	40	36	32	29
343	**345**	68	64	60	56	52	48	45	41	37	33	29
345	**347**	68	64	60	57	53	49	45	41	37	33	30
347	**349**	69	65	61	57	53	49	46	42	38	34	30
349	**351**	69	65	61	58	54	50	46	42	38	34	31
351	**353**	70	66	62	58	54	50	47	43	39	35	31
353	**355**	70	66	62	59	55	51	47	43	39	35	32
355	**357**	71	67	63	59	55	51	48	44	40	36	32
357	**359**	71	67	63	60	56	52	48	44	40	36	33
359	**361**	72	68	64	60	56	52	49	45	41	37	33
361	**363**	72	68	64	61	57	53	49	45	41	37	34
363	**365**	73	69	65	61	57	53	50	46	42	38	34
365	**367**	73	69	65	62	58	54	50	46	42	38	35
367	**369**	74	70	66	62	58	54	51	47	43	39	35
369	**371**	74	70	66	63	59	55	51	47	43	39	36
371	**373**	75	71	67	63	59	55	52	48	44	40	36
373	**375**	76	71	67	64	60	56	52	48	44	40	37
375	**377**	76	72	68	64	60	56	53	49	45	41	37
377	**379**	77	72	68	65	61	57	53	49	45	41	38
379	**381**	77	73	69	65	61	57	54	50	46	42	38
381	**383**	78	74	69	66	62	58	54	50	46	42	39
383	**385**	78	74	70	66	62	58	55	51	47	43	39
385	**387**	79	75	70	67	63	59	55	51	47	43	40
387	**389**	80	75	71	67	63	59	56	52	48	44	40
389	**391**	80	76	71	68	64	60	56	52	48	44	41
391	**393**	81	76	72	68	64	60	57	53	49	45	41
$393 and over		Use Table 8(a) for a **SINGLE person** on page 46. Also see the instructions on page 43.										

Publication 15 (2015)

Wage Bracket Method Tables for Income Tax Withholding

MARRIED Persons—**DAILY** Payroll Period

(For Wages Paid through December 31, 2015)

And the wages are–		And the number of withholding allowances claimed is—										
At least	But less than	0	1	2	3	4	5	6	7	8	9	10
		The amount of income tax to be withheld is—										
$0	**$39**	$0	$0	$0	$0	$0	$0	$0	$0	$0	$0	$0
39	**42**	1	0	0	0	0	0	0	0	0	0	0
42	**45**	1	0	0	0	0	0	0	0	0	0	0
45	**48**	1	0	0	0	0	0	0	0	0	0	0
48	**51**	2	0	0	0	0	0	0	0	0	0	0
51	**54**	2	0	0	0	0	0	0	0	0	0	0
54	**57**	2	1	0	0	0	0	0	0	0	0	0
57	**60**	3	1	0	0	0	0	0	0	0	0	0
60	**63**	3	1	0	0	0	0	0	0	0	0	0
63	**66**	3	2	0	0	0	0	0	0	0	0	0
66	**69**	3	2	0	0	0	0	0	0	0	0	0
69	**72**	4	2	1	0	0	0	0	0	0	0	0
72	**75**	4	3	1	0	0	0	0	0	0	0	0
75	**78**	4	3	1	0	0	0	0	0	0	0	0
78	**81**	5	3	2	0	0	0	0	0	0	0	0
81	**84**	5	3	2	0	0	0	0	0	0	0	0
84	**87**	5	4	2	1	0	0	0	0	0	0	0
87	**90**	6	4	2	1	0	0	0	0	0	0	0
90	**93**	6	4	3	1	0	0	0	0	0	0	0
93	**96**	6	5	3	2	0	0	0	0	0	0	0
96	**99**	6	5	3	2	0	0	0	0	0	0	0
99	**102**	7	5	4	2	1	0	0	0	0	0	0
102	**105**	7	6	4	2	1	0	0	0	0	0	0
105	**108**	7	6	4	3	1	0	0	0	0	0	0
108	**111**	8	6	5	3	1	0	0	0	0	0	0
111	**114**	8	6	5	3	2	0	0	0	0	0	0
114	**117**	9	7	5	4	2	1	0	0	0	0	0
117	**120**	9	7	5	4	2	1	0	0	0	0	0
120	**123**	10	7	6	4	3	1	0	0	0	0	0
123	**126**	10	8	6	5	3	1	0	0	0	0	0
126	**129**	11	8	6	5	3	2	0	0	0	0	0
129	**132**	11	9	7	5	4	2	1	0	0	0	0
132	**135**	12	9	7	5	4	2	1	0	0	0	0
135	**138**	12	10	7	6	4	3	1	0	0	0	0
138	**141**	12	10	8	6	4	3	1	0	0	0	0
141	**144**	13	11	8	6	5	3	2	0	0	0	0
144	**147**	13	11	9	7	5	4	2	0	0	0	0
147	**150**	14	11	9	7	5	4	2	1	0	0	0
150	**153**	14	12	10	7	6	4	3	1	0	0	0
153	**156**	15	12	10	8	6	4	3	1	0	0	0
156	**159**	15	13	11	8	6	5	3	2	0	0	0
159	**162**	16	13	11	9	7	5	4	2	0	0	0
162	**165**	16	14	11	9	7	5	4	2	1	0	0
165	**168**	16	14	12	10	7	6	4	3	1	0	0
168	**171**	17	15	12	10	8	6	4	3	1	0	0
171	**174**	17	15	13	10	8	6	5	3	2	0	0
174	**177**	18	16	13	11	9	7	5	3	2	0	0
177	**180**	18	16	14	11	9	7	5	4	2	1	0
180	**183**	19	16	14	12	9	7	6	4	3	1	0
183	**186**	19	17	15	12	10	8	6	4	3	1	0
186	**189**	20	17	15	13	10	8	6	5	3	2	0
189	**192**	20	18	15	13	11	9	7	5	3	2	0
192	**195**	21	18	16	14	11	9	7	5	4	2	1
195	**198**	21	19	16	14	12	9	7	6	4	2	1
198	**201**	21	19	17	14	12	10	8	6	4	3	1
201	**204**	22	20	17	15	13	10	8	6	5	3	2
204	**207**	22	20	18	15	13	11	8	6	5	3	2
207	**210**	23	20	18	16	14	11	9	7	5	4	2
210	**213**	23	21	19	16	14	12	9	7	6	4	2
213	**216**	24	21	19	17	14	12	10	8	6	4	3
216	**219**	24	22	20	17	15	13	10	8	6	5	3
219	**222**	25	22	20	18	15	13	11	8	6	5	3
222	**225**	25	23	20	18	16	13	11	9	7	5	4
225	**228**	25	23	21	19	16	14	12	9	7	5	4
228	**231**	26	24	21	19	17	14	12	10	7	6	4
231	**234**	26	24	22	19	17	15	13	10	8	6	5
234	**237**	27	25	22	20	18	15	13	11	8	6	5
237	**240**	27	25	23	20	18	16	13	11	9	7	5
240	**243**	28	25	23	21	18	16	14	12	9	7	5
243	**246**	28	26	24	21	19	17	14	12	10	7	6
246	**249**	29	26	24	22	19	17	15	12	10	8	6

Publication 15 (2015)

Wage Bracket Method Tables for Income Tax Withholding

MARRIED Persons—**DAILY** Payroll Period

(For Wages Paid through December 31, 2015)

And the wages are–		And the number of withholding allowances claimed is—										
At least	But less than	0	1	2	3	4	5	6	7	8	9	10
		The amount of income tax to be withheld is—										
$249	**$252**	$29	$27	$24	$22	$20	$18	$15	$13	$11	$8	$6
252	**255**	30	27	25	23	20	18	16	13	11	9	7
255	**258**	30	28	25	23	21	18	16	14	12	9	7
258	**261**	30	28	26	23	21	19	17	14	12	10	7
261	**264**	31	29	26	24	22	19	17	15	12	10	8
264	**267**	31	29	27	24	22	20	17	15	13	11	8
267	**270**	32	29	27	25	23	20	18	16	13	11	9
270	**273**	32	30	28	25	23	21	18	16	14	11	9
273	**276**	33	30	28	26	23	21	19	17	14	12	10
276	**279**	33	31	29	26	24	22	19	17	15	12	10
279	**282**	34	31	29	27	24	22	20	17	15	13	10
282	**285**	34	32	29	27	25	22	20	18	16	13	11
285	**288**	34	32	30	28	25	23	21	18	16	14	11
288	**291**	35	33	30	28	26	23	21	19	16	14	12
291	**294**	35	33	31	28	26	24	22	19	17	15	12
294	**297**	36	34	31	29	27	24	22	20	17	15	13
297	**300**	36	34	32	29	27	25	22	20	18	15	13
300	**303**	37	34	32	30	27	25	23	21	18	16	14
303	**306**	37	35	33	30	28	26	23	21	19	16	14
306	**309**	38	35	33	31	28	26	24	21	19	17	15
309	**312**	38	36	33	31	29	27	24	22	20	17	15
312	**315**	39	36	34	32	29	27	25	22	20	18	15
315	**318**	39	37	34	32	30	27	25	23	21	18	16
318	**321**	39	37	35	32	30	28	26	23	21	19	16
321	**324**	40	38	35	33	31	28	26	24	21	19	17
324	**327**	41	38	36	33	31	29	26	24	22	20	17
327	**330**	42	38	36	34	32	29	27	25	22	20	18
330	**333**	42	39	37	34	32	30	27	25	23	20	18
333	**336**	43	39	37	35	32	30	28	26	23	21	19
336	**339**	44	40	38	35	33	31	28	26	24	21	19
339	**341**	44	41	38	36	33	31	29	26	24	22	19
341	**343**	45	41	38	36	34	31	29	27	24	22	20
343	**345**	45	42	38	36	34	32	29	27	25	22	20
345	**347**	46	42	39	36	34	32	30	27	25	23	20
347	**349**	46	43	39	37	34	32	30	28	25	23	21
349	**351**	47	43	39	37	35	32	30	28	26	23	21
351	**353**	47	44	40	37	35	33	30	28	26	24	21
353	**355**	48	44	40	38	35	33	31	28	26	24	22
355	**357**	48	45	41	38	36	33	31	29	26	24	22
357	**359**	49	45	41	38	36	34	31	29	27	24	22
359	**361**	49	46	42	39	36	34	32	29	27	25	22
361	**363**	50	46	42	39	37	34	32	30	27	25	23
363	**365**	50	47	43	39	37	35	32	30	28	25	23
365	**367**	51	47	43	39	37	35	33	30	28	26	23
367	**369**	51	48	44	40	37	35	33	31	28	26	24
369	**371**	52	48	44	40	38	35	33	31	29	26	24
371	**373**	52	49	45	41	38	36	33	31	29	27	24
373	**375**	53	49	45	41	38	36	34	31	29	27	25
375	**377**	53	50	46	42	39	36	34	32	29	27	25
377	**379**	54	50	46	42	39	37	34	32	30	27	25
379	**381**	54	51	47	43	39	37	35	32	30	28	25
381	**383**	55	51	47	43	40	37	35	33	30	28	26
383	**385**	55	52	48	44	40	38	35	33	31	28	26
385	**387**	56	52	48	44	40	38	36	33	31	29	26
387	**389**	56	53	49	45	41	38	36	34	31	29	27
389	**391**	57	53	49	45	41	38	36	34	32	29	27
391	**393**	57	54	50	46	42	39	36	34	32	30	27
393	**395**	58	54	50	46	42	39	37	34	32	30	28
395	**397**	58	55	51	47	43	39	37	35	32	30	28
397	**399**	59	55	51	47	43	40	37	35	33	30	28
399	**401**	59	56	52	48	44	40	38	35	33	31	28
401	**403**	60	56	52	48	44	41	38	36	33	31	29
403	**405**	60	57	53	49	45	41	38	36	34	31	29
405	**407**	61	57	53	49	45	42	39	36	34	32	29
407	**409**	61	58	54	50	46	42	39	37	34	32	30

$409 and over — Use Table 8(b) for a **MARRIED person** on page 46. Also see the instructions on page 43.

Publication 15 (2015)

Table 10-4: Percentage Method – 2016 Amount for One Withholding Allowance

Payroll Period	One Withholding Allowance
Weekly	$ 77.90
Biweekly	155.80
Semimonthly	168.80
Monthly	337.50
Quarterly	1,012.50
Semiannually	2,025.00
Annually	4,050.00
Daily	15.60

Percentage Method Tables for Income Tax Withholding

(For Wages Paid in 2016)

TABLE 1—WEEKLY Payroll Period

(a) SINGLE person (including head of household)—

If the amount of wages (after subtracting withholding allowances) is: Not over $43 . . . . The amount of income tax to withhold is: $0

Over—	But not over—	The amount of income tax to withhold is:	of excess over—
$43	—$222	$0.00 plus 10%	—$43
$222	—$767	$17.90 plus 15%	—$222
$767	—$1,796	$99.65 plus 25%	—$767
$1,796	—$3,700	$356.90 plus 28%	—$1,796
$3,700	—$7,992	$890.02 plus 33%	—$3,700
$7,992	—$8,025	$2,306.38 plus 35%	—$7,992
$8,025	. . . .	$2,317.93 plus 39.6%	—$8,025

(b) MARRIED person—

If the amount of wages (after subtracting withholding allowances) is: Not over $164 . . . . The amount of income tax to withhold is: $0

Over—	But not over—	The amount of income tax to withhold is:	of excess over—
$164	—$521	$0.00 plus 10%	—$164
$521	—$1,613	$35.70 plus 15%	—$521
$1,613	—$3,086	$199.50 plus 25%	—$1,613
$3,086	—$4,615	$567.75 plus 28%	—$3,086
$4,615	—$8,113	$995.87 plus 33%	—$4,615
$8,113	—$9,144	$2,150.21 plus 35%	—$8,113
$9,144	. . . .	$2,511.06 plus 39.6%	—$9,144

TABLE 2—BIWEEKLY Payroll Period

(a) SINGLE person (including head of household)—

If the amount of wages (after subtracting withholding allowances) is: Not over $87 . . . . The amount of income tax to withhold is: $0

Over—	But not over—	The amount of income tax to withhold is:	of excess over—
$87	—$443	$0.00 plus 10%	—$87
$443	—$1,535	$35.60 plus 15%	—$443
$1,535	—$3,592	$199.40 plus 25%	—$1,535
$3,592	—$7,400	$713.65 plus 28%	—$3,592
$7,400	—$15,985	$1,779.89 plus 33%	—$7,400
$15,985	—$16,050	$4,612.94 plus 35%	—$15,985
$16,050	. . . .	$4,635.69 plus 39.6%	—$16,050

(b) MARRIED person—

If the amount of wages (after subtracting withholding allowances) is: Not over $329 . . . . The amount of income tax to withhold is: $0

Over—	But not over—	The amount of income tax to withhold is:	of excess over—
$329	—$1,042	$0.00 plus 10%	—$329
$1,042	—$3,225	$71.30 plus 15%	—$1,042
$3,225	—$6,171	$398.75 plus 25%	—$3,225
$6,171	—$9,231	$1,135.25 plus 28%	—$6,171
$9,231	—$16,227	$1,992.05 plus 33%	—$9,231
$16,227	—$18,288	$4,300.73 plus 35%	—$16,227
$18,288	. . . .	$5,022.08 plus 39.6%	—$18,288

TABLE 3—SEMIMONTHLY Payroll Period

(a) SINGLE person (including head of household)—

If the amount of wages (after subtracting withholding allowances) is: Not over $94 . . . . The amount of income tax to withhold is: $0

Over—	But not over—	The amount of income tax to withhold is:	of excess over—
$94	—$480	$0.00 plus 10%	—$94
$480	—$1,663	$38.60 plus 15%	—$480
$1,663	—$3,892	$216.05 plus 25%	—$1,663
$3,892	—$8,017	$773.30 plus 28%	—$3,892
$8,017	—$17,317	$1,928.30 plus 33%	—$8,017
$17,317	—$17,388	$4,997.30 plus 35%	—$17,317
$17,388	. . . .	$5,022.15 plus 39.6%	—$17,388

(b) MARRIED person—

If the amount of wages (after subtracting withholding allowances) is: Not over $356 . . . . The amount of income tax to withhold is: $0

Over—	But not over—	The amount of income tax to withhold is:	of excess over—
$356	—$1,129	$0.00 plus 10%	—$356
$1,129	—$3,494	$77.30 plus 15%	—$1,129
$3,494	—$6,685	$432.05 plus 25%	—$3,494
$6,685	—$10,000	$1,229.80 plus 28%	—$6,685
$10,000	—$17,579	$2,158.00 plus 33%	—$10,000
$17,579	—$19,813	$4,659.07 plus 35%	—$17,579
$19,813	. . . .	$5,440.97 plus 39.6%	—$19,813

TABLE 4—MONTHLY Payroll Period

(a) SINGLE person (including head of household)—

If the amount of wages (after subtracting withholding allowances) is: Not over $188 . . . . The amount of income tax to withhold is: $0

Over—	But not over—	The amount of income tax to withhold is:	of excess over—
$188	—$960	$0.00 plus 10%	—$188
$960	—$3,325	$77.20 plus 15%	—$960
$3,325	—$7,783	$431.95 plus 25%	—$3,325
$7,783	—$16,033	$1,546.45 plus 28%	—$7,783
$16,033	—$34,633	$3,856.45 plus 33%	—$16,033
$34,633	—$34,775	$9,994.45 plus 35%	—$34,633
$34,775	. . . .	$10,044.15 plus 39.6%	—$34,775

(b) MARRIED person—

If the amount of wages (after subtracting withholding allowances) is: Not over $713 . . . . The amount of income tax to withhold is: $0

Over—	But not over—	The amount of income tax to withhold is:	of excess over—
$713	—$2,258	$0.00 plus 10%	—$713
$2,258	—$6,988	$154.50 plus 15%	—$2,258
$6,988	—$13,371	$864.00 plus 25%	—$6,988
$13,371	—$20,000	$2,459.75 plus 28%	—$13,371
$20,000	—$35,158	$4,315.87 plus 33%	—$20,000
$35,158	—$39,625	$9,318.01 plus 35%	—$35,158
$39,625	. . . .	$10,881.46 plus 39.6%	—$39,625

Table 10-5: IRS Tables for Percentage Method of Withholding

Percentage Method Tables for Income Tax Withholding (continued)

(For Wages Paid in 2016)

TABLE 5—QUARTERLY Payroll Period

(a) SINGLE person (including head of household)—

If the amount of wages (after subtracting withholding allowances) is: Not over $563 . . . . The amount of income tax to withhold is: $0

Over—	But not over—		of excess over—
$563	—$2,881 . .	$0.00 plus 10%	—$563
$2,881	—$9,975 . .	$231.80 plus 15%	—$2,881
$9,975	—$23,350 . .	$1,295.90 plus 25%	—$9,975
$23,350	—$48,100 . .	$4,639.65 plus 28%	—$23,350
$48,100	—$103,900 . .	$11,569.65 plus 33%	—$48,100
$103,900	—$104,325 . .	$29,983.65 plus 35%	—$103,900
$104,325		$30,132.40 plus 39.6%	—$104,325

(b) MARRIED person—

If the amount of wages (after subtracting withholding allowances) is: Not over $2,138 . . . . The amount of income tax to withhold is: $0

Over—	But not over—		of excess over—
$2,138	—$6,775 . .	$0.00 plus 10%	—$2,138
$6,775	—$20,963 . .	$463.70 plus 15%	—$6,775
$20,963	—$40,113 . .	$2,591.90 plus 25%	—$20,963
$40,113	—$60,000 . .	$7,379.40 plus 28%	—$40,113
$60,000	—$105,475 . .	$12,947.76 plus 33%	—$60,000
$105,475	—$118,875 . .	$27,954.51 plus 35%	—$105,475
$118,875		$32,644.51 plus 39.6%	—$118,875

TABLE 6—SEMIANNUAL Payroll Period

(a) SINGLE person (including head of household)—

If the amount of wages (after subtracting withholding allowances) is: Not over $1,125 . . . . The amount of income tax to withhold is: $0

Over—	But not over—		of excess over—
$1,125	—$5,763 . .	$0.00 plus 10%	—$1,125
$5,763	—$19,950 . .	$463.80 plus 15%	—$5,763
$19,950	—$46,700 . .	$2,591.85 plus 25%	—$19,950
$46,700	—$96,200 . .	$9,279.35 plus 28%	—$46,700
$96,200	—$207,800 . .	$23,139.35 plus 33%	—$96,200
$207,800	—$208,650 . .	$59,967.35 plus 35%	—$207,800
$208,650		$60,264.85 plus 39.6%	—$208,650

(b) MARRIED person—

If the amount of wages (after subtracting withholding allowances) is: Not over $4,275 . . . . The amount of income tax to withhold is: $0

Over—	But not over—		of excess over—
$4,275	—$13,550 . .	$0.00 plus 10%	—$4,275
$13,550	—$41,925 . .	$927.50 plus 15%	—$13,550
$41,925	—$80,225 . .	$5,183.75 plus 25%	—$41,925
$80,225	—$120,000 . .	$14,758.75 plus 28%	—$80,225
$120,000	—$210,950 . .	$25,895.75 plus 33%	—$120,000
$210,950	—$237,750 . .	$55,909.25 plus 35%	—$210,950
$237,750		$65,289.25 plus 39.6%	—$237,750

TABLE 7—ANNUAL Payroll Period

(a) SINGLE person (including head of household)—

If the amount of wages (after subtracting withholding allowances) is: Not over $2,250 . . . . The amount of income tax to withhold is: $0

Over—	But not over—		of excess over—
$2,250	—$11,525 . .	$0.00 plus 10%	—$2,250
$11,525	—$39,900 . .	$927.50 plus 15%	—$11,525
$39,900	—$93,400 . .	$5,183.75 plus 25%	—$39,900
$93,400	—$192,400 . .	$18,558.75 plus 28%	—$93,400
$192,400	—$415,600 . .	$46,278.75 plus 33%	—$192,400
$415,600	—$417,300 . .	$119,934.75 plus 35%	—$415,600
$417,300		$120,529.75 plus 39.6%	—$417,300

(b) MARRIED person—

If the amount of wages (after subtracting withholding allowances) is: Not over $8,550 . . . . The amount of income tax to withhold is: $0

Over—	But not over—		of excess over—
$8,550	—$27,100 . .	$0.00 plus 10%	—$8,550
$27,100	—$83,850 . .	$1,855.00 plus 15%	—$27,100
$83,850	—$160,450 . .	$10,367.50 plus 25%	—$83,850
$160,450	—$240,000 . .	$29,517.50 plus 28%	—$160,450
$240,000	—$421,900 . .	$51,791.50 plus 33%	—$240,000
$421,900	—$475,500 . .	$111,818.50 plus 35%	—$421,900
$475,500		$130,578.50 plus 39.6%	—$475,500

TABLE 8—DAILY or MISCELLANEOUS Payroll Period

(a) SINGLE person (including head of household)—

If the amount of wages (after subtracting withholding allowances) divided by the number of days in the payroll period is: Not over $8.70 . . . . The amount of income tax to withhold per day is: $0

Over—	But not over—		of excess over—
$8.70	—$44.30 . .	$0.00 plus 10%	—$8.70
$44.30	—$153.50 . .	$3.56 plus 15%	—$44.30
$153.50	—$359.20 . .	$19.94 plus 25%	—$153.50
$359.20	—$740.00 . .	$71.37 plus 28%	—$359.20
$740.00	—$1,598.50 . .	$177.99 plus 33%	—$740.00
$1,598.50	—$1,605.00 . .	$461.30 plus 35%	—$1,598.50
$1,605.00		$463.58 plus 39.6%	—$1,605.00

(b) MARRIED person—

If the amount of wages (after subtracting withholding allowances) divided by the number of days in the payroll period is: Not over $32.90 . . . . The amount of income tax to withhold per day is: $0

Over—	But not over—		of excess over—
$32.90	—$104.20 . .	$0.00 plus 10%	—$32.90
$104.20	—$322.50 . .	$7.13 plus 15%	—$104.20
$322.50	—$617.10 . .	$39.88 plus 25%	—$322.50
$617.10	—$923.10 . .	$113.53 plus 28%	—$617.10
$923.10	—$1,622.70 . .	$199.21 plus 33%	—$923.10
$1,622.70	—$1,828.80 . .	$430.08 plus 35%	—$1,622.70
$1,828.80		$502.22 plus 39.6%	—$1,828.80

Publication 15 (2016)

Table 11-1: Sequential Numbers for Dates of the Year

Day of Month	JAN	FEB	MAR	APR	MAY	JUN	JUL	AUG	SEP	OCT	NOV	DEC
1	1	30	60	91	121	152	182	213	244	274	305	335
2	2	33	61	92	122	153	183	214	245	275	306	336
3	3	34	62	93	123	154	184	215	246	276	307	337
4	4	35	63	94	124	155	185	216	247	277	308	338
5	5	36	64	95	125	156	186	217	248	278	309	339
6	6	37	65	96	126	157	187	218	249	279	310	340
7	7	38	66	97	127	158	188	219	250	280	311	341
8	8	39	67	98	128	159	189	220	251	281	312	342
9	9	40	68	99	129	160	190	221	252	282	313	343
10	10	41	69	100	130	161	191	222	253	283	314	344
11	11	42	70	101	131	162	192	223	254	284	315	345
12	12	43	71	102	132	163	193	224	255	285	316	346
13	13	44	72	103	133	164	194	225	256	286	317	347
14	14	45	73	104	134	165	195	226	257	287	318	348
15	15	46	74	105	135	166	196	227	258	288	319	349
16	16	47	75	106	136	167	197	228	259	289	320	350
17	17	48	76	107	137	168	198	229	260	290	321	351
18	18	49	77	108	138	169	199	230	261	291	322	352
19	19	50	78	109	139	170	200	231	262	292	323	353
20	20	51	79	110	140	171	201	232	263	293	324	354
21	21	52	80	111	141	172	202	233	264	294	325	355
22	22	53	81	112	142	173	203	234	265	295	326	356
23	23	54	82	113	143	174	204	235	266	296	327	357
24	24	55	83	114	144	175	205	236	267	297	328	358
25	25	56	84	115	145	176	206	237	268	298	329	359
26	26	57	85	116	146	177	207	238	269	299	330	360
27	27	58	86	117	147	178	208	239	270	300	331	361
28	28	59	87	118	148	179	209	240	271	301	332	362
29	29	*	88	119	149	180	210	241	272	302	333	363
30	30		89	120	150	181	211	242	273	303	334	364
31	31		90		151		212	243		304		365

For leap years, add one to each sequential number AFTER February 28. For centennial years (those at the turn of the century), leap years occur only when the number of the year is divisable by 400. Thus, year 2000 was a leap year (2000/400 divides exactly), but 1700, 1800 and 1900 were not leap years.

Number of Monthly Payments	APR (Annual Percentage Rate)							
	10.00%	10.25%	10.50%	10.75%	11.00%	11.25%	11.50%	11.75%
1	0.83	0.85	0.87	0.90	0.92	0.94	0.96	0.98
2	1.25	1.28	1.31	1.35	1.38	1.41	1.44	1.47
3	1.67	1.71	1.76	1.80	1.84	1.88	1.92	1.96
4	2.09	2.14	2.20	2.25	2.30	2.35	2.41	2.46
5	2.51	2.58	2.64	2.70	2.77	2.83	2.89	2.96
6	2.94	3.01	3.08	3.16	3.23	3.31	3.38	3.45
7	3.36	3.45	3.53	3.62	3.70	3.78	3.87	3.95
8	3.79	3.88	3.98	4.07	4.17	4.26	4.36	4.46
9	4.21	4.32	4.43	4.53	4.64	4.75	4.85	4.96
10	4.64	4.76	4.88	4.99	5.11	5.23	5.35	5.46
11	5.07	5.20	5.33	5.45	5.58	5.71	5.84	5.97
12	5.50	5.64	5.78	5.92	6.06	6.20	6.34	6.48
13	5.93	6.08	6.23	6.38	6.53	6.68	6.84	6.99
14	6.36	6.52	6.69	6.85	7.01	7.17	7.34	7.50
15	6.80	6.97	7.14	7.32	7.49	7.66	7.84	8.01
16	7.23	7.41	7.60	7.78	7.97	8.15	8.34	8.53
17	7.67	7.86	8.06	8.25	8.45	8.65	8.84	9.04
18	8.10	8.31	8.52	8.73	8.93	9.14	9.35	9.56
19	8.54	8.76	8.98	9.20	9.42	9.64	9.86	10.08
20	8.98	9.21	9.44	9.67	9.90	10.13	10.37	10.60
21	9.42	9.66	9.90	10.15	10.39	10.63	10.88	11.12
22	9.86	10.12	10.37	10.62	10.88	11.13	11.39	11.64
23	10.30	10.57	10.84	11.10	11.37	11.63	11.90	12.17
24	10.75	11.02	11.30	11.58	11.86	12.14	12.42	12.70
25	11.19	11.48	11.77	12.06	12.35	12.64	12.93	13.22
26	11.64	11.94	12.24	12.54	12.85	13.15	13.45	13.75
27	12.09	12.40	12.71	13.03	13.34	13.66	13.97	14.29
28	12.53	12.86	13.18	13.51	13.84	14.16	14.49	14.82
29	12.98	13.32	13.66	14.00	14.33	14.67	15.01	15.35
30	13.43	13.78	14.13	14.48	14.83	15.19	15.54	15.89
31	13.89	14.25	14.61	14.97	15.33	15.70	16.06	16.43
32	14.34	14.71	15.09	15.46	15.84	16.21	16.59	16.97
33	14.79	15.18	15.57	15.95	16.34	16.73	17.12	17.51
34	15.25	15.65	16.05	16.44	16.85	17.25	17.65	18.05
35	15.70	16.11	16.53	16.94	17.35	17.77	18.18	18.60
36	16.16	16.58	17.01	17.43	17.86	18.29	18.71	19.14
37	16.62	17.06	17.49	17.93	18.37	18.81	19.25	19.69
38	17.08	17.53	17.98	18.43	18.88	19.33	19.78	20.24
39	17.54	18.00	18.46	18.93	19.39	19.86	20.32	20.79
40	18.00	18.48	18.95	19.43	19.90	20.38	20.86	21.34
41	18.47	18.95	19.44	19.93	20.42	20.91	21.40	21.89
42	18.93	19.43	19.93	20.43	20.93	21.44	21.94	22.45
43	19.40	19.91	20.42	20.94	21.45	21.97	22.49	23.01
44	19.86	20.39	20.91	21.44	21.97	22.50	23.03	23.57
45	20.33	20.87	21.41	21.95	22.49	23.03	23.58	24.12
46	20.80	21.35	21.90	22.46	23.01	23.57	24.13	24.69
47	21.27	21.83	22.40	22.79	23.53	24.10	24.68	25.25
48	21.74	22.32	22.90	23.48	24.06	24.64	25.23	25.81
49	22.21	22.80	23.39	23.99	24.58	25.18	25.78	26.38
50	22.69	23.29	23.89	24.50	25.11	25.72	26.33	26.95
51	23.16	23.78	24.40	25.02	25.64	26.26	26.89	27.52
52	23.64	24.27	24.90	25.53	26.17	26.81	27.45	28.09
53	24.11	24.76	25.40	26.05	26.70	27.35	28.00	28.66
54	24.59	25.25	25.91	26.57	27.23	27.90	28.56	29.23
55	25.07	25.74	26.41	27.09	27.77	28.44	29.13	29.81
56	25.55	26.23	26.92	27.61	28.30	28.99	29.69	30.39
57	26.03	26.73	27.43	28.13	28.84	29.54	30.25	30.97
58	26.51	27.23	27.94	28.66	29.37	30.10	30.82	31.55
59	27.00	27.72	28.45	29.18	29.91	30.65	31.39	32.13
60	27.48	28.22	28.96	29.71	30.45	31.20	31.96	32.71

Number of Monthly Payments	APR (Annual Percentage Rate)							
	12.00%	**12.25%**	**12.50%**	**12.75%**	**13.00%**	**13.25%**	**13.50%**	**13.75%**
1	1.00	1.02	1.04	1.06	1.08	1.10	1.12	1.15
2	1.50	1.53	1.57	1.60	1.63	1.66	1.69	1.72
3	2.01	2.05	2.09	2.13	2.17	2.22	2.26	2.30
4	2.51	2.57	2.62	2.67	2.72	2.78	2.83	2.88
5	3.02	3.08	3.15	3.21	3.27	3.34	3.40	3.46
6	3.53	3.60	3.68	3.75	3.83	3.90	3.97	4.05
7	4.04	4.12	4.21	4.29	4.38	4.47	4.55	4.64
8	4.55	4.65	4.74	4.84	4.94	5.03	5.13	5.22
9	5.07	5.17	5.28	5.39	5.49	5.60	5.71	5.82
10	5.58	5.70	5.82	5.94	6.05	6.17	6.29	6.41
11	6.10	6.23	6.36	6.49	6.62	6.75	6.88	7.01
12	6.62	6.76	6.90	7.04	7.18	7.32	7.46	7.60
13	7.14	7.29	7.44	7.59	7.75	7.90	8.05	8.20
14	7.66	7.82	7.99	8.15	8.31	8.48	8.64	8.81
15	8.19	8.36	8.53	8.71	8.88	9.06	9.23	9.41
16	8.71	8.90	9.08	9.27	9.46	9.64	8.98	10.02
17	9.24	9.44	9.63	9.83	10.03	10.23	10.44	10.63
18	9.77	9.98	10.19	10.40	10.61	10.82	11.03	11.24
19	10.30	10.52	10.74	10.96	11.18	11.41	11.63	11.85
20	10.83	11.06	11.30	11.53	11.76	12.00	12.23	12.46
21	11.36	11.61	11.85	12.10	12.34	12.59	12.84	13.08
22	11.90	12.16	12.41	12.67	12.93	13.19	13.44	13.70
23	12.44	12.71	12.97	13.24	13.51	13.78	14.05	14.32
24	12.98	13.26	13.54	13.82	14.10	14.38	14.66	14.95
25	13.52	13.81	14.10	14.40	14.69	14.98	15.28	15.57
26	14.06	14.36	14.67	14.97	15.28	15.59	15.89	16.20
27	14.60	14.92	15.24	15.56	15.87	16.19	16.51	16.83
28	15.15	15.48	15.81	16.14	16.47	16.80	17.13	17.46
29	15.70	16.04	16.38	16.72	17.07	17.41	17.75	18.10
30	16.24	16.60	16.95	17.31	17.66	18.02	18.38	18.74
31	16.79	17.16	17.53	17.90	18.27	18.63	19.00	19.38
32	17.35	17.73	18.11	18.49	18.87	19.25	19.63	20.02
33	17.90	18.29	18.69	19.08	19.47	19.87	20.26	20.66
34	18.46	18.86	19.27	19.67	20.08	20.49	20.90	21.31
35	19.01	19.43	19.85	20.27	20.69	21.11	21.53	21.95
36	19.57	20.00	20.43	20.87	21.30	21.73	22.17	22.60
37	20.13	20.58	21.02	21.46	21.91	22.36	22.81	23.25
38	20.69	21.15	21.61	22.07	22.52	22.99	23.45	23.91
39	21.26	21.73	22.20	22.67	23.14	23.61	24.09	24.56
40	21.82	22.30	22.79	23.27	23.70	24.25	24.73	25.22
41	22.39	22.88	23.38	23.88	24.38	24.88	25.38	25.88
42	22.96	23.47	23.98	24.49	25.00	25.51	26.03	26.55
43	23.53	24.05	24.57	25.10	25.62	26.15	26.68	27.21
44	24.10	24.64	25.17	25.71	26.25	26.79	27.33	27.88
45	24.67	25.22	25.77	26.32	26.88	27.43	27.99	28.55
46	25.25	25.81	26.37	26.94	27.51	28.08	28.65	29.22
47	25.82	26.40	26.98	27.56	28.14	28.72	29.31	29.89
48	26.40	26.99	27.58	28.18	28.77	29.37	29.97	30.57
49	26.98	27.59	28.19	28.80	29.41	30.02	30.63	31.24
50	27.56	28.18	28.80	29.42	30.04	30.67	31.29	31.92
51	28.15	28.78	29.41	30.05	30.68	31.32	31.96	32.60
52	28.73	29.38	30.02	30.67	31.32	31.98	32.63	33.29
53	29.32	29.98	30.64	31.30	31.97	32.63	33.30	33.97
54	29.91	30.58	31.25	31.93	32.61	33.29	33.98	34.66
55	30.50	31.18	31.87	32.56	33.26	33.95	34.65	35.35
56	31.09	31.79	32.49	33.20	33.91	34.62	35.33	36.04
57	31.68	32.39	33.11	33.83	34.56	35.28	36.01	36.74
58	32.27	33.00	33.74	34.47	35.21	35.95	36.69	37.43
59	32.87	33.61	34.36	25.11	35.86	36.62	37.37	38.13
60	33.47	34.23	44.99	35.75	36.52	37.29	38.06	38.83

Number of Monthly Payments	APR (Annual Percentage Rate)							
	14.00%	**14.25%**	**14.50%**	**14.75%**	**15.00%**	**15.25%**	**15.50%**	**15.75%**
1	1.17	1.19	1.21	1.23	1.25	1.27	1.29	1.31
2	1.75	1.78	1.82	1.85	1.88	1.91	1.94	1.97
3	2.34	2.38	2.43	2.47	2.51	2.55	2.59	2.64
4	2.93	2.99	3.04	3.09	3.14	3.20	3.25	3.30
5	3.53	3.59	3.65	3.72	3.78	3.84	3.91	3.97
6	4.12	4.20	4.27	4.35	4.42	4.49	4.57	4.64
7	4.72	4.81	4.89	4.98	5.06	5.15	5.23	5.32
8	5.32	5.42	5.51	5.61	5.71	5.80	5.90	6.00
9	5.92	6.03	6.14	6.25	6.35	6.46	6.57	6.68
10	6.53	6.65	6.77	6.88	7.00	7.12	7.24	7.36
11	7.14	7.27	7.40	7.53	7.66	7.79	7.92	8.05
12	7.74	7.89	8.03	8.17	8.31	8.45	8.59	8.74
13	8.36	8.51	8.66	8.81	8.97	9.12	9.27	9.43
14	8.97	9.13	9.30	9.46	9.63	9.79	9.96	10.12
15	9.59	9.76	9.94	10.11	10.29	10.47	10.64	10.82
16	10.20	10.39	10.58	10.77	10.95	11.14	11.33	11.52
17	10.82	11.02	11.22	11.42	11.62	11.82	12.02	12.22
18	11.45	11.66	11.87	12.08	12.29	12.50	12.72	12.93
19	12.07	12.30	12.52	12.74	12.97	13.19	13.41	13.64
20	12.70	12.93	13.17	13.41	13.64	13.88	14.11	14.35
21	13.33	13.58	13.82	14.07	14.32	14.57	14.82	15.06
22	13.96	14.22	14.48	14.74	15.00	15.26	15.52	15.78
23	14.59	14.87	15.14	15.41	15.68	15.96	16.23	16.50
24	15.23	15.51	15.80	16.08	16.37	16.65	16.94	17.22
25	15.87	16.17	16.46	16.76	17.06	17.35	17.65	17.95
26	16.51	16.82	17.13	17.44	17.75	18.06	18.37	18.68
27	17.15	17.47	17.80	18.12	18.44	18.76	19.09	19.41
28	17.80	18.13	18.47	18.80	19.14	19.47	19.81	20.15
29	18.45	18.79	19.14	19.49	19.83	20.18	20.53	20.88
30	19.10	19.45	19.81	20.17	20.54	20.90	21.26	21.62
31	19.75	20.12	20.49	20.87	21.24	21.61	21.99	22.37
32	20.40	20.79	21.17	21.56	21.95	22.33	22.72	23.11
33	21.06	21.46	21.85	22.25	22.65	23.06	23.46	23.86
34	21.72	22.13	22.54	22.95	23.37	23.78	24.19	24.61
35	22.38	22.80	23.23	23.65	24.08	24.51	24.94	25.36
36	23.04	23.48	23.92	24.35	24.80	25.24	25.68	26.12
37	23.70	24.16	24.69	25.06	25.51	25.97	26.42	26.88
38	24.37	24.84	25.30	25.77	26.24	26.70	27.17	27.64
39	25.04	25.52	26.00	26.48	26.96	27.44	27.92	28.41
40	25.71	26.20	26.70	27.19	27.69	28.18	28.68	29.18
41	26.39	26.89	27.40	27.91	28.41	28.92	29.44	29.95
42	27.06	27.58	28.10	28.62	29.15	29.67	30.19	30.72
43	27.74	28.27	28.81	29.34	29.88	30.42	30.96	31.50
44	28.42	28.97	29.52	30.07	30.62	31.17	31.72	32.28
45	29.11	29.67	30.23	30.79	31.36	31.92	32.49	33.06
46	29.79	30.36	30.94	31.52	32.10	32.68	33.26	33.84
47	30.48	31.07	31.66	32.25	32.84	33.44	34.03	34.63
48	31.17	31.77	32.37	32.98	33.59	34.20	34.81	35.42
49	31.86	32.48	33.09	33.71	34.34	34.96	35.59	36.21
50	32.55	33.18	33.82	34.45	35.09	35.73	36.37	37.01
51	33.25	33.89	34.54	35.19	35.84	36.49	37.15	37.81
52	33.95	34.61	35.27	35.93	36.60	37.27	37.94	38.61
53	34.65	35.32	36.00	36.68	37.36	38.04	38.72	39.41
54	35.35	36.04	36.73	37.42	38.12	38.82	39.52	40.22
55	36.05	36.76	37.46	38.17	38.88	39.60	40.31	41.03
56	36.76	37.48	38.20	38.92	39.65	40.38	41.11	41.84
57	37.47	38.20	38.94	39.68	40.42	41.16	41.91	42.65
58	38.18	38.93	39.68	40.43	41.19	41.95	42.71	43.47
59	38.89	39.66	40.42	41.19	41.96	42.74	43.51	44.29
60	39.61	40.39	41.17	41.95	42.74	43.53	44.32	45.11

Number of Monthly Payments	APR (Annual Percentage Rate)							
	16.00%	16.25%	16.50%	16.75%	17.00%	17.25%	17.50%	17.75%
1	1.33	1.35	1.37	1.40	1.42	1.44	1.46	1.48
2	2.00	2.04	2.07	2.10	2.13	2.16	2.17	2.22
3	2.68	2.72	2.76	2.80	2.85	2.89	2.93	2.97
4	3.36	3.41	3.46	3.51	3.57	3.62	3.67	3.73
5	4.04	4.10	4.16	4.23	4.29	4.35	4.42	4.48
6	4.72	4.79	4.87	4.94	5.02	5.01	5.17	5.24
7	5.40	5.49	5.58	5.66	5.75	5.83	5.92	6.00
8	6.09	6.19	6.29	6.38	6.48	6.58	6.67	6.77
9	6.78	6.89	7.00	7.11	7.22	7.32	7.43	7.54
10	7.48	7.60	7.72	7.84	7.96	8.08	8.19	8.31
11	8.18	8.31	8.44	8.57	8.70	8.83	8.96	9.09
12	8.88	9.02	9.16	9.30	9.45	9.59	9.73	9.87
13	9.58	9.73	9.89	10.04	10.20	10.35	10.50	10.66
14	10.29	10.45	10.67	10.78	10.95	11.11	11.28	11.45
15	11.00	11.17	11.35	11.53	11.71	11.88	12.06	12.24
16	11.71	11.90	12.09	12.28	12.46	12.65	12.84	13.03
17	12.42	12.62	12.83	13.03	13.23	13.43	13.63	13.83
18	13.14	13.35	13.57	13.78	13.99	14.21	14.42	14.64
19	13.86	14.09	14.31	14.54	14.76	14.99	15.22	15.44
20	14.59	14.82	15.06	15.30	15.54	15.77	16.01	16.25
21	15.31	15.56	15.81	16.06	16.31	16.56	16.81	17.07
22	16.04	16.30	16.57	16.83	17.09	17.36	17.62	17.88
23	16.78	17.00	17.32	17.60	17.88	18.15	18.43	18.70
24	17.51	17.80	18.09	18.37	18.66	18.95	19.24	19.53
25	18.25	18.55	18.85	19.15	19.45	19.75	20.05	20.36
26	18.99	19.30	19.62	19.93	20.24	20.56	20.87	21.19
27	19.74	20.06	20.39	20.71	21.04	21.37	21.69	22.02
28	20.48	20.82	21.16	21.50	21.84	22.18	22.52	22.86
29	21.23	21.58	21.94	22.29	22.64	22.99	23.35	23.70
30	21.99	22.35	22.72	23.08	23.45	23.81	24.18	24.55
31	22.74	23.12	23.50	23.88	24.26	24.64	25.02	25.40
32	23.50	23.89	24.28	24.68	25.07	25.46	25.86	26.25
33	24.26	24.67	25.07	25.48	25.88	26.29	26.70	27.11
34	25.03	25.44	25.86	26.28	26.70	27.12	27.54	27.97
35	25.79	26.23	26.66	27.09	27.52	27.96	28.39	28.83
36	26.57	27.01	27.46	27.90	28.35	28.80	29.25	29.70
37	27.34	27.80	28.26	28.72	29.18	29.64	30.10	30.57
38	28.11	28.59	29.06	29.53	30.01	30.49	30.96	31.44
39	28.89	29.38	29.87	30.36	30.85	31.34	31.83	32.32
40	29.68	30.18	30.68	31.18	31.68	32.19	32.69	33.20
41	30.46	30.97	31.49	32.01	32.52	33.04	33.56	34.08
42	31.25	31.78	32.31	32.84	33.37	33.90	34.44	34.97
43	32.04	32.58	33.13	33.67	34.22	34.76	35.31	35.86
44	32.83	33.39	33.95	34.51	35.07	35.63	36.19	36.78
45	33.63	34.20	34.77	35.35	35.92	36.50	37.08	37.66
46	34.43	35.01	35.60	36.19	36.78	37.37	37.96	38.56
47	35.23	35.83	36.43	37.04	37.64	38.25	38.86	39.46
48	36.03	36.65	37.27	37.88	38.50	39.13	39.75	40.37
49	36.84	37.47	38.10	38.74	39.37	40.01	40.65	41.29
50	37.65	38.30	38.94	39.59	40.24	40.89	41.55	42.20
51	38.46	39.17	39.79	40.45	41.11	41.78	42.45	43.12
52	39.28	39.96	40.63	41.31	41.99	42.67	43.36	44.04
53	40.10	40.79	41.48	42.17	42.87	43.57	44.27	44.97
54	40.92	41.63	42.33	43.04	43.75	44.47	45.18	45.90
55	41.74	42.47	43.19	43.91	44.64	45.37	46.10	46.83
56	42.57	43.31	44.05	44.79	45.53	46.27	47.02	47.77
57	43.40	44.15	44.91	45.66	46.42	47.18	47.97	47.71
58	44.23	45.00	45.77	46.54	47.32	48.09	48.87	49.65
59	45.07	45.85	46.64	47.42	48.21	49.01	49.80	50.60
60	45.91	46.71	47.51	48.31	49.12	49.92	50.70	51.55

Number of Monthly	APR (Annual Percentage Rate)							
Payments	**18.00%**	**18.25%**	**18.50%**	**18.75%**	**19.00%**	**19.25%**	**19.50%**	**19.75%**
1	1.50	1.52	1.54	1.56	1.58	1.60	1.62	1.65
2	2.26	2.29	2.32	2.35	2.38	2.41	2.44	2.48
3	3.01	3.06	3.10	3.14	3.18	3.23	3.27	3.31
4	3.78	3.83	3.88	3.94	3.99	4.04	4.10	4.15
5	4.54	4.61	4.67	4.74	4.80	4.86	4.93	4.99
6	5.32	5.39	5.46	5.54	5.61	5.69	5.76	5.84
7	6.09	6.18	6.26	6.35	6.43	6.52	6.60	6.69
8	6.87	6.96	7.06	7.16	7.26	7.35	7.45	7.55
9	7.65	7.76	7.87	7.97	8.08	8.19	8.30	8.41
10	8.43	8.55	8.67	8.79	8.91	9.03	9.15	9.27
11	9.22	9.35	9.49	9.62	9.75	9.88	10.01	10.14
12	10.02	10.16	10.30	10.44	10.59	10.73	10.87	11.02
13	10.81	10.97	11.12	11.28	11.43	11.59	11.74	11.90
14	11.61	11.78	11.95	12.11	12.28	12.45	12.61	12.78
15	12.42	12.59	12.77	12.95	13.13	13.31	13.49	13.67
16	13.22	13.41	13.60	13.80	13.99	14.18	14.37	14.56
17	14.04	14.24	14.44	14.64	14.85	15.05	15.25	15.46
18	14.85	15.07	15.28	15.49	15.71	15.93	16.14	16.36
19	15.67	15.90	16.12	16.35	16.58	16.81	17.03	17.26
20	16.49	16.73	16.97	17.21	17.45	17.69	17.93	18.17
21	17.32	17.57	17.82	18.07	18.33	18.58	18.83	19.09
22	18.15	18.41	18.68	18.94	19.21	19.47	19.74	20.01
23	18.98	19.26	19.54	19.81	20.09	20.37	20.65	20.93
24	19.82	20.11	20.40	20.69	20.98	21.27	21.56	21.86
25	20.66	20.96	21.27	21.57	21.87	22.18	22.48	22.79
26	21.50	21.82	22.14	22.45	22.77	23.09	23.41	23.73
27	22.35	22.68	23.01	23.44	23.67	24.00	24.33	24.67
28	23.20	23.55	23.89	24.23	24.58	24.92	25.27	25.61
29	24.06	24.41	24.27	25.13	25.49	25.84	26.20	26.56
30	24.92	25.29	25.66	26.03	26.40	26.77	27.14	27.52
31	25.78	26.16	26.55	26.93	27.32	27.70	28.09	28.47
32	26.65	27.04	27.44	27.84	28.24	28.64	29.04	29.44
33	27.52	27.93	28.34	28.75	29.16	29.57	29.99	30.40
34	28.39	28.81	29.24	29.66	30.09	30.52	30.95	31.37
35	29.27	29.71	30.14	30.58	31.02	31.47	31.91	32.35
36	30.15	30.60	31.05	31.51	31.96	32.42	32.87	33.33
37	31.03	31.50	31.97	32.43	32.90	33.37	33.84	34.32
38	31.92	32.40	32.88	33.37	33.85	34.33	34.82	35.30
39	32.81	33.31	33.80	34.30	34.80	35.30	35.80	36.30
40	33.71	34.22	34.73	35.24	35.75	36.26	36.78	37.29
41	34.61	35.13	35.66	36.18	36.71	37.24	37.77	38.30
42	35.51	36.05	36.59	37.13	37.67	38.21	38.76	39.30
43	36.42	36.97	37.52	38.08	38.63	39.19	39.75	40.31
44	37.33	37.89	38.46	39.03	39.60	40.18	40.75	41.33
45	38.24	38.82	39.41	39.99	40.58	41.17	41.75	42.35
46	39.16	39.75	40.35	40.95	41.55	42.16	42.76	43.37
47	40.08	40.69	41.30	41.92	42.54	43.15	43.77	44.40
48	41.00	41.63	42.26	42.89	43.52	44.15	44.79	45.43
49	41.93	42.57	43.22	43.86	44.51	45.16	45.81	46.46
50	42.86	43.52	44.18	44.84	45.50	46.17	46.83	47.50
51	43.79	44.47	45.14	45.82	46.50	47.18	47.86	48.55
52	44.73	45.42	46.11	46.80	47.50	48.20	48.89	49.59
53	45.67	46.38	47.08	47.79	48.50	49.22	49.93	50.65
54	46.62	47.34	48.06	48.79	49.51	50.24	50.97	51.70
55	47.57	48.30	49.04	49.78	50.52	51.27	52.02	52.76
56	48.52	49.27	50.03	50.78	51.54	52.30	53.06	53.83
57	49.47	50.24	51.01	51.79	52.56	53.34	54.12	54.90
58	50.43	51.22	52.00	52.79	53.58	54.38	55.17	55.97
59	51.39	52.20	53.00	53.80	54.61	55.42	56.23	57.05
60	52.36	53.18	54.00	54.82	55.64	56.47	57.30	58.13

Table 12-2: Sum-of-Digits for Numbers 1 to N*
(for Determining Interest Rebate Using the Rule of 78)

N	Sum of Digits	N	Sum of Digits	N	Sum of Digits	N	Sum of Digits
1	1	16	136	31	496	46	1,081
2	3	17	153	32	528	47	1,128
3	6	18	171	33	561	48	1,176
4	10	19	190	34	595	49	1,225
5	15	20	210	35	630	50	1,275
6	21	21	231	36	666	51	1,326
7	28	22	253	37	703	52	1,378
8	36	23	276	38	741	53	1,431
9	45	24	300	39	780	54	1,485
10	55	25	325	40	820	55	1,540
11	66	26	351	41	861	56	1,596
12	78	27	378	42	903	57	1,653
13	91	28	406	43	946	58	1,711
14	105	29	435	44	990	59	1,770
15	120	30	465	45	1,035	60	1,830

*Sum of Digits = $(N * (N + 1))/2$

	Rate per Period						
Periods	**0.25%**	**0.50%**	**0.75%**	**1.00%**	**1.25%**	**1.50%**	**1.75%**
1	1.00250	1.00500	1.00750	1.01000	1.01250	1.01500	1.01750
2	1.00501	1.01003	1.01506	1.02010	1.02516	1.03023	1.03531
3	1.00752	1.01508	1.02267	1.03030	1.03797	1.04568	1.05342
4	1.01004	1.02015	1.03034	1.04060	1.05095	1.06136	1.07186
5	1.01256	1.02525	1.03807	1.05101	1.06408	1.07728	1.09062
6	1.01509	1.03038	1.04585	1.06152	1.07738	1.09344	1.10970
7	1.01763	1.03553	1.05370	1.07214	1.09085	1.10984	1.12912
8	1.02018	1.04071	1.06160	1.08286	1.10449	1.12649	1.14888
9	1.02273	1.04591	1.06956	1.09369	1.11829	1.14339	1.16899
10	1.02528	1.05114	1.07758	1.10462	1.13227	1.16054	1.18944
11	1.02785	1.05640	1.08566	1.11567	1.14642	1.17795	1.21026
12	1.03042	1.06168	1.09381	1.12683	1.16075	1.19562	1.23144
13	1.03299	1.06699	1.10201	1.13809	1.17526	1.21355	1.25299
14	1.03557	1.07232	1.11028	1.14947	1.18995	1.23176	1.27492
15	1.03816	1.07768	1.11860	1.16097	1.20483	1.25023	1.29723
16	1.04076	1.08307	1.12699	1.17258	1.21989	1.26899	1.31993
17	1.04336	1.08849	1.13544	1.18430	1.23514	1.28802	1.34303
18	1.04597	1.09393	1.14396	1.19615	1.25058	1.30734	1.36653
19	1.04858	1.09940	1.15254	1.20811	1.26621	1.32695	1.39045
20	1.05121	1.10490	1.16118	1.22019	1.28204	1.34686	1.41478
21	1.05383	1.11042	1.16989	1.23239	1.29806	1.36706	1.43954
22	1.05647	1.11597	1.17867	1.24472	1.31429	1.38756	1.46473
23	1.05911	1.12155	1.18751	1.25716	1.33072	1.40838	1.49036
24	1.06176	1.12716	1.19641	1.26973	1.34735	1.42950	1.51644
25	1.06441	1.13280	1.20539	1.28243	1.36419	1.45095	1.54298
26	1.06707	1.13846	1.21443	1.29526	1.38125	1.47271	1.56998
27	1.06974	1.14415	1.22354	1.30821	1.39851	1.49480	1.59746
28	1.07241	1.14987	1.23271	1.32129	1.41599	1.51722	1.62541
29	1.07510	1.15562	1.24196	1.33450	1.43369	1.53998	1.65386
30	1.07778	1.16140	1.25127	1.34785	1.45161	1.56308	1.68280
35	1.09132	1.19073	1.29890	1.41660	1.54464	1.68388	1.83529
40	1.10503	1.22079	1.34835	1.48886	1.64362	1.81402	2.00160
45	1.11892	1.25162	1.39968	1.56481	1.74895	1.95421	2.18298
50	1.13297	1.28323	1.45296	1.64463	1.86102	2.10524	2.38079
55	1.14720	1.31563	1.50827	1.72852	1.98028	2.26794	2.59653
60	1.16162	1.34885	1.56568	1.81670	2.10718	2.44322	2.83182
65	1.17621	1.38291	1.62528	1.90937	2.24221	2.63204	3.08843
70	1.19099	1.41783	1.68715	2.00676	2.38590	2.83546	3.36829
75	1.20595	1.45363	1.75137	2.10913	2.53879	3.05459	3.67351
80	1.22110	1.49034	1.81804	2.21672	2.70148	3.29066	4.00639
85	1.23644	1.52797	1.88725	2.32979	2.87460	3.54498	4.36944
90	1.25197	1.56655	1.95909	2.44863	3.05881	3.81895	4.76538
95	1.26770	1.60611	2.03367	2.57354	3.25483	4.11409	5.19720
100	1.28362	1.64667	2.11108	2.70481	3.46340	4.43205	5.66816

Table shows future value (FV) of $1 compounded for N periods at R rate per period.
Table values can be generated using the formula: FV = $1 * (1 + R) ^N.

	Rate per Period					
Periods	**2.00%**	**2.25%**	**2.50%**	**2.75%**	**3.00%**	**3.25%**
1	1.02000	1.02250	1.02500	1.02750	1.03000	1.03250
2	1.04040	1.04551	1.05063	1.05576	1.06090	1.06606
3	1.06121	1.06903	1.07689	1.08479	1.09273	1.10070
4	1.08243	1.09308	1.10381	1.11462	1.12551	1.13648
5	1.10408	1.11768	1.13141	1.14527	1.15927	1.17341
6	1.12616	1.14283	1.15969	1.17677	1.19405	1.21155
7	1.14869	1.16854	1.18869	1.20913	1.22987	1.25092
8	1.17166	1.19483	1.21840	1.24238	1.26677	1.29158
9	1.19509	1.22171	1.24886	1.27655	1.30477	1.33355
10	1.21899	1.24920	1.28008	1.31165	1.34392	1.37689
11	1.24337	1.27731	1.31209	1.34772	1.38423	1.42164
12	1.26824	1.30605	1.34489	1.38478	1.42576	1.46785
13	1.29361	1.33544	1.37851	1.42287	1.46853	1.51555
14	1.31948	1.36548	1.41297	1.46199	1.51259	1.56481
15	1.34587	1.39621	1.44830	1.50220	1.55797	1.61566
16	1.37279	1.42762	1.48451	1.54351	1.60471	1.66817
17	1.40024	1.45974	1.52162	1.58596	1.65285	1.72239
18	1.42825	1.49259	1.55966	1.62957	1.70243	1.77837
19	1.45681	1.52617	1.59865	1.67438	1.75351	1.83616
20	1.48595	1.56051	1.63862	1.72043	1.80611	1.89584
21	1.51567	1.59562	1.67958	1.76774	1.86029	1.95745
22	1.54598	1.63152	1.72157	1.81635	1.91610	2.02107
23	1.57690	1.66823	1.76461	1.86630	1.97359	2.08675
24	1.60844	1.70577	1.80873	1.91763	2.03279	2.15457
25	1.64061	1.74415	1.85394	1.97036	2.09378	2.22460
26	1.67342	1.78339	1.90029	2.02455	2.15659	2.29690
27	1.70689	1.82352	1.94780	2.08022	2.22129	2.37155
28	1.74102	1.86454	1.99650	2.13743	2.28793	2.44862
29	1.77584	1.90650	2.04641	2.19621	2.35657	2.52820
30	1.81136	1.94939	2.09757	2.25660	2.42726	2.61037
35	1.99989	2.17879	2.37321	2.58443	2.81386	3.06304
40	2.20804	2.43519	2.68506	2.95987	3.26204	3.59420
45	2.43785	2.72176	3.03790	3.38986	3.78160	4.21748
50	2.69159	3.04205	3.43711	3.88232	4.38391	4.94884
55	2.97173	3.40003	3.88877	4.44632	5.08215	5.80702
60	3.28103	3.80013	4.39979	5.09225	5.89160	6.81402
65	3.62252	4.24733	4.97796	5.83202	6.82998	7.99565
70	3.99956	4.74714	5.63210	6.67926	7.91782	9.38219
75	4.41584	5.30577	6.37221	7.64957	9.17893	11.00917
80	4.87544	5.93015	7.20957	8.76085	10.64089	12.91828
85	5.38288	6.62799	8.15696	10.03357	12.33571	15.15846
90	5.94313	7.40796	9.22886	11.49118	14.30047	17.78711
95	6.56170	8.27971	10.44160	13.16055	16.57816	20.87160
100	7.24465	9.25405	11.81372	15.07242	19.21863	24.49097

Table shows future value (FV) of $1 compounded for N periods at R rate per period.
Table values can be generated using the formula: FV = $1 * (1 + R)^N.

			Rate per Period			
Periods	**3.50%**	**3.75%**	**4.00%**	**4.25%**	**4.50%**	**4.75%**
1	1.03500	1.03750	1.04000	1.04250	1.04500	1.04750
2	1.07123	1.07641	1.08160	1.08681	1.09203	1.09726
3	1.10872	1.11677	1.12486	1.13300	1.14117	1.14938
4	1.14752	1.15865	1.16986	1.18115	1.19252	1.20397
5	1.18769	1.20210	1.21665	1.23135	1.24618	1.26116
6	1.22926	1.24718	1.26532	1.28368	1.30226	1.32107
7	1.27228	1.29395	1.31593	1.33824	1.36086	1.38382
8	1.31681	1.34247	1.36857	1.39511	1.42210	1.44955
9	1.36290	1.39281	1.42331	1.45440	1.48610	1.51840
10	1.41060	1.44504	1.48024	1.51621	1.55297	1.59052
11	1.45997	1.49923	1.53945	1.58065	1.62285	1.66607
12	1.51107	1.55545	1.60103	1.64783	1.69588	1.74521
13	1.56396	1.61378	1.66507	1.71786	1.77220	1.82811
14	1.61869	1.67430	1.73168	1.79087	1.85194	1.91495
15	1.67535	1.73709	1.80094	1.86699	1.93528	2.00591
16	1.73399	1.80223	1.87298	1.94633	2.02237	2.10119
17	1.79468	1.86981	1.94790	2.02905	2.11338	2.20099
18	1.85749	1.93993	2.02582	2.11529	2.20848	2.30554
19	1.92250	2.01268	2.10685	2.20519	2.30786	2.41505
20	1.98979	2.08815	2.19112	2.29891	2.41171	2.52977
21	2.05943	2.16646	2.27877	2.39661	2.52024	2.64993
22	2.13151	2.24770	2.36992	2.49847	2.63365	2.77580
23	2.20611	2.33199	2.46472	2.60465	2.75217	2.90765
24	2.28333	2.41944	2.56330	2.71535	2.87601	3.04577
25	2.36324	2.51017	2.66584	2.83075	3.00543	3.19044
26	2.44596	2.60430	2.77247	2.95106	3.14068	3.34199
27	2.53157	2.70196	2.88337	3.07648	3.28201	3.50073
28	2.62017	2.80328	2.99870	3.20723	3.42970	3.66702
29	2.71188	2.90841	3.11865	3.34353	3.58404	3.84120
30	2.80679	3.01747	3.24340	3.48564	3.74532	4.02366
35	3.33359	3.62730	3.94609	4.29202	4.66735	5.07447
40	3.95926	4.36038	4.80102	5.28497	5.81636	6.39972
45	4.70236	5.24161	5.84118	6.50763	7.24825	8.07108
50	5.58493	6.30094	7.10668	8.01315	9.03264	10.17892
55	6.63314	7.57436	8.64637	9.86696	11.25631	12.83724
60	7.87809	9.10513	10.51963	12.14965	14.02741	16.18982
65	9.35670	10.94528	12.79874	14.96043	17.48070	20.41795
70	11.11283	13.15732	15.57162	18.42148	21.78414	25.75030
75	13.19855	15.81641	18.94525	22.68322	27.14700	32.47524
80	15.67574	19.01290	23.04980	27.93091	33.83010	40.95647
85	18.61786	22.85541	28.04360	34.39263	42.15846	51.65266
90	22.11218	27.47448	34.11933	42.34925	52.53711	65.14226
95	26.26233	33.02707	41.51139	52.14661	65.47079	82.15481
100	31.19141	39.70183	50.50495	64.21055	81.58852	103.61036

Table shows future value (FV) of $1 compounded for N periods at R rate per period.
Table values can be generated using the formula: FV = $1 * (1 + R) ^N.

Periods	5.00%	5.25%	5.50%	5.75%	6.00%	6.25%
			Rate per Period			
1	1.05000	1.05250	1.05500	1.05750	1.06000	1.06250
2	1.10250	1.10776	1.11303	1.11831	1.12360	1.12891
3	1.15763	1.16591	1.17424	1.18261	1.19102	1.19946
4	1.21551	1.22712	1.23882	1.25061	1.26248	1.27443
5	1.27628	1.29155	1.30696	1.32252	1.33823	1.35408
6	1.34010	1.35935	1.37884	1.39856	1.41852	1.43871
7	1.40710	1.43072	1.45468	1.47898	1.50363	1.52863
8	1.47746	1.50583	1.53469	1.56402	1.59385	1.62417
9	1.55133	1.58489	1.61909	1.65395	1.68948	1.72568
10	1.62889	1.66810	1.70814	1.74906	1.79085	1.83354
11	1.71034	1.75567	1.80209	1.84963	1.89830	1.94813
12	1.79586	1.84784	1.90121	1.95598	2.01220	2.06989
13	1.88565	1.94486	2.00577	2.06845	2.13293	2.19926
14	1.97993	2.04696	2.11609	2.18739	2.26090	2.33671
15	2.07893	2.15443	2.23248	2.31316	2.39656	2.48276
16	2.18287	2.26753	2.35526	2.44617	2.54035	2.63793
17	2.29202	2.38658	2.48480	2.58682	2.69277	2.80280
18	2.40662	2.51187	2.62147	2.73556	2.85434	2.97797
19	2.52695	2.64375	2.76565	2.89286	3.02560	3.16410
20	2.65330	2.78254	2.91776	3.05920	3.20714	3.36185
21	2.78596	2.92863	3.07823	3.23510	3.39956	3.57197
22	2.92526	3.08238	3.24754	3.42112	3.60354	3.79522
23	3.07152	3.24421	3.42615	3.61783	3.81975	4.03242
24	3.22510	3.41453	3.61459	3.82586	4.04893	4.28444
25	3.38635	3.59379	3.81339	4.04585	4.29187	4.55222
26	3.55567	3.78246	4.02313	4.27848	4.54938	4.83674
27	3.73346	3.98104	4.24440	4.52450	4.82235	5.13903
28	3.92013	4.19005	4.47784	4.78465	5.11169	5.46022
29	4.11614	4.41002	4.72412	5.05977	5.41839	5.80149
30	4.32194	4.64155	4.98395	5.35071	5.74349	6.16408
35	5.51602	5.99479	6.51383	7.07641	7.68609	8.34666
40	7.03999	7.74255	8.51331	9.35869	10.28572	11.30206
45	8.98501	9.99988	11.12655	12.37704	13.76461	15.30390
50	11.46740	12.91532	14.54196	16.36887	18.42015	20.72273
55	14.63563	16.68076	19.00576	21.64814	24.65032	28.06026
60	18.67919	21.54400	24.83977	28.63008	32.98769	37.99586
65	23.83990	27.82510	32.46459	37.86382	44.14497	51.44948
70	30.42643	35.93745	42.42992	50.07562	59.07593	69.66678
75	38.83269	46.41494	55.45420	66.22595	79.05692	94.33447
80	49.56144	59.94713	72.47643	87.58507	105.79599	127.73653
85	63.25435	77.42458	94.72379	115.83291	141.57890	172.96562
90	80.73037	99.99756	123.80021	153.19121	189.46451	234.20949
95	103.03468	129.15164	161.80192	202.59827	253.54625	317.13865
100	131.50126	166.80553	211.46864	267.94003	339.30208	429.43147

Table shows future value (FV) of $1 compounded for N periods at R rate per period.
Table values can be generated using the formula: FV = $1 * (1 + R)^N.

	Rate per Period					
Periods	**6.50%**	**6.75%**	**7.00%**	**7.25%**	**7.50%**	**7.75%**
1	1.06500	1.06750	1.07000	1.07250	1.07500	1.07750
2	1.13423	1.13956	1.14490	1.15026	1.15563	1.16101
3	1.20795	1.21648	1.22504	1.23365	1.24230	1.25098
4	1.28647	1.29859	1.31080	1.32309	1.33547	1.34794
5	1.37009	1.38624	1.40255	1.41901	1.43563	1.45240
6	1.45914	1.47981	1.50073	1.52189	1.54330	1.56496
7	1.55399	1.57970	1.60578	1.63223	1.65905	1.68625
8	1.65500	1.68633	1.71819	1.75057	1.78348	1.81693
9	1.76257	1.80016	1.83846	1.87748	1.91724	1.95774
10	1.87714	1.92167	1.96715	2.01360	2.06103	2.10947
11	1.99915	2.05138	2.10485	2.15959	2.21561	2.27295
12	2.12910	2.18985	2.25219	2.31615	2.38178	2.44910
13	2.26749	2.33767	2.40985	2.48408	2.56041	2.63891
14	2.41487	2.49546	2.57853	2.66417	2.75244	2.84343
15	2.57184	2.66390	2.75903	2.85732	2.95888	3.06379
16	2.73901	2.84372	2.95216	3.06448	3.18079	3.30124
17	2.91705	3.03567	3.15882	3.28665	3.41935	3.55708
18	3.10665	3.24057	3.37993	3.52494	3.67580	3.83275
19	3.30859	3.45931	3.61653	3.78050	3.95149	4.12979
20	3.52365	3.69282	3.86968	4.05458	4.24785	4.44985
21	3.75268	3.94208	4.14056	4.34854	4.56644	4.79472
22	3.99661	4.20817	4.43040	4.66381	4.90892	5.16631
23	4.25639	4.49222	4.74053	5.00193	5.27709	5.56669
24	4.53305	4.79545	5.07237	5.36457	5.67287	5.99811
25	4.82770	5.11914	5.42743	5.75351	6.09834	6.46297
26	5.14150	5.46468	5.80735	6.17063	6.55572	6.96385
27	5.47570	5.83355	6.21387	6.61801	7.04739	7.50355
28	5.83162	6.22731	6.64884	7.09781	7.57595	8.08507
29	6.21067	6.64766	7.11426	7.61240	8.14414	8.71166
30	6.61437	7.09637	7.61226	8.16430	8.75496	9.38682
35	9.06225	9.83730	10.67658	11.58525	12.56887	13.63342
40	12.41607	13.63689	14.97446	16.43963	18.04424	19.80118
45	17.01110	18.90405	21.00245	23.32806	25.90484	28.75925
50	23.30668	26.20560	29.45703	33.10282	37.18975	41.76995
55	31.93217	36.32734	41.31500	46.97335	53.39069	60.66669
60	43.74984	50.35853	57.94643	66.65582	76.64924	88.11234
65	59.94107	69.80916	81.27286	94.58550	110.03990	127.97441
70	82.12446	96.77248	113.98939	134.21809	157.97650	185.87009
75	112.51763	134.15019	159.87602	190.45727	226.79570	269.95782
80	154.15891	185.96478	224.23439	270.26143	325.59456	392.08688
85	211.21106	257.79240	314.50033	383.50460	467.43310	569.46718
90	289.37746	357.36296	441.10298	544.19817	671.06066	827.09443
95	396.47220	495.39196	618.66975	772.22451	963.39437	1201.27237
100	543.20127	686.73372	867.71633	1095.79695	1383.07721	1744.72861

Table shows future value (FV) of $1 compounded for N periods at R rate per period.

Table values can be generated using the formula: FV = $1 * (1 + R)^N.

	Rate per Period					
Periods	**8.00%**	**8.25%**	**8.50%**	**8.75%**	**9.00%**	**9.25%**
1	1.08000	1.08250	1.08500	1.08750	1.09000	1.09250
2	1.16640	1.17181	1.17723	1.18266	1.18810	1.19356
3	1.25971	1.26848	1.27729	1.28614	1.29503	1.30396
4	1.36049	1.37313	1.38586	1.39868	1.41158	1.42458
5	1.46933	1.48641	1.50366	1.52106	1.53862	1.55635
6	1.58687	1.60904	1.63147	1.65415	1.67710	1.70031
7	1.71382	1.74179	1.77014	1.79889	1.82804	1.85759
8	1.85093	1.88549	1.92060	1.95629	1.99256	2.02942
9	1.99900	2.04104	2.08386	2.12747	2.17189	2.21714
10	2.15892	2.20942	2.26098	2.31362	2.36736	2.42222
11	2.33164	2.39170	2.45317	2.51607	2.58043	2.64628
12	2.51817	2.58902	2.66169	2.73622	2.81266	2.89106
13	2.71962	2.80261	2.88793	2.97564	3.06580	3.15848
14	2.93719	3.03383	3.13340	3.23601	3.34173	3.45064
15	3.17217	3.28412	3.39974	3.51916	3.64248	3.76983
16	3.42594	3.55506	3.68872	3.82709	3.97031	4.11854
17	3.70002	3.84835	4.00226	4.16196	4.32763	4.49950
18	3.99602	4.16584	4.34245	4.52613	4.71712	4.91571
19	4.31570	4.50952	4.71156	4.92216	5.14166	5.37041
20	4.66096	4.88155	5.11205	5.35285	5.60441	5.86717
21	5.03383	5.28428	5.54657	5.82123	6.10881	6.40989
22	5.43654	5.72024	6.01803	6.33058	6.65860	7.00280
23	5.87146	6.19215	6.52956	6.88451	7.25787	7.65056
24	6.34118	6.70301	7.08457	7.48691	7.91108	8.35824
25	6.84848	7.25601	7.68676	8.14201	8.62308	9.13137
26	7.39635	7.85463	8.34014	8.85444	9.39916	9.97603
27	7.98806	8.50263	9.04905	9.62920	10.24508	10.89881
28	8.62711	9.20410	9.81822	10.47175	11.16714	11.90695
29	9.31727	9.96344	10.65277	11.38803	12.17218	13.00834
30	10.06266	10.78542	11.55825	12.38449	13.26768	14.21161
35	14.78534	16.03159	17.37964	18.83754	20.41397	22.11824
40	21.72452	23.82957	26.13302	28.65303	31.40942	34.42372
45	31.92045	35.42058	39.29508	43.58298	48.32729	53.57535
50	46.90161	52.64962	59.08632	66.29233	74.35752	83.38200
55	68.91386	78.25909	88.84553	100.83461	114.40826	129.77156
60	101.25706	116.32533	133.59318	153.37548	176.03129	201.96994
65	148.77985	172.90750	200.87828	233.29330	270.84596	314.33589
70	218.60641	257.01197	302.05197	354.85309	416.73009	489.21661
75	321.20453	382.02596	454.18247	539.75282	641.19089	761.39220
80	471.95483	567.84839	682.93450	820.99639	986.55167	1184.99264
85	693.45649	844.05729	1026.89903	1248.78473	1517.93203	1844.26311
90	1018.91509	1254.61782	1544.10360	1899.47642	2335.52658	2870.31862
95	1497.12055	1864.88037	2321.80171	2889.21749	3593.49715	4467.21995
100	2199.76126	2771.98262	3491.19268	4394.67297	5529.04079	6952.55710

Table shows future value (FV) of $1 compounded for N periods at R rate per period.
Table values can be generated using the formula: FV = $1 * (1 + R)^N.

	Rate per Period					
Periods	**9.50%**	**9.75%**	**10.00%**	**10.25%**	**10.50%**	**10.75%**
1	1.09500	1.09750	1.10000	1.10250	1.10500	1.10750
2	1.19903	1.20451	1.21000	1.21551	1.22103	1.22656
3	1.31293	1.32195	1.33100	1.34010	1.34923	1.35841
4	1.43766	1.45084	1.46410	1.47746	1.49090	1.50444
5	1.57424	1.59229	1.61051	1.62889	1.64745	1.66617
6	1.72379	1.74754	1.77156	1.79586	1.82043	1.84528
7	1.88755	1.91793	1.94872	1.97993	2.01157	2.04365
8	2.06687	2.10492	2.14359	2.18287	2.22279	2.26334
9	2.26322	2.31015	2.35795	2.40662	2.45618	2.50665
10	2.47823	2.53539	2.59374	2.65330	2.71408	2.77611
11	2.71366	2.78259	2.85312	2.92526	2.99906	3.07455
12	2.97146	3.05390	3.13843	3.22510	3.31396	3.40506
13	3.25375	3.35165	3.45227	3.55567	3.66193	3.77110
14	3.56285	3.67844	3.79750	3.92013	4.04643	4.17650
15	3.90132	4.03709	4.17725	4.32194	4.47130	4.62547
16	4.27195	4.43070	4.59497	4.76494	4.94079	5.12271
17	4.67778	4.86269	5.05447	5.25335	5.45957	5.67340
18	5.12217	5.33681	5.55992	5.79182	6.03283	6.28329
19	5.60878	5.85715	6.11591	6.38548	6.66628	6.95875
20	6.14161	6.42822	6.72750	7.03999	7.36623	7.70681
21	6.72507	7.05497	7.40025	7.76159	8.13969	8.53529
22	7.36395	7.74283	8.14027	8.55715	8.99436	9.45284
23	8.06352	8.49775	8.95430	9.43426	9.93876	10.46902
24	8.82956	9.32629	9.84973	10.40127	10.98233	11.59444
25	9.66836	10.23560	10.83471	11.46740	12.13548	12.84084
26	10.58686	11.23357	11.91818	12.64281	13.40971	14.22123
27	11.59261	12.32884	13.10999	13.93870	14.81772	15.75001
28	12.69391	13.53090	14.42099	15.36741	16.37359	17.44314
29	13.89983	14.85017	15.86309	16.94257	18.09281	19.31827
30	15.22031	16.29806	17.44940	18.67919	19.99256	21.39499
35	23.96041	25.95126	28.10244	30.42643	32.93667	35.64763
40	37.71940	41.32198	45.25926	49.56144	54.26142	59.39493
45	59.37934	65.79665	72.89048	80.73037	89.39279	98.96191
50	93.47726	104.76747	117.39085	131.50126	147.26987	164.88712
55	147.15552	166.82037	189.05914	214.20169	242.61927	274.72958
60	231.65792	265.62670	304.48164	348.91199	399.70233	457.74551
65	364.68487	422.95521	490.37073	568.34086	658.48831	762.68072
70	574.10105	673.46809	789.74696	925.76737	1084.82444	1270.75387
75	903.77212	1072.35769	1271.89537	1507.97750	1787.19052	2117.28888
80	1422.75308	1707.50629	2048.40021	2456.33644	2944.30124	3527.75805
85	2239.75302	2718.84818	3298.96903	4001.11323	4850.57955	5877.83602
90	3525.90597	4329.19953	5313.02261	6517.39184	7991.07160	9793.45970
95	5550.61777	6893.34868	8556.67605	10616.14455	13164.86506	16317.54485
100	8737.99753	10976.22223	13780.61234	17292.58082	21688.41437	27187.76388

Table shows future value (FV) of $1 compounded for N periods at R rate per period.

Table values can be generated using the formula: FV = $1 * (1 + R)^N.

	Rate per Period					
Periods	**11.00%**	**11.25%**	**11.50%**	**11.75%**	**12.00%**	**12.25%**
1	1.11000	1.11250	1.11500	1.11750	1.12000	1.12250
2	1.23210	1.23766	1.24323	1.24881	1.25440	1.26001
3	1.36763	1.37689	1.38620	1.39554	1.40493	1.41436
4	1.51807	1.53179	1.54561	1.55952	1.57352	1.58762
5	1.68506	1.70412	1.72335	1.74276	1.76234	1.78210
6	1.87041	1.89583	1.92154	1.94753	1.97382	2.00041
7	2.07616	2.10911	2.14252	2.17637	2.21068	2.24546
8	2.30454	2.34639	2.38891	2.43209	2.47596	2.52052
9	2.55804	2.61036	2.66363	2.71786	2.77308	2.82929
10	2.83942	2.90402	2.96995	3.03721	3.10585	3.17588
11	3.15176	3.23073	3.31149	3.39409	3.47855	3.56492
12	3.49845	3.59418	3.69231	3.79289	3.89598	4.00162
13	3.88328	3.99853	4.11693	4.23856	4.36349	4.49182
14	4.31044	4.44836	4.59037	4.73659	4.88711	5.04207
15	4.78459	4.94880	5.11827	5.29314	5.47357	5.65972
16	5.31089	5.50554	5.70687	5.91508	6.13039	6.35304
17	5.89509	6.12492	6.36316	6.61010	6.86604	7.13129
18	6.54355	6.81397	7.09492	7.38679	7.68997	8.00487
19	7.26334	7.58054	7.91084	8.25473	8.61276	8.98547
20	8.06231	8.43336	8.82058	9.22467	9.64629	10.08619
21	8.94917	9.38211	9.83495	10.30856	10.80385	11.32174
22	9.93357	10.43759	10.96597	11.51982	12.10031	12.70866
23	11.02627	11.61182	12.22706	12.87340	13.55235	14.26547
24	12.23916	12.91815	13.63317	14.38602	15.17863	16.01299
25	13.58546	14.37145	15.20098	16.07638	17.00006	17.97458
26	15.07986	15.98823	16.94910	17.96536	19.04007	20.17647
27	16.73865	17.78691	18.89824	20.07629	21.32488	22.64808
28	18.57990	19.78794	21.07154	22.43525	23.88387	25.42247
29	20.62369	22.01408	23.49477	25.07139	26.74993	28.53673
30	22.89230	24.49067	26.19667	28.01728	29.95992	32.03247
35	38.57485	41.73503	45.14611	48.82740	52.79962	57.08503
40	65.00087	71.12148	77.80270	85.09446	93.05097	101.73116
45	109.53024	121.19952	134.08155	148.29924	163.98760	181.29496
50	184.56483	206.53848	231.06990	258.45003	289.00219	323.08551
55	311.00247	351.96630	398.21508	450.41646	509.32061	575.77026
60	524.05724	599.79270	686.26530	784.96792	897.59693	1026.07943
65	883.06693	1022.11857	1182.67762	1368.01093	1581.87249	1828.57479
70	1488.01913	1741.81239	2038.17146	2384.11514	2787.79983	3258.70073
75	2507.39877	2968.25682	3512.48965	4154.94123	4913.05584	5807.32626
80	4225.11275	5058.26493	6053.26087	7241.06664	8658.48310	10349.22846
85	7119.56070	8619.88894	10431.90750	12619.44349	15259.20568	18443.34637
90	11996.87381	14689.32260	17977.86292	21992.66517	26891.93422	32867.86320
95	20215.43005	25032.36410	30982.21058	38327.94383	47392.77662	58573.77561
100	34064.17527	42658.14492	53393.29692	66796.41902	83522.26573	104384.24817

Table shows future value (FV) of $1 compounded for N periods at R rate per period.
Table values can be generated using the formula: FV = $1 * (1 + R)^N.

TABLE 13-2:
Compound Interest on $100, Compounded Daily (365 Days)
(Exact Time, Exact Interest Basis)

pg. 1

Days	Annual rate 0.50%	0.75%	1.00%	1.25%	1.50%	1.75%	2.00%	2.25%
1	0.001370	0.002055	0.002740	0.003425	0.004110	0.004795	0.005479	0.006164
2	0.002740	0.004110	0.005480	0.006849	0.008219	0.009589	0.010959	0.012329
3	0.004110	0.006165	0.008219	0.010274	0.012329	0.014384	0.016439	0.018494
4	0.005480	0.008219	0.010959	0.013699	0.016439	0.019179	0.021920	0.024660
5	0.006850	0.010274	0.013699	0.017124	0.020550	0.023975	0.027400	0.030826
6	0.008219	0.012329	0.016439	0.020550	0.024660	0.028771	0.032881	0.036992
7	0.009589	0.014384	0.019180	0.023975	0.028771	0.033566	0.038362	0.043159
8	0.010959	0.016440	0.021920	0.027401	0.032881	0.038363	0.043844	0.049326
9	0.012329	0.018495	0.024660	0.030826	0.036992	0.043159	0.049326	0.055493
10	0.013699	0.020550	0.027401	0.034252	0.041103	0.047956	0.054808	0.061661
11	0.015070	0.022605	0.030141	0.037678	0.045215	0.052752	0.060290	0.067829
12	0.016440	0.024660	0.032882	0.041104	0.049326	0.057549	0.065773	0.073998
13	0.017810	0.026716	0.035622	0.044530	0.053438	0.062347	0.071256	0.080167
14	0.019180	0.028771	0.038363	0.047956	0.057550	0.067144	0.076740	0.086336
15	0.020550	0.030826	0.041104	0.051382	0.061662	0.071942	0.082223	0.092506
16	0.021920	0.032882	0.043845	0.054809	0.065774	0.076740	0.087707	0.098676
17	0.023290	0.034937	0.046586	0.058235	0.069886	0.081538	0.093192	0.104846
18	0.024660	0.036993	0.049327	0.061662	0.073998	0.086337	0.098676	0.111017
19	0.026031	0.039048	0.052068	0.065089	0.078111	0.091135	0.104161	0.117188
20	0.027401	0.041104	0.054809	0.068515	0.082224	0.095934	0.109646	0.123360
21	0.028771	0.043160	0.057550	0.071942	0.086337	0.100733	0.115132	0.129532
22	0.030141	0.045215	0.060291	0.075370	0.090450	0.105533	0.120617	0.135704
23	0.031512	0.047271	0.063033	0.078797	0.094563	0.110332	0.126103	0.141877
24	0.032882	0.049327	0.065774	0.082224	0.098677	0.115132	0.131590	0.148050
25	0.034252	0.051383	0.068516	0.085652	0.102790	0.119932	0.137076	0.154224
26	0.035623	0.053438	0.071257	0.089079	0.106904	0.124732	0.142563	0.160398
27	0.036993	0.055494	0.073999	0.092507	0.111018	0.129533	0.148051	0.166572
28	0.038363	0.057550	0.076741	0.095935	0.115132	0.134334	0.153538	0.172746
29	0.039734	0.059606	0.079483	0.099363	0.119247	0.139134	0.159026	0.178921
30	0.041104	0.061662	0.082224	0.102791	0.123361	0.143936	0.164514	0.185097
31	0.042474	0.063718	0.084966	0.106219	0.127476	0.148737	0.170003	0.191273
32	0.043845	0.065774	0.087708	0.109647	0.131591	0.153539	0.175491	0.197449
33	0.045215	0.067831	0.090451	0.113076	0.135706	0.158341	0.180981	0.203625
34	0.046586	0.069887	0.093193	0.116504	0.139821	0.163143	0.186470	0.209802
35	0.047956	0.071943	0.095935	0.119933	0.143936	0.167945	0.191960	0.215980
40	0.054809	0.082225	0.109648	0.137078	0.164515	0.191960	0.219412	0.246872
45	0.061662	0.092508	0.123362	0.154226	0.185099	0.215981	0.246873	0.277774
50	0.068516	0.102791	0.137078	0.171377	0.205686	0.240008	0.274341	0.308685
55	0.075370	0.113076	0.150796	0.188530	0.226278	0.264040	0.301816	0.339606
60	0.082225	0.123362	0.164516	0.205687	0.246875	0.288078	0.329299	0.370536
90	0.123363	0.185101	0.246876	0.308689	0.370540	0.432429	0.494355	0.556319
120	0.164518	0.246877	0.329304	0.411797	0.494358	0.576987	0.659683	0.742446
150	0.205689	0.308691	0.411799	0.515011	0.618330	0.721753	0.825282	0.928917
180	0.246878	0.370544	0.494362	0.618332	0.742453	0.866728	0.991154	1.115733
240	0.329306	0.494364	0.659692	0.825291	0.991161	1.157303	1.323717	1.490404
360	0.494365	0.742461	0.991168	1.240487	1.490419	1.740967	1.992132	2.243915
365	0.501249	0.752812	1.005003	1.257823	1.511275	1.765360	2.020078	2.275432
730	1.005010	1.511291	2.020106	2.531468	3.045390	3.561884	4.080963	4.602641
1095	1.511296	2.275480	3.045411	3.821133	4.602689	5.390124	6.183480	6.982803
1825	2.531494	3.821160	5.127038	6.449332	7.788249	9.143998	10.516789	11.906838
3650	5.127074	7.788332	10.516940	13.314603	16.183066	19.124122	22.139607	25.231403

Table shows interest (I) on $100 compounded daily for N days at an annual rate of R.
*Table values can be generated using the formula: I = 100 * (1 + R/365)^N - 100.*

TABLE 13-2

Compound Interest on $100, Compounded Daily (365 Days) (Exact Time, Exact Interest Basis) -- Continued

pg. 2

	Annual rate							
Days	**2.50%**	**2.75%**	**3.00%**	**3.25%**	**2.50%**	**3.75%**	**4.00%**	**4.25%**
1	0.006849	0.007534	0.008219	0.008904	0.006849	0.010274	0.010959	0.011644
2	0.013699	0.015069	0.016439	0.017809	0.013699	0.020549	0.021919	0.023289
3	0.020549	0.022604	0.024660	0.026715	0.020549	0.030825	0.032880	0.034936
4	0.027400	0.030140	0.032881	0.035621	0.027400	0.041102	0.043843	0.046583
5	0.034251	0.037677	0.041103	0.044528	0.034251	0.051380	0.054807	0.058233
6	0.041103	0.045214	0.049325	0.053437	0.041103	0.061660	0.065771	0.069883
7	0.047955	0.052752	0.057548	0.062345	0.047955	0.071940	0.076738	0.081535
8	0.054808	0.060290	0.065772	0.071255	0.054808	0.082221	0.087705	0.093189
9	0.061661	0.067829	0.073997	0.080166	0.061661	0.092504	0.098673	0.104843
10	0.068514	0.075368	0.082222	0.089077	0.068514	0.102787	0.109643	0.116499
11	0.075368	0.082908	0.090448	0.097989	0.075368	0.113072	0.120614	0.128157
12	0.082223	0.090448	0.098675	0.106902	0.082223	0.123357	0.131586	0.139816
13	0.089078	0.097989	0.106902	0.115815	0.089078	0.133644	0.142559	0.151476
14	0.095933	0.105531	0.115130	0.124730	0.095933	0.143932	0.153534	0.163137
15	0.102789	0.113073	0.123359	0.133645	0.102789	0.154220	0.164510	0.174800
16	0.109645	0.120616	0.131588	0.142561	0.109645	0.164510	0.175487	0.186464
17	0.116502	0.128159	0.139818	0.151478	0.116502	0.174801	0.186465	0.198130
18	0.123359	0.135703	0.148049	0.160395	0.123359	0.185093	0.197444	0.209797
19	0.130217	0.143248	0.156280	0.169314	0.130217	0.195386	0.208425	0.221465
20	0.137075	0.150793	0.164512	0.178233	0.137075	0.205680	0.219406	0.233134
21	0.143934	0.158338	0.172745	0.187153	0.143934	0.215975	0.230389	0.244805
22	0.150793	0.165885	0.180978	0.196074	0.150793	0.226271	0.241374	0.256478
23	0.157653	0.173431	0.189212	0.204995	0.157653	0.236569	0.252359	0.268152
24	0.164513	0.180979	0.197447	0.213918	0.164513	0.246867	0.263345	0.279827
25	0.171374	0.188527	0.205682	0.222841	0.171374	0.257166	0.274333	0.291503
26	0.178235	0.196075	0.213918	0.231765	0.178235	0.267467	0.285322	0.303181
27	0.185096	0.203624	0.222155	0.240689	0.185096	0.277768	0.296312	0.314860
28	0.191958	0.211174	0.230393	0.249615	0.191958	0.288071	0.307304	0.326540
29	0.198821	0.218724	0.238631	0.258541	0.198821	0.298374	0.318296	0.338222
30	0.205684	0.226274	0.246869	0.267468	0.205684	0.308679	0.329290	0.349905
31	0.212547	0.233826	0.255109	0.276396	0.212547	0.318984	0.340285	0.361590
32	0.219411	0.241378	0.263349	0.285325	0.219411	0.329291	0.351281	0.373276
33	0.226275	0.248930	0.271590	0.294255	0.226275	0.339599	0.362279	0.384963
34	0.233140	0.256483	0.279831	0.303185	0.233140	0.349908	0.373277	0.396652
35	0.240005	0.264037	0.288074	0.312116	0.240005	0.360218	0.384277	0.408342
40	0.274339	0.301813	0.329295	0.356783	0.274339	0.411783	0.439294	0.466813
45	0.308684	0.339604	0.370533	0.401471	0.308684	0.463375	0.494342	0.525317
50	0.343041	0.377409	0.411788	0.446178	0.343041	0.514994	0.549419	0.583856
55	0.377410	0.415228	0.453059	0.490905	0.377410	0.566639	0.604527	0.642428
60	0.411790	0.453061	0.494348	0.535652	0.411790	0.618310	0.659664	0.701035
90	0.618321	0.680361	0.742438	0.804553	0.618321	0.928898	0.991127	1.053394
120	0.825276	0.908175	0.991140	1.074174	0.825276	1.240444	1.323681	1.406985
150	1.032658	1.136504	1.240457	1.344515	1.032658	1.552952	1.657329	1.761814
180	1.240465	1.365350	1.490388	1.615580	1.240465	1.866424	1.992077	2.117884
240	1.657364	1.824597	1.992104	2.159886	1.657364	2.496275	2.664882	2.833766
360	2.496318	2.749342	3.002989	3.257261	2.496318	3.767683	4.023837	4.280622
365	2.531424	2.788055	3.045326	3.303240	2.531424	3.821000	4.080849	4.341347
730	5.126930	5.653843	6.183393	6.715594	5.126930	7.788000	8.328232	8.871168
1095	7.788138	8.599530	9.417024	10.240666	7.788138	11.906579	12.748944	13.597644
1825	13.314360	14.739576	16.182708	17.643981	13.314360	20.621863	22.138937	23.675081
3650	28.401442	31.651704	34.984217	38.401062	28.401442	45.496339	49.179200	52.955258

Table shows interest (I) on $100 compounded daily for N days at an annual rate of R.
*Table values can be generated using the formula: I = 100 * (1 + R/365)^N - 100.*

TABLE 13-2
Compound Interest on $100, Compounded Daily (365 Days) (Exact Time, Exact Interest Basis) -- Continued

				Annual rate				
Days	**4.50%**	**4.75%**	**5.00%**	**5.25%**	**5.50%**	**5.75%**	**6.00%**	**6.25%**
1	0.012329	0.013014	0.013699	0.014384	0.015068	0.015753	0.016438	0.017123
2	0.006756	0.026029	0.027399	0.028769	0.030139	0.031509	0.032879	0.034250
3	0.010134	0.039046	0.041102	0.043157	0.045212	0.047268	0.049323	0.051379
4	0.013512	0.052065	0.054806	0.057547	0.060288	0.063029	0.065770	0.068511
5	0.016890	0.065085	0.068512	0.071938	0.075365	0.078792	0.082219	0.085646
6	0.020268	0.078108	0.082220	0.086332	0.090445	0.094558	0.098671	0.102784
7	0.023647	0.091131	0.095930	0.100728	0.105527	0.110326	0.115125	0.119925
8	0.027025	0.104157	0.109642	0.115126	0.120612	0.126097	0.131583	0.137068
9	0.030404	0.117184	0.123355	0.129527	0.135698	0.141870	0.148043	0.154215
10	0.033783	0.130213	0.137071	0.143929	0.150787	0.157646	0.164505	0.171365
11	0.037161	0.143244	0.150788	0.158333	0.165878	0.173424	0.180971	0.188518
12	0.040540	0.156276	0.164507	0.172739	0.180972	0.189205	0.197439	0.205673
13	0.043920	0.169310	0.178229	0.187148	0.196068	0.204988	0.213910	0.222832
14	0.047299	0.182346	0.191952	0.201558	0.211166	0.220774	0.230383	0.239993
15	0.050678	0.195383	0.205677	0.215971	0.226266	0.236562	0.246859	0.257157
16	0.054058	0.208423	0.219403	0.230385	0.241369	0.252353	0.263338	0.274325
17	0.057437	0.221463	0.233132	0.244802	0.256473	0.268146	0.279820	0.291495
18	0.060817	0.234506	0.246863	0.259221	0.271581	0.283942	0.296304	0.308668
19	0.064197	0.247550	0.260595	0.273642	0.286690	0.299740	0.312791	0.325844
20	0.067577	0.260596	0.274329	0.288065	0.301802	0.315540	0.329281	0.343023
21	0.070957	0.273644	0.288066	0.302490	0.316916	0.331344	0.345774	0.360205
22	0.074337	0.286693	0.301804	0.316917	0.332032	0.347149	0.362269	0.377390
23	0.077717	0.299744	0.315544	0.331346	0.347150	0.362957	0.378767	0.394578
24	0.081097	0.312797	0.329286	0.345777	0.362271	0.378768	0.395267	0.411769
25	0.084478	0.325851	0.343029	0.360210	0.377394	0.394581	0.411771	0.428963
26	0.087858	0.338907	0.356775	0.374646	0.392520	0.410397	0.428277	0.446160
27	0.091239	0.351965	0.370522	0.389083	0.407647	0.426215	0.444785	0.463359
28	0.094620	0.365024	0.384272	0.403523	0.422777	0.442035	0.461297	0.480562
29	0.098001	0.378086	0.398023	0.417964	0.437909	0.457858	0.477811	0.497768
30	0.101382	0.391149	0.411776	0.432408	0.453044	0.473684	0.494328	0.514976
31	0.104763	0.404213	0.425531	0.446854	0.468181	0.489512	0.510848	0.532188
32	0.108144	0.417279	0.439288	0.461302	0.483320	0.505342	0.527370	0.549402
33	0.111526	0.430347	0.453047	0.475752	0.498461	0.521175	0.543895	0.566619
34	0.114907	0.443417	0.127683	0.134071	0.140460	0.146849	0.153238	0.159628
35	0.118289	0.456489	0.131441	0.138017	0.144594	0.151171	0.157749	0.164327
40	0.135199	0.521871	0.549411	0.576959	0.604514	0.632077	0.659646	0.687223
45	0.152112	0.587296	0.618300	0.649313	0.680335	0.711367	0.742408	0.773458
50	0.169027	0.652764	0.687235	0.721718	0.756213	0.790719	0.825237	0.859766
55	0.185945	0.718274	0.756218	0.794176	0.832148	0.870134	0.908134	0.946148
60	0.202867	0.783827	0.825248	0.866686	0.908140	0.949612	0.991099	1.032604
90	0.304454	1.178042	1.240422	1.302841	1.365298	1.427794	1.490327	1.552898
120	0.406145	1.573798	1.657306	1.740883	1.824528	1.908241	1.992022	2.075871
150	0.507939	1.971102	2.075907	2.180819	2.285838	2.390964	2.496197	2.601538
180	0.609836	2.369961	2.496231	2.622657	2.749237	2.875973	3.002864	3.129911
240	0.813940	3.172364	3.342080	3.512073	3.682344	3.852895	4.023725	4.194835
360	1.223390	4.796089	5.054775	5.314097	5.574058	5.834658	6.095900	6.357785
365	1.240487	4.864296	5.126750	5.389858	5.653624	5.918047	6.183131	6.448876
730	2.496362	9.965206	10.516335	11.070222	11.626882	12.186328	12.748573	13.313633
1095	3.767816	15.314239	16.182231	17.056750	17.937846	18.825568	19.719965	20.621089
1825	6.358236	26.805540	28.400343	30.015193	31.650340	33.306041	34.982553	36.680138
3650	13.120744	60.796450	64.866481	69.039503	73.318120	77.705005	82.202895	86.814600

Table shows interest (I) on $100 compounded daily for N days at an annual rate of R.
*Table values can be generated using the formula: I = 100 * (1 + R/365)^N - 100.*

TABLE 13-2
Compound Interest on $100, Compounded Daily (365 Days)
(Exact Time, Exact Interest Basis) -- Continued

				Annual rate				*pg. 4*
Days	**6.50%**	**6.75%**	**7.00%**	**7.25%**	**7.50%**	**7.75%**	**8.00%**	**8.25%**
1	0.017808	0.018493	0.019178	0.019863	0.020548	0.021233	0.021918	0.022603
2	0.035620	0.036990	0.038360	0.039730	0.041100	0.042470	0.043840	0.045211
3	0.053434	0.055490	0.057545	0.059601	0.061657	0.063712	0.065768	0.067824
4	0.071252	0.073993	0.076734	0.079476	0.082217	0.084959	0.087700	0.090442
5	0.089073	0.092500	0.095927	0.099355	0.102782	0.106209	0.109637	0.113065
6	0.106897	0.111010	0.115124	0.119237	0.123351	0.127465	0.131579	0.135693
7	0.124724	0.129524	0.134324	0.139124	0.143924	0.148725	0.153526	0.158327
8	0.142555	0.148041	0.153528	0.159015	0.164502	0.169989	0.175477	0.180965
9	0.160388	0.166562	0.172735	0.178909	0.185084	0.191258	0.197433	0.203609
10	0.178225	0.185085	0.191946	0.198808	0.205670	0.212532	0.219394	0.226257
11	0.196065	0.203613	0.211161	0.218710	0.226260	0.233810	0.241360	0.248911
12	0.213908	0.222144	0.230380	0.238617	0.246854	0.255092	0.263331	0.271570
13	0.231754	0.240678	0.249602	0.258527	0.267453	0.276379	0.285307	0.294234
14	0.249604	0.259216	0.268828	0.278442	0.288056	0.297671	0.307287	0.316904
15	0.267457	0.277757	0.288058	0.298360	0.308663	0.318967	0.329272	0.339578
16	0.285312	0.296301	0.307291	0.318282	0.329274	0.340268	0.351262	0.362258
17	0.303171	0.314849	0.326528	0.338208	0.349890	0.361573	0.373257	0.384942
18	0.321034	0.333400	0.345769	0.358139	0.370510	0.382882	0.395256	0.407632
19	0.338899	0.351955	0.365013	0.378073	0.391134	0.404197	0.417261	0.430327
20	0.356768	0.370514	0.384261	0.398011	0.411762	0.425515	0.439270	0.453027
21	0.374639	0.389075	0.403513	0.417953	0.432395	0.446838	0.461284	0.475732
22	0.392514	0.407640	0.422769	0.437899	0.453031	0.468166	0.483303	0.498442
23	0.410392	0.426209	0.442028	0.457849	0.473672	0.489498	0.505327	0.521158
24	0.428274	0.444781	0.461291	0.477803	0.494318	0.510835	0.527355	0.543878
25	0.446158	0.463356	0.480557	0.497761	0.514967	0.532177	0.549389	0.566604
26	0.464046	0.481935	0.499827	0.517723	0.535621	0.553523	0.571427	0.589335
27	0.481937	0.500517	0.519101	0.537688	0.556279	0.574873	0.593470	0.612071
28	0.499831	0.519103	0.538379	0.557658	0.576941	0.596228	0.615518	0.634812
29	0.517728	0.537692	0.557660	0.577632	0.597608	0.617587	0.637571	0.657558
30	0.535628	0.556285	0.576945	0.597610	0.618279	0.638951	0.659628	0.680309
31	0.553532	0.574881	0.596234	0.617592	0.638954	0.660320	0.681691	0.703066
32	0.571439	0.593480	0.615526	0.637577	0.659633	0.681693	0.703758	0.725827
33	0.589349	0.612083	0.634823	0.657567	0.680316	0.703071	0.725830	0.748594
34	0.607262	0.630690	0.654122	0.677561	0.701004	0.724453	0.747907	0.771366
35	0.625178	0.649299	0.673426	0.697558	0.721696	0.745839	0.769989	0.794143
40	0.714808	0.742400	0.769999	0.797606	0.825220	0.852841	0.880470	0.908106
45	0.804518	0.835587	0.866665	0.897753	0.928850	0.959956	0.991072	1.022197
50	0.894307	0.928859	0.963424	0.997999	1.032586	1.067185	1.101796	1.136418
55	0.984176	1.022219	1.060275	1.098345	1.136430	1.174528	1.212641	1.250768
60	1.074126	1.115664	1.157219	1.198791	1.240380	1.281985	1.323608	1.365247
90	1.615507	1.678155	1.740841	1.803565	1.866327	1.929128	1.991967	2.054844
120	2.159789	2.243775	2.327830	2.411953	2.496145	2.580405	2.664734	2.749132
150	2.706986	2.812542	2.918205	3.023977	3.129857	3.235844	3.341940	3.448144
180	3.257114	3.384472	3.511987	3.639658	3.767486	3.895471	4.023613	4.151911
240	4.366225	4.537896	4.709848	4.882081	5.054597	5.227396	5.400477	5.573842
360	6.620315	6.883491	7.147315	7.411788	7.676912	7.942689	8.209120	8.476207
365	6.715285	6.982358	7.250098	7.518507	7.787585	8.057334	8.327757	8.598855
730	13.881520	14.452250	15.025836	15.602292	16.181634	16.763875	17.349030	17.937113
1095	21.528989	22.443716	23.365322	24.293858	25.229377	26.171931	27.121572	28.078354
1825	38.399060	40.139588	41.901993	43.686550	45.493537	47.323235	49.175931	51.051913
3650	91.542998	96.391041	101.361756	106.458246	111.683692	117.041357	122.534585	128.166805

Table shows interest (I) on $100 compounded daily for N days at an annual rate of R.
*Table values can be generated using the formula: I = 100 * (1 + R/365)^N - 100.*

TABLE 13-2

Compound Interest on $100, Compounded Daily (365 Days) (Exact Time, Exact Interest Basis) -- Continued

	Annual rate							
Days	**8.50%**	**8.75%**	**9.00%**	**9.25%**	**9.50%**	**9.75%**	**10%**	**12%**
1	0.023288	0.023973	0.024658	0.025342	0.026027	0.026712	0.027397	0.032877
2	0.046581	0.047951	0.049321	0.050691	0.052062	0.053432	0.054802	0.065764
3	0.069879	0.071935	0.073991	0.076047	0.078103	0.080158	0.082214	0.098663
4	0.093183	0.095925	0.098667	0.101408	0.104150	0.106892	0.109634	0.131572
5	0.116493	0.119920	0.123348	0.126777	0.130205	0.133633	0.137061	0.164492
6	0.139807	0.143922	0.148036	0.152151	0.156266	0.160381	0.164496	0.197422
7	0.163128	0.167929	0.172730	0.177532	0.182334	0.187136	0.191939	0.230364
8	0.186453	0.191942	0.197431	0.202920	0.208409	0.213899	0.219388	0.263317
9	0.209784	0.215960	0.222137	0.228314	0.234491	0.240668	0.246846	0.296280
10	0.233121	0.239985	0.246849	0.253714	0.260579	0.267445	0.274311	0.329254
11	0.256463	0.264015	0.271568	0.279121	0.286674	0.294228	0.301783	0.362239
12	0.279810	0.288051	0.296292	0.304534	0.312776	0.321019	0.329263	0.395235
13	0.303163	0.312092	0.321023	0.329953	0.338885	0.347817	0.356750	0.428241
14	0.326521	0.336140	0.345759	0.355380	0.365001	0.374623	0.384245	0.461259
15	0.349885	0.360193	0.370502	0.380812	0.391123	0.401435	0.411748	0.494287
16	0.373254	0.384252	0.395251	0.406251	0.417252	0.428255	0.439258	0.527326
17	0.396629	0.408317	0.420006	0.431696	0.443388	0.455081	0.466776	0.560377
18	0.420009	0.432387	0.444767	0.457148	0.469531	0.481915	0.494301	0.593437
19	0.443394	0.456464	0.469534	0.482607	0.495681	0.508756	0.521833	0.626509
20	0.466785	0.480546	0.494308	0.508071	0.521837	0.535604	0.549374	0.659592
21	0.490182	0.504633	0.519087	0.533543	0.548000	0.562460	0.576921	0.692686
22	0.513583	0.528727	0.543873	0.559020	0.574170	0.589322	0.604477	0.725790
23	0.536991	0.552826	0.568664	0.584504	0.600347	0.616192	0.632040	0.758905
24	0.560403	0.576931	0.593462	0.609995	0.626531	0.643069	0.659610	0.792032
25	0.583822	0.601042	0.618266	0.635492	0.652721	0.669953	0.687188	0.825169
26	0.607245	0.625159	0.643076	0.660996	0.678919	0.696845	0.714774	0.858317
27	0.630674	0.649281	0.667892	0.686506	0.705123	0.723743	0.742367	0.891476
28	0.654109	0.673410	0.692714	0.712022	0.731334	0.750649	0.769967	0.924645
29	0.677549	0.697544	0.717542	0.737545	0.757551	0.777562	0.797576	0.957826
30	0.700994	0.721684	0.742377	0.763074	0.783776	0.804482	0.825191	0.991018
31	0.724445	0.745829	0.767217	0.788610	0.810007	0.831409	0.852815	1.024220
32	0.747902	0.769981	0.792064	0.814153	0.836246	0.858343	0.880446	1.057434
33	0.771363	0.794138	0.816917	0.839701	0.862491	0.885285	0.908084	1.090658
34	0.794831	0.818301	0.841776	0.865257	0.888742	0.912234	0.935730	1.123893
35	0.818304	0.842470	0.866641	0.890818	0.915001	0.939190	0.963384	1.157139
40	0.935749	0.963400	0.991059	1.018724	1.046397	1.074078	1.101766	1.323535
45	1.053332	1.084476	1.115630	1.146792	1.177964	1.209146	1.240337	1.490203
50	1.171052	1.205697	1.240354	1.275023	1.309703	1.344395	1.379098	1.657146
55	1.288909	1.327063	1.365233	1.403416	1.441613	1.479824	1.518050	1.824364
60	1.406903	1.448575	1.490265	1.531972	1.573695	1.615435	1.657192	1.991856
90	2.117759	2.180713	2.243705	2.306736	2.369805	2.432912	2.496058	3.002614
120	2.833599	2.918135	3.002739	3.087412	3.172155	3.256966	3.341847	4.023388
150	3.554457	3.660878	3.767407	3.874046	3.980793	4.087650	4.194615	5.054278
180	4.280368	4.408981	4.537753	4.666682	4.795770	4.925016	5.054420	6.095384
240	5.747491	5.921424	6.095642	6.270146	6.444935	6.620011	6.795373	8.208652
360	8.743951	9.012354	9.281418	9.551144	9.821533	10.092589	10.364311	12.562306
365	8.870629	9.143082	9.416214	9.690029	9.964526	10.239709	10.515578	12.747462
730	18.528139	19.122123	19.719080	20.319024	20.921970	21.527934	22.136930	27.119901
1095	29.042331	30.013557	30.992085	31.977972	32.971272	33.972041	34.980335	43.324461
1825	52.951474	54.874909	56.822519	58.794608	60.791482	62.813453	64.860837	82.193913
3650	133.941534	139.862375	145.933026	152.157274	158.539006	165.082205	171.790955	231.946220

Table shows interest (I) on $100 compounded daily for N days at an annual rate of R.
*Table values can be generated using the formula: I = 100 * (1 + R/365)^N - 100.*

Table 13-3: ***Present Value of $1.00***

	Rate per Period					
Periods	**0.25%**	**0.50%**	**0.75%**	**1.00%**	**1.25%**	**1.50%**
1	0.99751	0.99502	0.99256	0.99010	0.98765	0.98522
2	0.99502	0.99007	0.98517	0.98030	0.97546	0.97066
3	0.99254	0.98515	0.97783	0.97059	0.96342	0.95632
4	0.99006	0.98025	0.97055	0.96098	0.95152	0.94218
5	0.98759	0.97537	0.96333	0.95147	0.93978	0.92826
6	0.98513	0.97052	0.95616	0.94205	0.92817	0.91454
7	0.98267	0.96569	0.94904	0.93272	0.91672	0.90103
8	0.98022	0.96089	0.94198	0.92348	0.90540	0.88771
9	0.97778	0.95610	0.93496	0.91434	0.89422	0.87459
10	0.97534	0.95135	0.92800	0.90529	0.88318	0.86167
11	0.97291	0.94661	0.92109	0.89632	0.87228	0.84893
12	0.97048	0.94191	0.91424	0.88745	0.86151	0.83639
13	0.96806	0.93722	0.90743	0.87866	0.85087	0.82403
14	0.96565	0.93256	0.90068	0.86996	0.84037	0.81185
15	0.96324	0.92792	0.89397	0.86135	0.82999	0.79985
16	0.96084	0.92330	0.88732	0.85282	0.81975	0.78803
17	0.95844	0.91871	0.88071	0.84438	0.80963	0.77639
18	0.95605	0.91414	0.87416	0.83602	0.79963	0.76491
19	0.95367	0.90959	0.86765	0.82774	0.78976	0.75361
20	0.95129	0.90506	0.86119	0.81954	0.78001	0.74247
21	0.94892	0.90056	0.85478	0.81143	0.77038	0.73150
22	0.94655	0.89608	0.84842	0.80340	0.76087	0.72069
23	0.94419	0.89162	0.84210	0.79544	0.75147	0.71004
24	0.94184	0.88719	0.83583	0.78757	0.74220	0.69954
25	0.93949	0.88277	0.82961	0.77977	0.73303	0.68921
26	0.93714	0.87838	0.82343	0.77205	0.72398	0.67902
27	0.93481	0.87401	0.81730	0.76440	0.71505	0.66899
28	0.93248	0.86966	0.81122	0.75684	0.70622	0.65910
29	0.93015	0.86533	0.80518	0.74934	0.69750	0.64936
30	0.92783	0.86103	0.79919	0.74192	0.68889	0.63976
35	0.91632	0.83982	0.76988	0.70591	0.64740	0.59387
40	0.90495	0.81914	0.74165	0.67165	0.60841	0.55126
45	0.89372	0.79896	0.71445	0.63905	0.57177	0.51171
50	0.88263	0.77929	0.68825	0.60804	0.53734	0.47500
55	0.87168	0.76009	0.66301	0.57853	0.50498	0.44093
60	0.86087	0.74137	0.63870	0.55045	0.47457	0.40930
65	0.85019	0.72311	0.61528	0.52373	0.44599	0.37993
70	0.83964	0.70530	0.59272	0.49831	0.41913	0.35268
75	0.82922	0.68793	0.57098	0.47413	0.39389	0.32738
80	0.81894	0.67099	0.55004	0.45112	0.37017	0.30389
85	0.80877	0.65446	0.52987	0.42922	0.34787	0.28209
90	0.79874	0.63834	0.51044	0.40839	0.32692	0.26185
95	0.78883	0.62262	0.49172	0.38857	0.30724	0.24307
100	0.77904	0.60729	0.47369	0.36971	0.28873	0.22563

Table shows the lump sum amount of money, present value (PV), that should be invested now so that the accumulated amount will be $1 after a specified number of periods, N, at a specified rate per period, R. Table values can be generated by using the formula: PV = $1/(1 + R)^N.

Table 13-3: Present Value of $1.00

Periods	1.75%	2.00%	Rate per Period 2.25%	2.50%	2.75%	3.00%
1	0.98280	0.98039	0.97800	0.97561	0.97324	0.97087
2	0.96590	0.96117	0.95647	0.95181	0.94719	0.94260
3	0.94929	0.94232	0.93543	0.92860	0.92184	0.91514
4	0.93296	0.92385	0.91484	0.90595	0.89717	0.88849
5	0.91691	0.90573	0.89471	0.88385	0.87315	0.86261
6	0.90114	0.88797	0.87502	0.86230	0.84978	0.83748
7	0.88564	0.87056	0.85577	0.84127	0.82704	0.81309
8	0.87041	0.85349	0.83694	0.82075	0.80491	0.78941
9	0.85544	0.83676	0.81852	0.80073	0.78336	0.76642
10	0.84073	0.82035	0.80051	0.78120	0.76240	0.74409
11	0.82627	0.80426	0.78289	0.76214	0.74199	0.72242
12	0.81206	0.78849	0.76567	0.74356	0.72213	0.70138
13	0.79809	0.77303	0.74882	0.72542	0.70281	0.68095
14	0.78436	0.75788	0.73234	0.70773	0.68400	0.66112
15	0.77087	0.74301	0.71623	0.69047	0.66569	0.64186
16	0.75762	0.72845	0.70047	0.67362	0.64787	0.62317
17	0.74459	0.71416	0.68505	0.65720	0.63053	0.60502
18	0.73178	0.70016	0.66998	0.64117	0.61366	0.58739
19	0.71919	0.68643	0.65523	0.62553	0.59723	0.57029
20	0.70682	0.67297	0.64082	0.61027	0.58125	0.55368
21	0.69467	0.65978	0.62672	0.59539	0.56569	0.53755
22	0.68272	0.64684	0.61292	0.58086	0.55055	0.52189
23	0.67098	0.63416	0.59944	0.56670	0.53582	0.50669
24	0.65944	0.62172	0.58625	0.55288	0.52148	0.49193
25	0.64810	0.60953	0.57335	0.53939	0.50752	0.47761
26	0.63695	0.59758	0.56073	0.52623	0.49394	0.46369
27	0.62599	0.58586	0.54839	0.51340	0.48072	0.45019
28	0.61523	0.57437	0.53632	0.50088	0.46785	0.43708
29	0.60465	0.56311	0.52452	0.48866	0.45533	0.42435
30	0.59425	0.55207	0.51298	0.47674	0.44314	0.41199
35	0.54487	0.50003	0.45897	0.42137	0.38693	0.35538
40	0.49960	0.45289	0.41065	0.37243	0.33785	0.30656
45	0.45809	0.41020	0.36741	0.32917	0.29500	0.26444
50	0.42003	0.37153	0.32873	0.29094	0.25758	0.22811
55	0.38513	0.33650	0.29412	0.25715	0.22491	0.19677
60	0.35313	0.30478	0.26315	0.22728	0.19638	0.16973
65	0.32379	0.27605	0.23544	0.20089	0.17147	0.14641
70	0.29689	0.25003	0.21065	0.17755	0.14972	0.12630
75	0.27222	0.22646	0.18847	0.15693	0.13073	0.10895
80	0.24960	0.20511	0.16863	0.13870	0.11414	0.09398
85	0.22886	0.18577	0.15088	0.12259	0.09967	0.08107
90	0.20985	0.16826	0.13499	0.10836	0.08702	0.06993
95	0.19241	0.15240	0.12078	0.09577	0.07598	0.06032
100	0.17642	0.13803	0.10806	0.08465	0.06635	0.05203

Table shows the lump sum amount of money, present value (PV), that should be invested now so that the accumulated amount will be $1 after a specified number of periods, N, at a specified rate per period, R. Table values can be generated by using the formula: PV = $1/(1 + R)^N.

	Rate per Period					
Periods	**3.25%**	**3.50%**	**3.75%**	**4.00%**	**4.25%**	**4.50%**
1	0.96852	0.96618	0.96386	0.96154	0.95923	0.95694
2	0.93804	0.93351	0.92902	0.92456	0.92013	0.91573
3	0.90851	0.90194	0.89544	0.88900	0.88262	0.87630
4	0.87991	0.87144	0.86307	0.85480	0.84663	0.83856
5	0.85222	0.84197	0.83188	0.82193	0.81212	0.80245
6	0.82539	0.81350	0.80181	0.79031	0.77901	0.76790
7	0.79941	0.78599	0.77283	0.75992	0.74725	0.73483
8	0.77425	0.75941	0.74490	0.73069	0.71679	0.70319
9	0.74988	0.73373	0.71797	0.70259	0.68757	0.67290
10	0.72627	0.70892	0.69202	0.67556	0.65954	0.64393
11	0.70341	0.68495	0.66701	0.64958	0.63265	0.61620
12	0.68127	0.66178	0.64290	0.62460	0.60686	0.58966
13	0.65983	0.63940	0.61966	0.60057	0.58212	0.56427
14	0.63906	0.61778	0.59726	0.57748	0.55839	0.53997
15	0.61894	0.59689	0.57568	0.55526	0.53562	0.51672
16	0.59946	0.57671	0.55487	0.53391	0.51379	0.49447
17	0.58059	0.55720	0.53481	0.51337	0.49284	0.47318
18	0.56231	0.53836	0.51548	0.49363	0.47275	0.45280
19	0.54461	0.52016	0.49685	0.47464	0.45348	0.43330
20	0.52747	0.50257	0.47889	0.45639	0.43499	0.41464
21	0.51087	0.48557	0.46158	0.43883	0.41726	0.39679
22	0.49479	0.46915	0.44490	0.42196	0.40025	0.37970
23	0.47921	0.45329	0.42882	0.40573	0.38393	0.36335
24	0.46413	0.43796	0.41332	0.39012	0.36828	0.34770
25	0.44952	0.42315	0.39838	0.37512	0.35326	0.33273
26	0.43537	0.40884	0.38398	0.36069	0.33886	0.31840
27	0.42167	0.39501	0.37010	0.34682	0.32505	0.30469
28	0.40839	0.38165	0.35672	0.33348	0.31180	0.29157
29	0.39554	0.36875	0.34383	0.32065	0.29908	0.27902
30	0.38309	0.35628	0.33140	0.30832	0.28689	0.26700
35	0.32647	0.29998	0.27569	0.25342	0.23299	0.21425
40	0.27823	0.25257	0.22934	0.20829	0.18922	0.17193
45	0.23711	0.21266	0.19078	0.17120	0.15367	0.13796
50	0.20207	0.17905	0.15871	0.14071	0.12479	0.11071
55	0.17221	0.15076	0.13202	0.11566	0.10135	0.08884
60	0.14676	0.12693	0.10983	0.09506	0.08231	0.07129
65	0.12507	0.10688	0.09136	0.07813	0.06684	0.05721
70	0.10658	0.08999	0.07600	0.06422	0.05428	0.04590
75	0.09083	0.07577	0.06323	0.05278	0.04409	0.03684
80	0.07741	0.06379	0.05260	0.04338	0.03580	0.02956
85	0.06597	0.05371	0.04375	0.03566	0.02908	0.02372
90	0.05622	0.04522	0.03640	0.02931	0.02361	0.01903
95	0.04791	0.03808	0.03028	0.02409	0.01918	0.01527
100	0.04083	0.03206	0.02519	0.01980	0.01557	0.01226

Table shows the lump sum amount of money, present value (PV), that should be invested now so that the accumulated amount will be $1 after a specified number of periods, N, at a specified rate per period, R. Table values can be generated by using the formula: PV = $1/(1 + R)^N.

Periods	4.75%	5.00%	5.25%	5.50%	5.75%	6.00%
			Rate per Period			
1	0.95465	0.95238	0.95012	0.94787	0.94563	0.94340
2	0.91136	0.90703	0.90273	0.89845	0.89421	0.89000
3	0.87004	0.86384	0.85770	0.85161	0.84559	0.83962
4	0.83058	0.82270	0.81491	0.80722	0.79961	0.79209
5	0.79292	0.78353	0.77426	0.76513	0.75613	0.74726
6	0.75697	0.74622	0.73564	0.72525	0.71502	0.70496
7	0.72264	0.71068	0.69895	0.68744	0.67614	0.66506
8	0.68987	0.67684	0.66408	0.65160	0.63938	0.62741
9	0.65859	0.64461	0.63096	0.61763	0.60461	0.59190
10	0.62872	0.61391	0.59949	0.58543	0.57174	0.55839
11	0.60021	0.58468	0.56958	0.55491	0.54065	0.52679
12	0.57300	0.55684	0.54117	0.52598	0.51125	0.49697
13	0.54701	0.53032	0.51418	0.49856	0.48345	0.46884
14	0.52221	0.50507	0.48853	0.47257	0.45717	0.44230
15	0.49853	0.48102	0.46416	0.44793	0.43231	0.41727
16	0.47592	0.45811	0.44101	0.42458	0.40880	0.39365
17	0.45434	0.43630	0.41901	0.40245	0.38657	0.37136
18	0.43374	0.41552	0.39811	0.38147	0.36556	0.35034
19	0.41407	0.39573	0.37825	0.36158	0.34568	0.33051
20	0.39529	0.37689	0.35938	0.34273	0.32688	0.31180
21	0.37737	0.35894	0.34146	0.32486	0.30911	0.29416
22	0.36026	0.34185	0.32442	0.30793	0.29230	0.27751
23	0.34392	0.32557	0.30824	0.29187	0.27641	0.26180
24	0.32832	0.31007	0.29287	0.27666	0.26138	0.24698
25	0.31344	0.29530	0.27826	0.26223	0.24717	0.23300
26	0.29922	0.28124	0.26438	0.24856	0.23373	0.21981
27	0.28565	0.26785	0.25119	0.23560	0.22102	0.20737
28	0.27270	0.25509	0.23866	0.22332	0.20900	0.19563
29	0.26034	0.24295	0.22676	0.21168	0.19764	0.18456
30	0.24853	0.23138	0.21545	0.20064	0.18689	0.17411
35	0.19706	0.18129	0.16681	0.15352	0.14131	0.13011
40	0.15626	0.14205	0.12916	0.11746	0.10685	0.09722
45	0.12390	0.11130	0.10000	0.08988	0.08079	0.07265
50	0.09824	0.08720	0.07743	0.06877	0.06109	0.05429
55	0.07790	0.06833	0.05995	0.05262	0.04619	0.04057
60	0.06177	0.05354	0.04642	0.04026	0.03493	0.03031
65	0.04898	0.04195	0.03594	0.03080	0.02641	0.02265
70	0.03883	0.03287	0.02783	0.02357	0.01997	0.01693
75	0.03079	0.02575	0.02154	0.01803	0.01510	0.01265
80	0.02442	0.02018	0.01668	0.01380	0.01142	0.00945
85	0.01936	0.01581	0.01292	0.01056	0.00863	0.00706
90	0.01535	0.01239	0.01000	0.00808	0.00653	0.00528
95	0.01217	0.00971	0.00774	0.00618	0.00494	0.00394
100	0.00965	0.00760	0.00600	0.00473	0.00373	0.00295

Table shows the lump sum amount of money, present value (PV), that should be invested now so that the accumulated amount will be $1 after a specified number of periods, N, at a specified rate per period, R. Table values can be generated by using the formula: PV = $1/(1 + R)^N.

Table 13-3: Present Value of $1.00

Periods	6.25%	6.50%	6.75%	7.00%	7.25%	7.50%
			Rate per Period			
1	0.95465	0.95238	0.95012	0.94787	0.94563	0.94340
2	0.91136	0.90703	0.90273	0.89845	0.89421	0.89000
3	0.87004	0.86384	0.85770	0.85161	0.84559	0.83962
4	0.83058	0.82270	0.81491	0.80722	0.79961	0.79209
5	0.79292	0.78353	0.77426	0.76513	0.75613	0.74726
6	0.75697	0.74622	0.73564	0.72525	0.71502	0.70496
7	0.72264	0.71068	0.69895	0.68744	0.67614	0.66506
8	0.68987	0.67684	0.66408	0.65160	0.63938	0.62741
9	0.65859	0.64461	0.63096	0.61763	0.60461	0.59190
10	0.62872	0.61391	0.59949	0.58543	0.57174	0.55839
11	0.60021	0.58468	0.56958	0.55491	0.54065	0.52679
12	0.57300	0.55684	0.54117	0.52598	0.51125	0.49697
13	0.54701	0.53032	0.51418	0.49856	0.48345	0.46884
14	0.52221	0.50507	0.48853	0.47257	0.45717	0.44230
15	0.49853	0.48102	0.46416	0.44793	0.43231	0.41727
16	0.47592	0.45811	0.44101	0.42458	0.40880	0.39365
17	0.45434	0.43630	0.41901	0.40245	0.38657	0.37136
18	0.43374	0.41552	0.39811	0.38147	0.36556	0.35034
19	0.41407	0.39573	0.37825	0.36158	0.34568	0.33051
20	0.39529	0.37689	0.35938	0.34273	0.32688	0.31180
21	0.37737	0.35894	0.34146	0.32486	0.30911	0.29416
22	0.36026	0.34185	0.32442	0.30793	0.29230	0.27751
23	0.34392	0.32557	0.30824	0.29187	0.27641	0.26180
24	0.32832	0.31007	0.29287	0.27666	0.26138	0.24698
25	0.31344	0.29530	0.27826	0.26223	0.24717	0.23300
26	0.29922	0.28124	0.26438	0.24856	0.23373	0.21981
27	0.28565	0.26785	0.25119	0.23560	0.22102	0.20737
28	0.27270	0.25509	0.23866	0.22332	0.20900	0.19563
29	0.26034	0.24295	0.22676	0.21168	0.19764	0.18456
30	0.24853	0.23138	0.21545	0.20064	0.18689	0.17411
35	0.19706	0.18129	0.16681	0.15352	0.14131	0.13011
40	0.15626	0.14205	0.12916	0.11746	0.10685	0.09722
45	0.12390	0.11130	0.10000	0.08988	0.08079	0.07265
50	0.09824	0.08720	0.07743	0.06877	0.06109	0.05429
55	0.07790	0.06833	0.05995	0.05262	0.04619	0.04057
60	0.06177	0.05354	0.04642	0.04026	0.03493	0.03031
65	0.04898	0.04195	0.03594	0.03080	0.02641	0.02265
70	0.03883	0.03287	0.02783	0.02357	0.01997	0.01693
75	0.03079	0.02575	0.02154	0.01803	0.01510	0.01265
80	0.02442	0.02018	0.01668	0.01380	0.01142	0.00945
85	0.01936	0.01581	0.01292	0.01056	0.00863	0.00706
90	0.01535	0.01239	0.01000	0.00808	0.00653	0.00528
95	0.01217	0.00971	0.00774	0.00618	0.00494	0.00394
100	0.00965	0.00760	0.00600	0.00473	0.00373	0.00295

Table shows the lump sum amount of money, present value (PV), that should be invested now so that the accumulated amount will be $1 after a specified number of periods, N, at a specified rate per period, R. Table values can be generated by using the formula: PV = $1/(1 + R)^N.

Table 13-3: Present Value of $1.00

Periods	7.75%	8.00%	8.25%	8.50%	8.75%	9.00%
1	0.92807	0.92593	0.92379	0.92166	0.91954	0.91743
2	0.86132	0.85734	0.85338	0.84946	0.84555	0.84168
3	0.79937	0.79383	0.78834	0.78291	0.77752	0.77218
4	0.74188	0.73503	0.72826	0.72157	0.71496	0.70843
5	0.68852	0.68058	0.67276	0.66505	0.65744	0.64993
6	0.63899	0.63017	0.62149	0.61295	0.60454	0.59627
7	0.59303	0.58349	0.57412	0.56493	0.55590	0.54703
8	0.55038	0.54027	0.53037	0.52067	0.51117	0.50187
9	0.51079	0.50025	0.48995	0.47988	0.47004	0.46043
10	0.47405	0.46319	0.45261	0.44229	0.43222	0.42241
11	0.43996	0.42888	0.41811	0.40764	0.39745	0.38753
12	0.40831	0.39711	0.38625	0.37570	0.36547	0.35553
13	0.37894	0.36770	0.35681	0.34627	0.33606	0.32618
14	0.35169	0.34046	0.32962	0.31914	0.30902	0.29925
15	0.32639	0.31524	0.30450	0.29414	0.28416	0.27454
16	0.30292	0.29189	0.28129	0.27110	0.26130	0.25187
17	0.28113	0.27027	0.25985	0.24986	0.24027	0.23107
18	0.26091	0.25025	0.24005	0.23028	0.22094	0.21199
19	0.24214	0.23171	0.22175	0.21224	0.20316	0.19449
20	0.22473	0.21455	0.20485	0.19562	0.18682	0.17843
21	0.20856	0.19866	0.18924	0.18029	0.17179	0.16370
22	0.19356	0.18394	0.17482	0.16617	0.15796	0.15018
23	0.17964	0.17032	0.16149	0.15315	0.14525	0.13778
24	0.16672	0.15770	0.14919	0.14115	0.13357	0.12640
25	0.15473	0.14602	0.13782	0.13009	0.12282	0.11597
26	0.14360	0.13520	0.12731	0.11990	0.11294	0.10639
27	0.13327	0.12519	0.11761	0.11051	0.10385	0.09761
28	0.12368	0.11591	0.10865	0.10185	0.09549	0.08955
29	0.11479	0.10733	0.10037	0.09387	0.08781	0.08215
30	0.10653	0.09938	0.09272	0.08652	0.08075	0.07537
35	0.07335	0.06763	0.06238	0.05754	0.05309	0.04899
40	0.05050	0.04603	0.04196	0.03827	0.03490	0.03184
45	0.03477	0.03133	0.02823	0.02545	0.02294	0.02069
50	0.02394	0.02132	0.01899	0.01692	0.01508	0.01345
55	0.01648	0.01451	0.01278	0.01126	0.00992	0.00874
60	0.01135	0.00988	0.00860	0.00749	0.00652	0.00568
65	0.00781	0.00672	0.00578	0.00498	0.00429	0.00369
70	0.00538	0.00457	0.00389	0.00331	0.00282	0.00240
75	0.00370	0.00311	0.00262	0.00220	0.00185	0.00156
80	0.00255	0.00212	0.00176	0.00146	0.00122	0.00101
85	0.00176	0.00144	0.00118	0.00097	0.00080	0.00066
90	0.00121	0.00098	0.00080	0.00065	0.00053	0.00043
95	0.00083	0.00067	0.00054	0.00043	0.00035	0.00028
100	0.00057	0.00045	0.00036	0.00029	0.00023	0.00018

(Column headers 7.75%–9.00% are under the spanning heading "Rate per Period".)

Table shows the lump sum amount of money, present value (PV), that should be invested now so that the accumulated amount will be $1 after a specified number of periods, N, at a specified rate per period, R. Table values can be generated by using the formula: PV = $1/(1 + R)^N.

Table 13-3: Present Value of $1.00

Periods	9.25%	9.50%	Rate per Period 9.75%	10.00%	10.25%	10.50%
1	0.91533	0.91324	0.91116	0.90909	0.90703	0.90498
2	0.83783	0.83401	0.83022	0.82645	0.82270	0.81898
3	0.76689	0.76165	0.75646	0.75131	0.74622	0.74116
4	0.70196	0.69557	0.68926	0.68301	0.67684	0.67073
5	0.64253	0.63523	0.62803	0.62092	0.61391	0.60700
6	0.58813	0.58012	0.57223	0.56447	0.55684	0.54932
7	0.53833	0.52979	0.52140	0.51316	0.50507	0.49712
8	0.49275	0.48382	0.47508	0.46651	0.45811	0.44989
9	0.45103	0.44185	0.43287	0.42410	0.41552	0.40714
10	0.41284	0.40351	0.39442	0.38554	0.37689	0.36845
11	0.37789	0.36851	0.35938	0.35049	0.34185	0.33344
12	0.34589	0.33654	0.32745	0.31863	0.31007	0.30175
13	0.31661	0.30734	0.29836	0.28966	0.28124	0.27308
14	0.28980	0.28067	0.27185	0.26333	0.25509	0.24713
15	0.26526	0.25632	0.24770	0.23939	0.23138	0.22365
16	0.24280	0.23409	0.22570	0.21763	0.20987	0.20240
17	0.22225	0.21378	0.20565	0.19784	0.19035	0.18316
18	0.20343	0.19523	0.18738	0.17986	0.17266	0.16576
19	0.18621	0.17829	0.17073	0.16351	0.15661	0.15001
20	0.17044	0.16282	0.15556	0.14864	0.14205	0.13575
21	0.15601	0.14870	0.14174	0.13513	0.12884	0.12285
22	0.14280	0.13580	0.12915	0.12285	0.11686	0.11118
23	0.13071	0.12402	0.11768	0.11168	0.10600	0.10062
24	0.11964	0.11326	0.10722	0.10153	0.09614	0.09106
25	0.10951	0.10343	0.09770	0.09230	0.08720	0.08240
26	0.10024	0.09446	0.08902	0.08391	0.07910	0.07457
27	0.09175	0.08626	0.08111	0.07628	0.07174	0.06749
28	0.08398	0.07878	0.07390	0.06934	0.06507	0.06107
29	0.07687	0.07194	0.06734	0.06304	0.05902	0.05527
30	0.07036	0.06570	0.06136	0.05731	0.05354	0.05002
35	0.04521	0.04174	0.03853	0.03558	0.03287	0.03036
40	0.02905	0.02651	0.02420	0.02209	0.02018	0.01843
45	0.01867	0.01684	0.01520	0.01372	0.01239	0.01119
50	0.01199	0.01070	0.00954	0.00852	0.00760	0.00679
55	0.00771	0.00680	0.00599	0.00529	0.00467	0.00412
60	0.00495	0.00432	0.00376	0.00328	0.00287	0.00250
65	0.00318	0.00274	0.00236	0.00204	0.00176	0.00152
70	0.00204	0.00174	0.00148	0.00127	0.00108	0.00092
75	0.00131	0.00111	0.00093	0.00079	0.00066	0.00056
80	0.00084	0.00070	0.00059	0.00049	0.00041	0.00034
85	0.00054	0.00045	0.00037	0.00030	0.00025	0.00021
90	0.00035	0.00028	0.00023	0.00019	0.00015	0.00013
95	0.00022	0.00018	0.00015	0.00012	0.00009	0.00008
100	0.00014	0.00011	0.00009	0.00007	0.00006	0.00005

Table shows the lump sum amount of money, present value (PV), that should be invested now so that the accumulated amount will be $1 after a specified number of periods, N, at a specified rate per period, R. Table values can be generated by using the formula: PV = $1/(1 + R)^N.

Periods	10.75%	11.00%	Rate per Period 11.25%	11.50%	11.75%	12.00%
1	0.90293	0.90090	0.89888	0.89686	0.89485	0.89286
2	0.81529	0.81162	0.80798	0.80436	0.80076	0.79719
3	0.73615	0.73119	0.72627	0.72140	0.71657	0.71178
4	0.66470	0.65873	0.65283	0.64699	0.64122	0.63552
5	0.60018	0.59345	0.58681	0.58026	0.57380	0.56743
6	0.54192	0.53464	0.52747	0.52042	0.51347	0.50663
7	0.48932	0.48166	0.47413	0.46674	0.45948	0.45235
8	0.44182	0.43393	0.42619	0.41860	0.41117	0.40388
9	0.39894	0.39092	0.38309	0.37543	0.36794	0.36061
10	0.36022	0.35218	0.34435	0.33671	0.32925	0.32197
11	0.32525	0.31728	0.30953	0.30198	0.29463	0.28748
12	0.29368	0.28584	0.27823	0.27083	0.26365	0.25668
13	0.26517	0.25751	0.25009	0.24290	0.23593	0.22917
14	0.23944	0.23199	0.22480	0.21785	0.21112	0.20462
15	0.21619	0.20900	0.20207	0.19538	0.18892	0.18270
16	0.19521	0.18829	0.18164	0.17523	0.16906	0.16312
17	0.17626	0.16963	0.16327	0.15715	0.15128	0.14564
18	0.15915	0.15282	0.14676	0.14095	0.13538	0.13004
19	0.14370	0.13768	0.13192	0.12641	0.12114	0.11611
20	0.12976	0.12403	0.11858	0.11337	0.10841	0.10367
21	0.11716	0.11174	0.10659	0.10168	0.09701	0.09256
22	0.10579	0.10067	0.09581	0.09119	0.08681	0.08264
23	0.09552	0.09069	0.08612	0.08179	0.07768	0.07379
24	0.08625	0.08170	0.07741	0.07335	0.06951	0.06588
25	0.07788	0.07361	0.06958	0.06579	0.06220	0.05882
26	0.07032	0.06631	0.06255	0.05900	0.05566	0.05252
27	0.06349	0.05974	0.05622	0.05291	0.04981	0.04689
28	0.05733	0.05382	0.05054	0.04746	0.04457	0.04187
29	0.05176	0.04849	0.04543	0.04256	0.03989	0.03738
30	0.04674	0.04368	0.04083	0.03817	0.03569	0.03338
35	0.02805	0.02592	0.02396	0.02215	0.02048	0.01894
40	0.01684	0.01538	0.01406	0.01285	0.01175	0.01075
45	0.01010	0.00913	0.00825	0.00746	0.00674	0.00610
50	0.00606	0.00542	0.00484	0.00433	0.00387	0.00346
55	0.00364	0.00322	0.00284	0.00251	0.00222	0.00196
60	0.00218	0.00191	0.00167	0.00146	0.00127	0.00111
65	0.00131	0.00113	0.00098	0.00085	0.00073	0.00063
70	0.00079	0.00067	0.00057	0.00049	0.00042	0.00036
75	0.00047	0.00040	0.00034	0.00028	0.00024	0.00020
80	0.00028	0.00024	0.00020	0.00017	0.00014	0.00012
85	0.00017	0.00014	0.00012	0.00010	0.00008	0.00007
90	0.00010	0.00008	0.00007	0.00006	0.00005	0.00004
95	0.00006	0.00005	0.00004	0.00003	0.00003	0.00002
100	0.00004	0.00003	0.00002	0.00002	0.00001	0.00001

Table shows the lump sum amount of money, present value (PV), that should be invested now so that the accumulated amount will be $1 after a specified number of periods, N, at a specified rate per period, R. Table values can be generated by using the formula: PV = $1/(1 + R)^N.

TABLE 14-1

Future Value of $1.00 Ordinary Annuity (*Annuity Due)

	Rate per period								
Periods	**0.25%**	**0.50%**	**0.75%**	**1.00%**	**1.25%**	**1.50%**	**1.75%**	**2.00%**	**2.25%**
1	1.000	1.000	1.000	1.000	1.000	1.000	1.000	1.000	1.000
2	2.002	2.005	2.008	2.010	2.013	2.015	2.018	2.020	2.022
3	3.008	3.015	3.023	3.030	3.038	3.045	3.053	3.060	3.068
4	4.015	4.030	4.045	4.060	4.076	4.091	4.106	4.122	4.137
5	5.025	5.050	5.076	5.101	5.127	5.152	5.178	5.204	5.230
6	6.038	6.076	6.114	6.152	6.191	6.230	6.269	6.308	6.348
7	7.053	7.106	7.159	7.214	7.268	7.323	7.378	7.434	7.491
8	8.070	8.141	8.213	8.286	8.359	8.433	8.508	8.583	8.659
9	9.091	9.182	9.275	9.369	9.463	9.559	9.656	9.755	9.854
10	10.113	10.228	10.344	10.462	10.582	10.703	10.825	10.950	11.076
11	11.139	11.279	11.422	11.567	11.714	11.863	12.015	12.169	12.325
12	12.166	12.336	12.508	12.683	12.860	13.041	13.225	13.412	13.602
13	13.197	13.397	13.601	13.809	14.021	14.237	14.457	14.680	14.908
14	14.230	14.464	14.703	14.947	15.196	15.450	15.710	15.974	16.244
15	15.265	15.537	15.814	16.097	16.386	16.682	16.984	17.293	17.609
16	16.304	16.614	16.932	17.258	17.591	17.932	18.282	18.639	19.005
17	17.344	17.697	18.059	18.430	18.811	19.201	19.602	20.012	20.433
18	18.388	18.786	19.195	19.615	20.046	20.489	20.945	21.412	21.893
19	19.434	19.880	20.339	20.811	21.297	21.797	22.311	22.841	23.385
20	20.482	20.979	21.491	22.019	22.563	23.124	23.702	24.297	24.912
21	21.533	22.084	22.652	23.239	23.845	24.471	25.116	25.783	26.472
22	22.587	23.194	23.822	24.472	25.143	25.838	26.556	27.299	28.068
23	23.644	24.310	25.001	25.716	26.457	27.225	28.021	28.845	29.699
24	24.703	25.432	26.188	26.973	27.788	28.634	29.511	30.422	31.367
25	25.765	26.559	27.385	28.243	29.135	30.063	31.027	32.030	33.073
26	26.829	27.692	28.590	29.526	30.500	31.514	32.570	33.671	34.817
27	27.896	28.830	29.805	30.821	31.881	32.987	34.140	35.344	36.601
28	28.966	29.975	31.028	32.129	33.279	34.481	35.738	37.051	38.424
29	30.038	31.124	32.261	33.450	34.695	35.999	37.363	38.792	40.289
30	31.113	32.280	33.503	34.785	36.129	37.539	39.017	40.568	42.195
35	36.529	38.145	39.854	41.660	43.571	45.592	47.731	49.994	52.391
36	37.621	39.336	41.153	43.077	45.116	47.276	49.566	51.994	54.570
40	42.013	44.159	46.446	48.886	51.490	54.268	57.234	60.402	63.786
42	44.226	46.607	49.153	51.879	54.797	57.923	61.272	64.862	68.711
48	50.931	54.098	57.521	61.223	65.228	69.565	74.263	79.354	84.873
54	57.738	61.817	66.272	71.141	76.467	82.295	88.678	95.673	103.343
60	64.647	69.770	75.424	81.670	88.575	96.215	104.675	114.052	124.450
66	71.660	77.965	84.996	92.846	101.619	111.435	122.427	134.749	148.573
72	78.779	86.409	95.007	104.710	115.674	128.077	142.126	158.057	176.141
78	86.006	95.109	105.477	117.304	130.815	146.275	163.987	184.306	207.646
84	93.342	104.074	116.427	130.672	147.129	166.173	188.245	213.867	243.651
90	100.788	113.311	127.879	144.863	164.705	187.930	215.165	247.157	284.798
96	108.347	122.829	139.856	159.927	183.641	211.720	245.037	284.647	331.822
100	113.450	129.334	148.145	170.481	197.072	228.803	266.752	312.232	366.847
102	116.020	132.635	152.383	175.918	204.042	237.734	278.187	326.866	385.563
120	139.741	163.879	193.514	230.039	275.217	331.288	401.096	488.258	597.379
126	147.888	174.933	208.501	250.343	302.705	368.474	451.366	556.166	689.048
132	156.158	186.323	224.175	271.896	332.320	409.135	507.151	632.641	793.809

Table values show the future value, or accumulated amount of the investment and interest, of a $1 investment for a given number of periods at a given rate per period. Table values can be generated using the formula: FV = ((1_R)^N)-1)/R when FV is the future value, R is the interest rate per period, and N is the number of periods.

****Annuity Due: To use table values for an annuity due, multiply the value of an ordinary annuity by the sum of 1 and the period interest rate (1 + R).***

TABLE 14-1 -- Continued

*Future Value of $1.00 Ordinary Annuity (*Annuity Due)* *pg. 2*

	Rate per period								
Periods	**2.50%**	**2.75%**	**3.00%**	**3.25%**	**3.50%**	**3.75%**	**4.00%**	**4.25%**	**4.50%**
1	1.000	1.000	1.000	1.000	1.000	1.000	1.000	1.000	1.000
2	2.025	2.028	2.030	2.033	2.035	2.038	2.040	2.043	2.045
3	3.076	3.083	3.091	3.099	3.106	3.114	3.122	3.129	3.137
4	4.153	4.168	4.184	4.199	4.215	4.231	4.246	4.262	4.278
5	5.256	5.283	5.309	5.336	5.362	5.389	5.416	5.443	5.471
6	6.388	6.428	6.468	6.509	6.550	6.591	6.633	6.675	6.717
7	7.547	7.605	7.662	7.721	7.779	7.839	7.898	7.958	8.019
8	8.736	8.814	8.892	8.972	9.052	9.133	9.214	9.297	9.380
9	9.955	10.056	10.159	10.263	10.368	10.475	10.583	10.692	10.802
10	11.203	11.333	11.464	11.597	11.731	11.868	12.006	12.146	12.288
11	12.483	12.644	12.808	12.974	13.142	13.313	13.486	13.662	13.841
12	13.796	13.992	14.192	14.395	14.602	14.812	15.026	15.243	15.464
13	15.140	15.377	15.618	15.863	16.113	16.368	16.627	16.891	17.160
14	16.519	16.800	17.086	17.379	17.677	17.981	18.292	18.609	18.932
15	17.932	18.262	18.599	18.943	19.296	19.656	20.024	20.400	20.784
16	19.380	19.764	20.157	20.559	20.971	21.393	21.825	22.267	22.719
17	20.865	21.307	21.762	22.227	22.705	23.195	23.698	24.213	24.742
18	22.386	22.893	23.414	23.950	24.500	25.065	25.645	26.242	26.855
19	23.946	24.523	25.117	25.728	26.357	27.005	27.671	28.357	29.064
20	25.545	26.197	26.870	27.564	28.280	29.017	29.778	30.563	31.371
21	27.183	27.918	28.676	29.460	30.269	31.106	31.969	32.861	33.783
22	28.863	29.686	30.537	31.418	32.329	33.272	34.248	35.258	36.303
23	30.584	31.502	32.453	33.439	34.460	35.520	36.618	37.756	38.937
24	32.349	33.368	34.426	35.525	36.667	37.852	39.083	40.361	41.689
25	34.158	35.286	36.459	37.680	38.950	40.271	41.646	43.076	44.565
26	36.012	37.256	38.553	39.905	41.313	42.781	44.312	45.907	47.571
27	37.912	39.281	40.710	42.201	43.759	45.386	47.084	48.858	50.711
28	39.860	41.361	42.931	44.573	46.291	48.088	49.968	51.935	53.993
29	41.856	43.498	45.219	47.022	48.911	50.891	52.966	55.142	57.423
30	43.903	45.695	47.575	49.550	51.623	53.799	56.085	58.486	61.007
35	54.928	57.615	60.462	63.478	66.674	70.061	73.652	77.459	81.497
36	57.301	60.200	63.276	66.541	70.008	73.689	77.598	81.751	86.164
40	67.403	71.268	75.401	79.822	84.550	89.610	95.026	100.823	107.030
42	72.840	77.269	82.023	87.127	92.607	98.494	104.820	111.617	118.925
48	90.860	97.356	104.408	112.067	120.388	129.431	139.263	149.956	161.588
54	111.757	120.993	131.137	142.284	154.538	168.016	182.845	199.170	217.146
60	135.992	148.809	163.053	178.893	196.517	216.137	237.991	262.345	289.498
66	164.096	181.542	201.163	223.247	248.120	276.153	307.767	343.441	383.719
72	196.689	220.061	246.667	276.983	311.552	351.003	396.057	447.543	506.418
78	234.487	265.388	301.002	342.087	389.528	444.355	507.771	581.176	666.205
84	278.321	318.729	365.881	420.964	485.379	560.782	649.125	752.718	874.289
90	329.154	381.498	443.349	516.527	603.205	705.986	827.983	972.924	1145.269
96	388.106	455.362	535.850	632.305	748.043	887.082	1054.296	1255.596	1498.155
100	432.549	511.724	607.288	722.799	862.612	1032.049	1237.624	1487.307	1790.856
102	456.471	542.284	646.302	772.577	926.086	1112.941	1340.654	1618.457	1957.704
120	734.326	906.583	1123.700	1397.874	1744.695	2184.092	2741.564	3449.742	4350.404
126	857.981	1073.266	1348.224	1700.100	2151.225	2730.544	3475.586	4435.035	5672.074
132	1001.382	1269.413	1616.319	2066.261	2650.956	3412.068	4404.358	5699.836	7393.233

Table values show the future value, or accumulated amount of the investment and interest, of a $1 investment for a given number of periods at a given rate per period. Table values can be generated using the formula: FV = ((1_R)^N)-1)/R when FV is the future value, R is the interest rate per period, and N is the number of periods.

****Annuity Due: To use table values for an annuity due, multiply the value of an ordinary annuity by the sum of 1 and the period interest rate (1 + R).***

TABLE 14-1 -- Continued

Future Value of $1.00 Ordinary Annuity (*Annuity Due)

Periods	Rate per period								
	4.75%	**5.00%**	**5.25%**	**5.50%**	**5.75%**	**6.00%**	**6.50%**	**7.00%**	**7.50%**
1	1.000	1.000	1.000	1.000	1.000	1.000	1.000	1.000	1.000
2	2.048	2.050	2.053	2.055	2.058	2.060	2.065	2.070	2.075
3	3.145	3.153	3.160	3.168	3.176	3.184	3.199	3.215	3.231
4	4.294	4.310	4.326	4.342	4.358	4.375	4.407	4.440	4.473
5	5.498	5.526	5.553	5.581	5.609	5.637	5.694	5.751	5.808
6	6.759	6.802	6.845	6.888	6.932	6.975	7.064	7.153	7.244
7	8.080	8.142	8.204	8.267	8.330	8.394	8.523	8.654	8.787
8	9.464	9.549	9.635	9.722	9.809	9.897	10.077	10.260	10.446
9	10.914	11.027	11.141	11.256	11.373	11.491	11.732	11.978	12.230
10	12.432	12.578	12.726	12.875	13.027	13.181	13.494	13.816	14.147
11	14.023	14.207	14.394	14.583	14.776	14.972	15.372	15.784	16.208
12	15.689	15.917	16.149	16.386	16.626	16.870	17.371	17.888	18.424
13	17.434	17.713	17.997	18.287	18.582	18.882	19.500	20.141	20.806
14	19.262	19.599	19.942	20.293	20.650	21.015	21.767	22.550	23.366
15	21.177	21.579	21.989	22.409	22.838	23.276	24.182	25.129	26.118
16	23.183	23.657	24.143	24.641	25.151	25.673	26.754	27.888	29.077
17	25.284	25.840	26.411	26.996	27.597	28.213	29.493	30.840	32.258
18	27.485	28.132	28.798	29.481	30.184	30.906	32.410	33.999	35.677
19	29.791	30.539	31.309	32.103	32.919	33.760	35.517	37.379	39.353
20	32.206	33.066	33.953	34.868	35.812	36.786	38.825	40.995	43.305
21	34.735	35.719	36.736	37.786	38.871	39.993	42.349	44.865	47.553
22	37.385	38.505	39.664	40.864	42.106	43.392	46.102	49.006	52.119
23	40.161	41.430	42.747	44.112	45.528	46.996	50.098	53.436	57.028
24	43.069	44.502	45.991	47.538	49.145	50.816	54.355	58.177	62.305
25	46.115	47.727	49.406	51.153	52.971	54.865	58.888	63.249	67.978
26	49.305	51.113	52.999	54.966	57.017	59.156	63.715	68.676	74.076
27	52.647	54.669	56.782	58.989	61.296	63.706	68.857	74.484	80.632
28	56.148	58.403	60.763	63.234	65.820	68.528	74.333	80.698	87.679
29	59.815	62.323	64.953	67.711	70.605	73.640	80.164	87.347	95.255
30	63.656	66.439	69.363	72.435	75.664	79.058	86.375	94.461	103.399
35	85.778	90.320	95.139	100.251	105.677	111.435	124.035	138.237	154.252
36	90.853	95.836	101.134	106.765	112.753	119.121	133.097	148.913	166.820
40	113.678	120.800	128.430	136.606	145.369	154.762	175.632	199.635	227.257
42	126.782	135.232	144.321	154.100	164.624	175.951	201.271	230.632	264.698
48	174.246	188.025	203.028	219.368	237.169	256.565	300.747	353.270	415.753
54	236.950	258.774	282.832	309.363	338.627	370.917	445.896	537.316	648.877
60	319.786	353.584	391.314	433.450	480.523	533.128	657.690	813.520	1008.657
66	429.217	480.638	538.779	604.548	678.974	763.228	966.727	1228.028	1563.905
72	573.783	650.903	739.237	840.465	956.520	1089.629	1417.656	1850.092	2420.821
78	764.763	879.074	1011.730	1165.757	1344.685	1552.634	2075.625	2783.643	3743.301
84	1017.061	1184.845	1382.144	1614.283	1887.559	2209.417	3035.696	4184.651	5784.286
90	1350.363	1594.607	1885.668	2232.731	2646.804	3141.075	4436.576	6287.185	8934.142
96	1790.677	2143.728	2570.135	3085.473	3708.655	4462.651	6480.660	9442.523	13795.319
100	2160.218	2610.025	3158.201	3826.702	4642.435	5638.368	8341.558	12381.662	18427.696
102	2372.360	2879.603	3500.569	4261.271	5193.722	6337.330	9463.269	14177.835	21297.581
120	5497.055	6958.240	8821.786	11200.258	14237.939	18119.796	29431.515	47954.120	78321.414
126	7268.727	9331.509	11998.777	15450.283	19919.596	25710.252	42951.832	71973.356	120880.802
132	9609.220	12511.916	16317.433	21310.400	27865.756	36477.459	62679.899	108019.754	186562.770

Table values show the future value, or accumulated amount of the investment and interest, of a $1 investment for a given number of periods at a given rate per period. Table values can be generated using the formula: FV = ((1_R)^N)-1)/R when FV is the future value, R is the interest rate per period, and N is the number of periods.

****Annuity Due: To use table values for an annuity due, multiply the value of an ordinary annuity by the sum of 1 and the period interest rate (1 + R).***

TABLE 14-1 -- Continued

*Future Value of $1.00 Ordinary Annuity (*Annuity Due)*

Periods	Rate per period								
	8.00%	8.50%	9.00%	9.50%	10.00%	10.50%	11.00%	11.50%	12.00%
1	1.000	1.000	1.000	1.000	1.000	1.000	1.000	1.000	1.000
2	2.080	2.085	2.090	2.095	2.100	2.105	2.110	2.115	2.120
3	3.246	3.262	3.278	3.294	3.310	3.326	3.342	3.358	3.374
4	4.506	4.540	4.573	4.607	4.641	4.675	4.710	4.744	4.779
5	5.867	5.925	5.985	6.045	6.105	6.166	6.228	6.290	6.353
6	7.336	7.429	7.523	7.619	7.716	7.814	7.913	8.013	8.115
7	8.923	9.060	9.200	9.343	9.487	9.634	9.783	9.935	10.089
8	10.637	10.831	11.028	11.230	11.436	11.646	11.859	12.077	12.300
9	12.488	12.751	13.021	13.297	13.579	13.868	14.164	14.466	14.776
10	14.487	14.835	15.193	15.560	15.937	16.325	16.722	17.130	17.549
11	16.645	17.096	17.560	18.039	18.531	19.039	19.561	20.100	20.655
12	18.977	19.549	20.141	20.752	21.384	22.038	22.713	23.411	24.133
13	21.495	22.211	22.953	23.724	24.523	25.352	26.212	27.104	28.029
14	24.215	25.099	26.019	26.977	27.975	29.014	30.095	31.221	32.393
15	27.152	28.232	29.361	30.540	31.772	33.060	34.405	35.811	37.280
16	30.324	31.632	33.003	34.442	35.950	37.531	39.190	40.929	42.753
17	33.750	35.321	36.974	38.714	40.545	42.472	44.501	46.636	48.884
18	37.450	39.323	41.301	43.391	45.599	47.932	50.396	52.999	55.750
19	41.446	43.665	46.018	48.513	51.159	53.965	56.939	60.094	63.440
20	45.762	48.377	51.160	54.122	57.275	60.631	64.203	68.005	72.052
21	50.423	53.489	56.765	60.264	64.002	67.997	72.265	76.826	81.699
22	55.457	59.036	62.873	66.989	71.403	76.137	81.214	86.661	92.503
23	60.893	65.054	69.532	74.353	79.543	85.131	91.148	97.627	104.603
24	66.765	71.583	76.790	82.416	88.497	95.070	102.174	109.854	118.155
25	73.106	78.668	84.701	91.246	98.347	106.052	114.413	123.487	133.334
26	79.954	86.355	93.324	100.914	109.182	118.188	127.999	138.688	150.334
27	87.351	94.695	102.723	111.501	121.100	131.597	143.079	155.637	169.374
28	95.339	103.744	112.968	123.094	134.210	146.415	159.817	174.535	190.699
29	103.966	113.562	124.135	135.788	148.631	162.789	178.397	195.607	214.583
30	113.283	124.215	136.308	149.688	164.494	180.881	199.021	219.101	241.333
35	172.317	192.702	215.711	241.688	271.024	304.159	341.590	383.879	431.663
36	187.102	210.081	236.125	265.649	299.127	337.095	380.164	429.025	484.463
40	259.057	295.683	337.882	386.520	442.593	507.252	581.826	667.850	767.091
42	304.244	350.170	403.528	465.542	537.637	621.472	718.978	832.402	964.359
48	490.132	578.720	684.280	810.116	960.172	1139.159	1352.700	1607.507	1911.590
54	785.114	951.592	1155.130	1404.091	1708.719	2081.571	2538.022	3096.901	3781.255
60	1253.213	1559.920	1944.792	2427.978	3034.816	3797.165	4755.066	5958.829	7471.641
66	1996.028	2552.387	3269.134	4192.947	5384.078	6920.282	8901.857	11458.135	14755.810
72	3174.781	4171.566	5490.189	7235.384	9545.938	12605.693	16658.076	22025.267	29133.468
78	5045.315	6813.204	9215.120	12479.912	16918.927	22955.579	31165.421	42330.423	57512.414
84	8013.617	11122.950	15462.202	21520.385	29980.628	41796.807	58300.170	81347.573	113527.423
90	12723.939	18154.160	25939.184	37104.273	53120.226	76095.920	109053.398	156320.547	224091.119
96	20198.627	29625.351	43510.132	63967.647	94113.437	138535.009	203982.976	300384.042	442324.248
100	27484.516	41061.090	61422.675	91968.395	137796.123	206546.804	309665.230	464280.843	696010.548
102	32060.019	48340.227	72978.371	110274.500	166735.409	252200.916	381540.640	577207.666	873077.751
120	128149.912	209954.565	344289.064	564888.330	927080.688	1521532.891	2496681.757	4095296.249	6713993.792
126	203365.140	342541.480	577414.751	973757.277	1642387.707	2769849.921	4669837.803	7869279.488	13252241.370
132	322722.255	558852.724	968389.865	1678562.059	2909597.724	5042322.039	8734540.496	15121135.483	26157582.760

Table values show the future value, or accumulated amount of the investment and interest, of a $1 investment for a given number of periods at a given rate per period. Table values can be generated using the formula: FV = ((1_R)^N)-1)/R when FV is the future value, R is the interest rate per period, and N is the number of periods.

****Annuity Due: To use table values for an annuity due, multiply the value of an ordinary annuity by the sum of 1 and the period interest rate (1 + R).***

Table 14-2: $1.00 Sinking Fund Payments

			Rate per Period			
Period	**0.50%**	**1.00%**	**1.50%**	**2.00%**	**2.50%**	**3.00%**
1	1.0000000	1.0000000	1.0000000	1.0000000	1.0000000	1.0000000
2	0.4987531	0.4975124	0.4962779	0.4950495	0.4938272	0.4926108
3	0.3316722	0.3300221	0.3283830	0.3267547	0.3251372	0.3235304
4	0.2481328	0.2462811	0.2444448	0.2426238	0.2408179	0.2390270
5	0.1980100	0.1960398	0.1940893	0.1921584	0.1902469	0.1883546
6	0.1645955	0.1625484	0.1605252	0.1585258	0.1565500	0.1545975
7	0.1407285	0.1386283	0.1365562	0.1345120	0.1324954	0.1305064
8	0.1228289	0.1206903	0.1185840	0.1165098	0.1144673	0.1124564
9	0.1089074	0.1067404	0.1046098	0.1025154	0.1004569	0.0984339
10	0.0977706	0.0955821	0.0934342	0.0913265	0.0892588	0.0872305
11	0.0886590	0.0864541	0.0842938	0.0821779	0.0801060	0.0780774
12	0.0810664	0.0788488	0.0766800	0.0745596	0.0724871	0.0704621
13	0.0746422	0.0724148	0.0702404	0.0681184	0.0660483	0.0640295
14	0.0691361	0.0669012	0.0647233	0.0626020	0.0605365	0.0585263
15	0.0643644	0.0621238	0.0599444	0.0578255	0.0557665	0.0537666
16	0.0601894	0.0579446	0.0557651	0.0536501	0.0515990	0.0496108
17	0.0565058	0.0542581	0.0520797	0.0499698	0.0479278	0.0459525
18	0.0532317	0.0509820	0.0488058	0.0467021	0.0446701	0.0427087
19	0.0503025	0.0480518	0.0458785	0.0437818	0.0417606	0.0398139
20	0.0476665	0.0454153	0.0432457	0.0411567	0.0391471	0.0372157
21	0.0452816	0.0430308	0.0408655	0.0387848	0.0367873	0.0348718
22	0.0431138	0.0408637	0.0387033	0.0366314	0.0346466	0.0327474
23	0.0411347	0.0388858	0.0367308	0.0346681	0.0326964	0.0308139
24	0.0393206	0.0370735	0.0349241	0.0328711	0.0309128	0.0290474
25	0.0376519	0.0354068	0.0332635	0.0312204	0.0292759	0.0274279
26	0.0361116	0.0338689	0.0317320	0.0296992	0.0277687	0.0259383
27	0.0346856	0.0324455	0.0303153	0.0282931	0.0263769	0.0245642
28	0.0333617	0.0311244	0.0290011	0.0269897	0.0250879	0.0232932
29	0.0321291	0.0298950	0.0277788	0.0257784	0.0238913	0.0221147
30	0.0309789	0.0287481	0.0266392	0.0246499	0.0227776	0.0210193
35	0.0262155	0.0240037	0.0219336	0.0200022	0.0182056	0.0165393
40	0.0226455	0.0204556	0.0184271	0.0165557	0.0148362	0.0132624
45	0.0198712	0.0177050	0.0157198	0.0139096	0.0122675	0.0107852
50	0.0176538	0.0155127	0.0135717	0.0118232	0.0102581	0.0088655
55	0.0158414	0.0137264	0.0118302	0.0101434	0.0086542	0.0073491
60	0.0143328	0.0122444	0.0103934	0.0087680	0.0073534	0.0061330
65	0.0130579	0.0109967	0.0091909	0.0076262	0.0062846	0.0051458
70	0.0119666	0.0099328	0.0081724	0.0066676	0.0053971	0.0043366
75	0.0110221	0.0090161	0.0073007	0.0058551	0.0046536	0.0036680
80	0.0101970	0.0082189	0.0065483	0.0051607	0.0040260	0.0031117
85	0.0094702	0.0075200	0.0058940	0.0045632	0.0034931	0.0026465
90	0.0088253	0.0069031	0.0053211	0.0040460	0.0030381	0.0022556
95	0.0082493	0.0063551	0.0048168	0.0035960	0.0026479	0.0019258
100	0.0077319	0.0058657	0.0043706	0.0032027	0.0023119	0.0016467

Table values show the sinking fund payment earning a given rate for a given number of periods so that the accumulated amount at the end of the time will be $1. The formula for generating the table values is TV = R/((1+R) ^N - 1) where the TV is the table value, R is the rate per period, and N is the number of periods or payments.

Period	Rate per Period 3.50%	4.00%	4.50%	5.00%	5.50%	6.00%
1	1.0000000	1.0000000	1.0000000	1.0000000	1.0000000	1.0000000
2	0.4914005	0.4901961	0.4889976	0.4878049	0.4866180	0.4854369
3	0.3219342	0.3203485	0.3187734	0.3172086	0.3156541	0.3141098
4	0.2372511	0.2354900	0.2337436	0.2320118	0.2302945	0.2285915
5	0.1864814	0.1846271	0.1827916	0.1809748	0.1791764	0.1773964
6	0.1526682	0.1507619	0.1488784	0.1470175	0.1451789	0.1433626
7	0.1285445	0.1266096	0.1247015	0.1228198	0.1209644	0.1191350
8	0.1104766	0.1085278	0.1066097	0.1047218	0.1028640	0.1010359
9	0.0964460	0.0944930	0.0925745	0.0906901	0.0888395	0.0870222
10	0.0852414	0.0832909	0.0813788	0.0795046	0.0776678	0.0758680
11	0.0760920	0.0741490	0.0722482	0.0703889	0.0685707	0.0667929
12	0.0684839	0.0665522	0.0646662	0.0628254	0.0610292	0.0592770
13	0.0620616	0.0601437	0.0582754	0.0564558	0.0546843	0.0529601
14	0.0565707	0.0546690	0.0528203	0.0510240	0.0492791	0.0475849
15	0.0518251	0.0499411	0.0481138	0.0463423	0.0446256	0.0429628
16	0.0476848	0.0458200	0.0440154	0.0422699	0.0405825	0.0389521
17	0.0440431	0.0421985	0.0404176	0.0386991	0.0370420	0.0354448
18	0.0408168	0.0389933	0.0372369	0.0355462	0.0339199	0.0323565
19	0.0379403	0.0361386	0.0344073	0.0327450	0.0311501	0.0296209
20	0.0353611	0.0335818	0.0318761	0.0302426	0.0286793	0.0271846
21	0.0330366	0.0312801	0.0296006	0.0279961	0.0264648	0.0250045
22	0.0309321	0.0291988	0.0275456	0.0259705	0.0244712	0.0230456
23	0.0290188	0.0273091	0.0256825	0.0241368	0.0226696	0.0212785
24	0.0272728	0.0255868	0.0239870	0.0224709	0.0210358	0.0196790
25	0.0256740	0.0240120	0.0224390	0.0209525	0.0195494	0.0182267
26	0.0242054	0.0225674	0.0210214	0.0195643	0.0181931	0.0169043
27	0.0228524	0.0212385	0.0197195	0.0182919	0.0169523	0.0156972
28	0.0216026	0.0200130	0.0185208	0.0171225	0.0158144	0.0145926
29	0.0204454	0.0188799	0.0174146	0.0160455	0.0147686	0.0135796
30	0.0193713	0.0178301	0.0163915	0.0150514	0.0138054	0.0126489
35	0.0149983	0.0135773	0.0122704	0.0110717	0.0099749	0.0089739
40	0.0118273	0.0105235	0.0093431	0.0082782	0.0073203	0.0064615
45	0.0094534	0.0082625	0.0072020	0.0062617	0.0054313	0.0047005
50	0.0076337	0.0065502	0.0056021	0.0047767	0.0040615	0.0034443
55	0.0062132	0.0052312	0.0043875	0.0036669	0.0030546	0.0025370
60	0.0050886	0.0042018	0.0034543	0.0028282	0.0023071	0.0018757
65	0.0041883	0.0033902	0.0027305	0.0021892	0.0017480	0.0013907
70	0.0034610	0.0027451	0.0021651	0.0016992	0.0013275	0.0010331
75	0.0028692	0.0022290	0.0017210	0.0013216	0.0010100	0.0007687
80	0.0023849	0.0018141	0.0013707	0.0010296	0.0007695	0.0005725
85	0.0019866	0.0014791	0.0010933	0.0008032	0.0005868	0.0004268
90	0.0016578	0.0012078	0.0008732	0.0006271	0.0004479	0.0003184
95	0.0013855	0.0009874	0.0006980	0.0004900	0.0003420	0.0002376
100	0.0011593	0.0008080	0.0005584	0.0003831	0.0002613	0.0001774

Table values show the sinking fund payment earning a given rate for a given number of periods so that the accumulated amount at the end of the time will be $1. The formula for generating the table values is $TV = R/((1+R)^N - 1)$ where the TV is the table value, R is the rate per period, and N is the number of periods or payments.

Table 14-2: $1.00 Sinking Fund Payments

Period	Rate per Period 6.50%	7.00%	7.50%	8.00%	8.50%	9.00%
1	1.0000000	1.0000000	1.0000000	1.0000000	1.0000000	1.0000000
2	0.4842615	0.4830918	0.4819277	0.4807692	0.4796163	0.4784689
3	0.3125757	0.3110517	0.3095376	0.3080335	0.3065392	0.3050548
4	0.2269027	0.2252281	0.2235675	0.2219208	0.2202879	0.2186687
5	0.1756345	0.1738907	0.1721647	0.1704565	0.1687658	0.1670925
6	0.1415683	0.1397958	0.1380449	0.1363154	0.1346071	0.1329198
7	0.1173314	0.1155532	0.1138003	0.1120724	0.1103692	0.1086905
8	0.0992373	0.0974678	0.0957270	0.0940148	0.0923307	0.0906744
9	0.0852380	0.0834865	0.0817672	0.0800797	0.0784237	0.0767988
10	0.0741047	0.0723775	0.0706859	0.0690295	0.0674077	0.0658201
11	0.0650552	0.0633569	0.0616975	0.0600763	0.0584929	0.0569467
12	0.0575682	0.0559020	0.0542778	0.0526950	0.0511529	0.0496507
13	0.0512826	0.0496508	0.0480642	0.0465218	0.0450229	0.0435666
14	0.0459405	0.0443449	0.0427974	0.0412969	0.0398424	0.0384332
15	0.0413528	0.0397946	0.0382872	0.0368295	0.0354205	0.0340589
16	0.0373776	0.0358576	0.0343912	0.0329769	0.0316135	0.0302999
17	0.0339063	0.0324252	0.0310000	0.0296294	0.0283120	0.0270462
18	0.0308546	0.0294126	0.0280290	0.0267021	0.0254304	0.0242123
19	0.0281558	0.0267530	0.0254109	0.0241276	0.0229014	0.0217304
20	0.0257564	0.0243929	0.0230922	0.0218522	0.0206710	0.0195465
21	0.0236133	0.0222890	0.0210294	0.0198323	0.0186954	0.0176166
22	0.0216912	0.0204058	0.0191869	0.0180321	0.0169389	0.0159050
23	0.0199608	0.0187139	0.0175353	0.0164222	0.0153719	0.0143819
24	0.0183977	0.0171890	0.0160501	0.0149780	0.0139698	0.0130226
25	0.0169815	0.0158105	0.0147107	0.0136788	0.0127117	0.0118063
26	0.0156948	0.0145610	0.0134996	0.0125071	0.0115802	0.0107154
27	0.0145229	0.0134257	0.0124020	0.0114481	0.0105603	0.0097349
28	0.0134531	0.0123919	0.0114052	0.0104889	0.0096391	0.0088520
29	0.0124744	0.0114487	0.0104981	0.0096185	0.0088058	0.0080557
30	0.0115774	0.0105864	0.0096712	0.0088274	0.0080506	0.0073364
35	0.0080623	0.0072340	0.0064829	0.0058033	0.0051894	0.0046358
40	0.0056937	0.0050091	0.0044003	0.0038602	0.0033820	0.0029596
45	0.0040597	0.0034996	0.0030115	0.0025873	0.0022196	0.0019017
50	0.0029139	0.0024598	0.0020724	0.0017429	0.0014633	0.0012269
55	0.0021014	0.0017363	0.0014316	0.0011780	0.0009676	0.0007936
60	0.0015205	0.0012292	0.0009914	0.0007979	0.0006411	0.0005142
65	0.0011028	0.0008720	0.0006878	0.0005413	0.0004253	0.0003335
70	0.0008012	0.0006195	0.0004778	0.0003676	0.0002823	0.0002165
75	0.0005829	0.0004406	0.0003322	0.0002498	0.0001876	0.0001406
80	0.0004244	0.0003136	0.0002311	0.0001699	0.0001246	0.0000913
85	0.0003092	0.0002233	0.0001608	0.0001155	0.0000829	0.0000593
90	0.0002254	0.0001591	0.0001119	0.0000786	0.0000551	0.0000386
95	0.0001644	0.0001133	0.0000779	0.0000535	0.0000366	0.0000251
100	0.0001199	0.0000808	0.0000543	0.0000364	0.0000244	0.0000163

Table values show the sinking fund payment earning a given rate for a given number of periods so that the accumulated amount at the end of the time will be $1. The formula for generating the table values is TV = R/((1+R) ^N - 1) where the TV is the table value, R is the rate per period, and N is the number of periods or payments.

			Rate per Perio			
Period	**9.50%**	**10.00%**	**10.50%**	**11.00%**	**11.50%**	**12.00%**
1	1.0000000	1.0000000	1.0000000	1.0000000	1.0000000	1.0000000
2	0.4773270	0.4761905	0.4750594	0.4739336	0.4728132	0.4716981
3	0.3035800	0.3021148	0.3006592	0.2992131	0.2977764	0.2963490
4	0.2170630	0.2154708	0.2138920	0.2123264	0.2107739	0.2092344
5	0.1654364	0.1637975	0.1621755	0.1605703	0.1589818	0.1574097
6	0.1312533	0.1296074	0.1279819	0.1263766	0.1247912	0.1232257
7	0.1070360	0.1054055	0.1037987	0.1022153	0.1006550	0.0991177
8	0.0890456	0.0874440	0.0858693	0.0843211	0.0827990	0.0813028
9	0.0752045	0.0736405	0.0721064	0.0706017	0.0691260	0.0676789
10	0.0642662	0.0627454	0.0612573	0.0598014	0.0583772	0.0569842
11	0.0554369	0.0539631	0.0525247	0.0511210	0.0497514	0.0484154
12	0.0481877	0.0467633	0.0453767	0.0440273	0.0427142	0.0414368
13	0.0421521	0.0407785	0.0394451	0.0381510	0.0368953	0.0356772
14	0.0370681	0.0357462	0.0344666	0.0332282	0.0320301	0.0308712
15	0.0327437	0.0314738	0.0302480	0.0290652	0.0279244	0.0268242
16	0.0290347	0.0278166	0.0266444	0.0255167	0.0244324	0.0233900
17	0.0258308	0.0246641	0.0235449	0.0224715	0.0214426	0.0204567
18	0.0230461	0.0219302	0.0208630	0.0198429	0.0188682	0.0179373
19	0.0206128	0.0195469	0.0185307	0.0175625	0.0166405	0.0157630
20	0.0184767	0.0174596	0.0164933	0.0155756	0.0147048	0.0138788
21	0.0165937	0.0156244	0.0147065	0.0138379	0.0130165	0.0122401
22	0.0149278	0.0140051	0.0131343	0.0123131	0.0115393	0.0108105
23	0.0134494	0.0125718	0.0117466	0.0109712	0.0102431	0.0095600
24	0.0121335	0.0112998	0.0105186	0.0097872	0.0091030	0.0084634
25	0.0109594	0.0101681	0.0094293	0.0087402	0.0080980	0.0075000
26	0.0099094	0.0091590	0.0084611	0.0078126	0.0072104	0.0066519
27	0.0089685	0.0082576	0.0075989	0.0069892	0.0064252	0.0059041
28	0.0081239	0.0074510	0.0068299	0.0062571	0.0057295	0.0052439
29	0.0073644	0.0067281	0.0061429	0.0056055	0.0051123	0.0046602
30	0.0066806	0.0060792	0.0055285	0.0050246	0.0045641	0.0041437
35	0.0041376	0.0036897	0.0032878	0.0029275	0.0026050	0.0023166
40	0.0025872	0.0022594	0.0019714	0.0017187	0.0014973	0.0013036
45	0.0016273	0.0013910	0.0011879	0.0010135	0.0008641	0.0007363
50	0.0010273	0.0008592	0.0007179	0.0005992	0.0004998	0.0004167
55	0.0006500	0.0005317	0.0004346	0.0003548	0.0002895	0.0002361
60	0.0004119	0.0003295	0.0002634	0.0002103	0.0001678	0.0001338
65	0.0002612	0.0002043	0.0001597	0.0001247	0.0000973	0.0000759
70	0.0001658	0.0001268	0.0000969	0.0000740	0.0000565	0.0000431
75	0.0001052	0.0000787	0.0000588	0.0000439	0.0000327	0.0000244
80	0.0000668	0.0000488	0.0000357	0.0000260	0.0000190	0.0000139
85	0.0000424	0.0000303	0.0000217	0.0000155	0.0000110	0.0000079
90	0.0000270	0.0000188	0.0000131	0.0000092	0.0000064	0.0000045
95	0.0000171	0.0000117	0.0000080	0.0000054	0.0000037	0.0000025
100	0.0000109	0.0000073	0.0000048	0.0000032	0.0000022	0.0000014

Table values show the sinking fund payment earning a given rate for a given number of periods so that the accumulated amount at the end of the time will be $1. The formula for generating the table values is TV = R/((1+R)^N - 1) where the TV is the table value, R is the rate per period, and N is the number of periods or payments.

Table 14-3: Present Value of a $1.00 Ordinary Annuity

Periods	0.50%	1.00%	1.50%	2.00%	2.50%	3.00%
	Rate per Period					
1	0.995	0.990	0.985	0.980	0.976	0.971
2	1.985	1.956	1.956	1.942	1.927	1.913
3	2.970	2.912	2.912	2.884	2.856	2.829
4	3.950	3.854	3.854	3.808	3.762	3.717
5	4.926	4.783	4.783	4.713	4.646	4.580
6	5.896	5.697	5.697	5.601	5.508	5.417
7	6.862	6.598	6.598	6.472	6.349	6.230
8	7.823	7.486	7.486	7.325	7.170	7.020
9	8.779	8.361	8.361	8.162	7.971	7.786
10	9.730	9.222	9.222	8.983	8.752	8.530
11	10.677	10.071	10.071	9.787	9.514	9.253
12	11.619	10.908	10.908	10.575	10.258	9.954
13	12.556	11.732	11.732	11.348	10.983	10.635
14	13.489	12.543	12.543	12.106	11.691	11.296
15	14.417	13.343	13.343	12.849	12.381	11.938
16	15.340	14.131	14.131	13.578	13.055	12.561
17	16.259	14.908	14.908	14.292	13.712	13.166
18	17.173	15.673	15.673	14.992	14.353	13.754
19	18.082	16.426	16.426	15.678	14.979	14.324
20	18.987	17.169	17.169	16.351	15.589	14.877
21	19.888	17.900	17.900	17.011	16.185	15.415
22	20.784	18.621	18.621	17.658	16.765	15.937
23	21.676	19.331	19.331	18.292	17.332	16.444
24	22.563	20.030	20.030	18.914	17.885	16.936
25	23.446	20.720	20.720	19.523	18.424	17.413
26	24.324	21.399	21.399	20.121	18.951	17.877
27	25.198	22.068	22.068	20.707	19.464	18.327
28	26.068	22.727	22.727	21.281	19.965	18.764
29	26.933	23.376	23.376	21.844	20.454	19.188
30	27.794	24.016	24.016	22.396	20.930	19.600
35	32.035	27.076	27.076	24.999	23.145	21.487
40	36.172	29.916	29.916	27.355	25.103	23.115
45	40.207	32.552	32.552	29.490	26.833	24.519
50	44.143	35.000	35.000	31.424	28.362	25.730
55	47.981	37.271	37.271	33.175	29.714	26.774
60	51.726	39.380	39.380	34.761	30.909	27.676
65	55.377	41.338	41.338	36.197	31.965	28.453
70	58.939	43.155	43.155	37.499	32.898	29.123
75	62.414	44.842	44.842	38.677	33.723	29.702
80	65.802	46.407	46.407	39.745	34.452	30.201
85	69.108	47.861	47.861	40.711	35.096	30.631
90	72.331	49.210	49.210	41.587	35.666	31.002
95	75.476	50.462	50.462	42.380	36.169	31.323
100	78.543	51.625	51.625	43.098	36.614	31.599

Table values show the present value of $1.00 ordinary annuity or the lump sum amount that, invested now, yields the same compounded amount as an annuity of $1.00 at a given rate per period for a given number of periods. Table values can be generated by using the formula: TV = ((1+R) ^N - 1)/(R * (1+R) ^N) where TV is the table value, R is the rate per period, and N is the number of periods.

Periods	Rate per Period 3.50%	4.00%	4.50%	5.00%	5.50%	6.00%
1	0.966	0.962	0.957	0.952	0.948	0.943
2	1.900	1.886	1.873	1.859	1.846	1.833
3	2.802	2.775	2.749	2.723	2.698	2.673
4	3.673	3.630	3.588	3.546	3.505	3.465
5	4.515	4.452	4.390	4.329	4.270	4.212
6	5.329	5.242	5.158	5.076	4.996	4.917
7	6.115	6.002	5.893	5.786	5.683	5.582
8	6.874	6.733	6.596	6.463	6.335	6.210
9	7.608	7.435	7.269	7.108	6.952	6.802
10	8.317	8.111	7.913	7.722	7.538	7.360
11	9.002	8.760	8.529	8.306	8.093	7.887
12	9.663	9.385	9.119	8.863	8.619	8.384
13	10.303	9.986	9.683	9.394	9.117	8.853
14	10.921	10.563	10.223	9.899	9.590	9.295
15	11.517	11.118	10.740	10.380	10.038	9.712
16	12.094	11.652	11.234	10.838	10.462	10.106
17	12.651	12.166	11.707	11.274	10.865	10.477
18	13.190	12.659	12.160	11.690	11.246	10.828
19	13.710	13.134	12.593	12.085	11.608	11.158
20	14.212	13.590	13.008	12.462	11.950	11.470
21	14.698	14.029	13.405	12.821	12.275	11.764
22	15.167	14.451	13.784	13.163	12.583	12.042
23	15.620	14.857	14.148	13.489	12.875	12.303
24	16.058	15.247	14.495	13.799	13.152	12.550
25	16.482	15.622	14.828	14.094	13.414	12.783
26	16.890	15.983	15.147	14.375	13.662	13.003
27	17.285	16.330	15.451	14.643	13.898	13.211
28	17.667	16.663	15.743	14.898	14.121	13.406
29	18.036	16.984	16.022	15.141	14.333	13.591
30	18.392	17.292	16.289	15.372	14.534	13.765
35	20.001	18.665	17.461	16.374	15.391	14.498
40	21.355	19.793	18.402	17.159	16.046	15.046
45	22.495	20.720	19.156	17.774	16.548	15.456
50	23.456	21.482	19.762	18.256	16.932	15.762
55	24.264	22.109	20.248	18.633	17.225	15.991
60	24.945	22.623	20.638	18.929	17.450	16.161
65	25.518	23.047	20.951	19.161	17.622	16.289
70	26.000	23.395	21.202	19.343	17.753	16.385
75	26.407	23.680	21.404	19.485	17.854	16.456
80	26.749	23.915	21.565	19.596	17.931	16.509
85	27.037	24.109	21.695	19.684	17.990	16.549
90	27.279	24.267	21.799	19.752	18.035	16.579
95	27.484	24.398	21.883	19.806	18.069	16.601
100	27.655	24.505	21.950	19.848	18.096	16.618

Table values show the present value of $1.00 ordinary annuity or the lump sum amount that, invested now, yields the same compounded amount as an annuity of $1.00 at a given rate per period for a given number of periods. Table values can be generated by using the formula: TV = ((1+R) ^N - 1)/(R * (1+R) ^N) where TV is the table value, R is the rate per period, and N is the number of periods.

Table 14-3: Present Value of a $1.00 Ordinary Annuity

Periods	Rate per Period 6.50%	7.00%	7.50%	8.00%	8.50%	9.00%
1	0.939	0.935	0.930	0.926	0.922	0.917
2	1.821	1.808	1.796	1.783	1.771	1.759
3	2.648	2.624	2.601	2.577	2.554	2.531
4	3.426	3.387	3.349	3.312	3.276	3.240
5	4.156	4.100	4.046	3.993	3.941	3.890
6	4.841	4.767	4.694	4.623	4.554	4.486
7	5.485	5.389	5.297	5.206	5.119	5.033
8	6.089	5.971	5.857	5.747	5.639	5.535
9	6.656	6.515	6.379	6.247	6.119	5.995
10	7.189	7.024	6.864	6.710	6.561	6.418
11	7.689	7.499	7.315	7.139	6.969	6.805
12	8.159	7.943	7.735	7.536	7.345	7.161
13	8.600	8.358	8.126	7.904	7.691	7.487
14	9.014	8.745	8.489	8.244	8.010	7.786
15	9.403	9.108	8.827	8.559	8.304	8.061
16	9.768	9.447	9.142	8.851	8.575	8.313
17	10.111	9.763	9.434	9.122	8.825	8.544
18	10.432	10.059	9.706	9.372	9.055	8.756
19	10.735	10.336	9.959	9.604	9.268	8.950
20	11.019	10.594	10.194	9.818	9.463	9.129
21	11.285	10.836	10.413	10.017	9.644	9.292
22	11.535	11.061	10.617	10.201	9.810	9.442
23	11.770	11.272	10.807	10.371	9.963	9.580
24	11.991	11.469	10.983	10.529	10.104	9.707
25	12.198	11.654	11.147	10.675	10.234	9.823
26	12.392	11.826	11.299	10.810	10.354	9.929
27	12.575	11.987	11.441	10.935	10.465	10.027
28	12.746	12.137	11.573	11.051	10.566	10.116
29	12.907	12.278	11.696	11.158	10.660	10.198
30	13.059	12.409	11.810	11.258	10.747	10.274
35	13.687	12.948	12.273	11.655	11.088	10.567
40	14.146	13.332	12.594	11.925	11.315	10.757
45	14.480	13.606	12.819	12.108	11.465	10.881
50	14.725	13.801	12.975	12.233	11.566	10.962
55	14.903	13.940	13.084	12.319	11.632	11.014
60	15.033	14.039	13.159	12.377	11.677	11.048
65	15.128	14.110	13.212	12.416	11.706	11.070
70	15.197	14.160	13.249	12.443	11.726	11.084
75	15.248	14.196	13.275	12.461	11.739	11.094
80	15.285	14.222	13.292	12.474	11.747	11.100
85	15.312	14.240	13.305	12.482	11.753	11.104
90	15.331	14.253	13.313	12.488	11.757	11.106
95	15.346	14.263	13.319	12.492	11.760	11.108
100	15.356	14.269	13.324	12.494	11.761	11.109

Table values show the present value of $1.00 ordinary annuity or the lump sum amount that, invested now, yields the same compounded amount as an annuity of $1.00 at a given rate per period for a given number of periods. Table values can be generated by using the formula: TV = ((1+R) ^N - 1)/(R * (1+R) ^N) where TV is the table value, R is the rate per period, and N is the number of periods.

Table 16-1: Monthly Payment of Principal and Interest per $1,000 of Amount Financed

Years Financed	Annual Interest Rate 5.00%	5.25%	5.50%	5.75%	6.00%	6.25%
10	10.61	10.73	10.85	10.98	11.10	11.23
12	9.25	9.37	9.50	9.63	9.76	9.89
15	7.91	8.04	8.17	8.30	8.44	8.57
17	7.29	7.42	7.56	7.69	7.83	7.97
20	6.60	6.74	6.88	7.02	7.16	7.31
22	6.25	6.39	6.54	6.68	6.83	6.98
25	5.85	5.99	6.14	6.29	6.44	6.60
30	5.37	5.52	5.68	5.84	6.00	6.16
35	5.05	5.21	5.37	5.54	5.70	5.87

Years Financed	Annual Interest Rate 6.50%	6.75%	7.00%	7.25%	7.50%	7.75%
10	11.35	11.48	11.61	11.74	11.87	12.00
12	10.02	10.15	10.28	10.42	10.55	10.69
15	8.71	8.85	8.99	9.13	9.27	9.41
17	8.11	8.25	8.40	8.54	8.69	8.83
20	7.46	7.60	7.75	7.90	8.06	8.21
22	7.13	7.28	7.43	7.59	7.75	7.90
25	6.75	6.91	7.07	7.23	7.39	7.55
30	6.32	6.49	6.65	6.82	6.99	7.16
35	6.04	6.21	6.39	6.56	6.74	6.92

Years Financed	Annual Interest Rate 8.00%	8.25%	8.50%	8.75%	9.00%	9.25%
10	12.13	12.27	12.40	12.53	12.67	12.80
12	10.82	10.96	11.10	11.24	11.38	11.52
15	9.56	9.70	9.85	9.99	10.14	10.29
17	8.98	9.13	9.28	9.43	9.59	9.74
20	8.36	8.52	8.68	8.84	9.00	9.16
22	8.06	8.22	8.38	8.55	8.71	8.88
25	7.72	7.88	8.05	8.22	8.39	8.56
30	7.34	7.51	7.69	7.87	8.05	8.23
35	7.10	7.28	7.47	7.65	7.84	8.03

Table values show the monthly payment of a $1,000 mortgage for the given number of years at the given annual interest rate if the interest is compounded monthly. Table values can be generated by using the formula: M = (1,000 * (R%)/12) / (1-(1+R%/12)^(-Y*12)), where M=monthly payment, R%=the annual interest rate, and Y=total number of years of the loan.

Table B-1. **Table of Class Lives and Recovery Periods**

Asset class	Description of assets included	Class Life (in years)	Recovery Periods (in years) GDS (MACRS)	ADS
	SPECIFIC DEPRECIABLE ASSETS USED IN ALL BUSINESS ACTIVITIES, EXCEPT AS NOTED:			
00.11	**Office Furniture, Fixtures, and Equipment:** Includes furniture and fixtures that are not a structural component of a building. Includes such assets as desks, files, safes, and communications equipment. Does not include communications equipment that is included in other classes.	10	7	10
00.12	**Information Systems:** Includes computers and their peripheral equipment used in administering normal business transactions and the maintenance of business records, their retrieval and analysis. Information systems are defined as: 1) Computers: A computer is a programmable electronically activated device capable of accepting information, applying prescribed processes to the information, and supplying the results of these processes with or without human intervention. It usually consists of a central processing unit containing extensive storage, logic, arithmetic, and control capabilities. Excluded from this category are adding machines, electronic desk calculators, etc., and other equipment described in class 00.13. 2) Peripheral equipment consists of the auxiliary machines which are designed to be placed under control of the central processing unit. Nonlimiting examples are: Card readers, card punches, magnetic tape feeds, high speed printers, optical character readers, tape cassettes, mass storage units, paper tape equipment, keypunches, data entry devices, teleprinters, terminals, tape drives, disc drives, disc files, disc packs, visual image projector tubes, card sorters, plotters, and collators. Peripheral equipment may be used on-line or off-line. Does not incude equipment that is an integral part of other capital equipment that is included in other classes of economic activity, i.e., computers used primarily for process or production control, switching, channeling, and automating distributive trades and services such as point of sale (POS) computer systems. Also, does not include equipment of a kind used primarily for amusement or entertainment of the user.	6	5	5
00.13	**Data Handling Equipment; except Computers:** Includes only typewriters, calculators, adding and accounting machines, copiers, and duplicating equipment.	6	5	6
00.21	**Airplanes (airframes and engines), except those used in commercial or contract carrying of passengers or freight, and all helicopters (airframes and engines)**	6	5	6
00.22	**Automobiles, Taxis**	3	5	5
00.23	**Buses**	9	5	9
00.241	**Light General Purpose Trucks:** Includes trucks for use over the road (actual weight less than 13,000 pounds)	4	5	5
00.242	**Heavy General Purpose Trucks:** Includes heavy general purpose trucks, concrete ready mix-trucks, and ore trucks, for use over the road (actual unloaded weight 13,000 pounds or more)	6	5	6
00.25	**Railroad Cars and Locomotives, except those owned by railroad transportation companies**	15	7	15
00.26	**Tractor Units for Use Over-The-Road**	4	3	4
00.27	**Trailers and Trailer-Mounted Containers**	6	5	6
00.28	**Vessels, Barges, Tugs, and Similar Water Transportation Equipment, except those used in marine construction**	18	10	18
00.3	**Land Improvements:** Includes improvements directly to or added to land, whether such improvements are section 1245 property or section 1250 property, provided such improvements are depreciable. Examples of such assets might include sidewalks, roads, canals, waterways, drainage facilities, sewers (not including municipal sewers in Class 51), wharves and docks, bridges, fences, landscaping shrubbery, or radio and television transmitting towers. Does not include land improvements that are explicitly included in any other class, and buildings and structural components as defined in section 1.48-1(e) of the regulations. Excludes public utility initial clearing and grading land improvements as specified in Rev. Rul. 72-403, 1972-2 C.B. 102.	20	15	20
00.4	**Industrial Steam and Electric Generation and/or Distribution Systems:** Includes assets, whether such assets are section 1245 property or 1250 property, providing such assets are depreciable, used in the production and/or distribution of electricity with rated total capacity in excess of 500 Kilowatts and/or assets used in the production and/or distribution of steam with rated total capacity in excess of 12,500 pounds per hour for use by the taxpayer in its industrial manufacturing process or plant activity and not ordinarily available for sale to others. Does not include buildings and structural components as defined in section 1.48-1(e) of the regulations. Assets used to generate and/or distribute electricity or steam of the type described above, but of lesser rated capacity, are not included, but are included in the appropriate manufacturing equipment classes elsewhere specified. Also includes electric generating and steam distribution assets, which may utilize steam produced by a waste reduction and resource recovery plant, used by the taxpayer in its industrial manufacturing process or plant activity. Steam and chemical recovery boiler systems used for the recovery and regeneration of chemicals used in manufacturing, with rated capacity in excess of that described above, with specifically related distribution and return systems are not included but are included in appropriate manufacturing equipment classes elsewhere specified. An example of an excluded steam and chemical recovery boiler system is that used in the pulp and paper manufacturing equipment classes elsewhere specified. An example of an excluded steam and chemical recovery boiler system is that used in the pulp and paper manufacturing industry.	22	15	22

Publication 946 (2015)

Table B-2. **Table of Class Lives and Recovery Periods**

Asset class	Description of assets included	Class Life (in years)	Recovery Periods (in years) GDS (MACRS)	ADS
	DEPRECIABLE ASSETS USED IN THE FOLLOWING ACTIVITIES:			
01.1	**Agriculture:** Includes machinery and equipment, grain bins, and fences but no other land improvements, that are used in the production of crops or plants, vines, and trees; livestock; the operation of farm dairies, nurseries, greenhouses, sod farms, mushroom cellars, cranberry bogs, apiaries, and fur farms; the performance of agriculture, animal husbandry, and horticultural services.	10	7	10
01.11	**Cotton Ginning Assets**	12	7	12
01.21	**Cattle, Breeding or Dairy**	7	5	7
01.221	**Any breeding or work horse that is 12 years old or less at the time it is placed in service****	10	7	10
01.222	**Any breeding or work horse that is more than 12 years old at the time it is placed in service****	10	3	10
01.223	**Any race horse that is more than 2 years old at the time it is placed in service****	*	3	12
01.224	**Any horse that is more than 12 years old at the time it is placed in service and that is neither a race horse nor a horse described in class 01.222****	*	3	12
01.225	**Any horse not described in classes 01.221, 01.222, 01.223, or 01.224**	*	7	12
01.23	**Hogs, Breeding**	3	3	3
01.24	**Sheep and Goats, Breeding**	5	5	5
01.3	**Farm buildings except structures included in Class 01.4**	25	20	25
01.4	**Single purpose agricultural or horticultural structures (within the meaning of section 168(i)(13) of the Code)**	15	10***	15
10.0	**Mining:** Includes assets used in the mining and quarrying of metallic and nonmetallic minerals (including sand, gravel, stone, and clay) and the milling, beneficiation and other primary preparation of such materials.	10	7	10
13.0	**Offshore Drilling:** Includes assets used in offshore drilling for oil and gas such as floating, self-propelled and other drilling vessels, barges, platforms, and drilling equipment and support vessels such as tenders, barges, towboats and crewboats. Excludes oil and gas production assets.	7.5	5	7.5
13.1	**Drilling of Oil and Gas Wells:** Includes assets used in the drilling of onshore oil and gas wells and the provision of geophysical and other exploration services; and the provision of such oil and gas field services as chemical treatment, plugging and abandoning of wells and cementing or perforating well casings. Does not include assets used in the performance of any of these activities and services by integrated petroleum and natural gas producers for their own account.	6	5	6
13.2	**Exploration for and Production of Petroleum and Natural Gas Deposits:** Includes assets used by petroleum and natural gas producers for drilling of wells and production of petroleum and natural gas, including gathering pipelines and related storage facilities. Also includes petroleum and natural gas offshore transportation facilities used by producers and others consisting of platforms (other than drilling platforms classified in Class 13.0), compression or pumping equipment, and gathering and transmission lines to the first onshore transshipment facility. The assets used in the first onshore transshipment facility are also included and consist of separation equipment (used for separation of natural gas, liquids, and in Class 49.23), and liquid holding or storage facilities (other than those classified in Class 49.25). Does not include support vessels.	14	7	14
13.3	**Petroleum Refining:** Includes assets used for the distillation, fractionation, and catalytic cracking of crude petroleum into gasoline and its other components.	16	10	16
15.0	**Construction:** Includes assets used in construction by general building, special trade, heavy and marine construction contractors, operative and investment builders, real estate subdividers and developers, and others except railroads.	6	5	6
20.1	**Manufacture of Grain and Grain Mill Products:** Includes assets used in the production of flours, cereals, livestock feeds, and other grain and grain mill products.	17	10	17
20.2	**Manufacture of Sugar and Sugar Products:** Includes assets used in the production of raw sugar, syrup, or finished sugar from sugar cane or sugar beets.	18	10	18
20.3	**Manufacture of Vegetable Oils and Vegetable Oil Products:** Includes assets used in the production of oil from vegetable materials and the manufacture of related vegetable oil products.	18	10	18
20.4	**Manufacture of Other Food and Kindred Products:** Includes assets used in the production of foods and beverages not included in classes 20.1, 20.2 and 20.3.	12	7	12
20.5	**Manufacture of Food and Beverages—Special Handling Devices:** Includes assets defined as specialized materials handling devices such as returnable pallets, palletized containers, and fish processing equipment including boxes, baskets, carts, and flaking trays used in activities as defined in classes 20.1, 20.2, 20.3 and 20.4. Does not include general purpose small tools such as wrenches and drills, both hand and power-driven, and other general purpose equipment such as conveyors, transfer equipment, and materials handling devices.	4	3	4

* Property described in asset classes 01.223, 01.224, and 01.225 are assigned recovery periods but have no class lives.
** A horse is more than 2 (or 12) years old after the day that is 24 (or 144) months after its actual birthdate.
*** 7 if property was placed in service before 1989.

Publication 946 (2015)

Table B-2. **Table of Class Lives and Recovery Periods**

Asset class	Description of assets included	Class Life (in years)	Recovery Periods (in years) GDS (MACRS)	ADS
21.0	**Manufacture of Tobacco and Tobacco Products:** Includes assets used in the production of cigarettes, cigars, smoking and chewing tobacco, snuff, and other tobacco products.	15	7	15
22.1	**Manufacture of Knitted Goods:** Includes assets used in the production of knitted and netted fabrics and lace. Assets used in yarn preparation, bleaching, dyeing, printing, and other similar finishing processes, texturing, and packaging, are elsewhere classified.	7.5	5	7.5
22.2	**Manufacture of Yarn, Thread, and Woven Fabric:** Includes assets used in the production of spun yarns including the preparing, blending, spinning, and twisting of fibers into yarns and threads, the preparation of yarns such as twisting, warping, and winding, the production of covered elastic yarn and thread, cordage, woven fabric, tire fabric, braided fabric, twisted jute for packaging, mattresses, pads, sheets, and industrial belts, and the processing of textile mill waste to recover fibers, flocks, and shoddies. Assets used to manufacture carpets, man-made fibers, and nonwovens, and assets used in texturing, bleaching, dyeing, printing, and other similar finishing processes, are elsewhere classified.	11	7	11
22.3	**Manufacture of Carpets and Dyeing, Finishing, and Packaging of Textile Products and Manufacture of Medical and Dental Supplies:** Includes assets used in the production of carpets, rugs, mats, woven carpet backing, chenille, and other tufted products, and assets used in the joining together of backing with carpet yarn or fabric. Includes assets used in washing, scouring, bleaching, dyeing, printing, drying, and similar finishing processes applied to textile fabrics, yarns, threads, and other textile goods. Includes assets used in the production and packaging of textile products, other than apparel, by creasing, forming, trimming, cutting, and sewing, such as the preparation of carpet and fabric samples, or similar joining together processes (other than the production of scrim reinforced paper products and laminated paper products) such as the sewing and folding of hosiery and panty hose, and the creasing, folding, trimming, and cutting of fabrics to produce nonwoven products, such as disposable diapers and sanitary products. Also includes assets used in the production of medical and dental supplies other than drugs and medicines. Assets used in the manufacture of nonwoven carpet backing, and hard surface floor covering such as tile, rubber, and cork, are elsewhere classified.	9	5	9
22.4	**Manufacture of Textile Yarns:** Includes assets used in the processing of yarns to impart bulk and/or stretch properties to the yarn. The principal machines involved are falsetwist, draw, beam-to-beam, and stuffer box texturing equipment and related highspeed twisters and winders. Assets, as described above, which are used to further process man-made fibers are elsewhere classified when located in the same plant in an integrated operation with man-made fiber producing assets. Assets used to manufacture man-made fibers and assets used in bleaching, dyeing, printing, and other similar finishing processes, are elsewhere classified.	8	5	8
22.5	**Manufacture of Nonwoven Fabrics:** Includes assets used in the production of nonwoven fabrics, felt goods including felt hats, padding, batting, wadding, oakum, and fillings, from new materials and from textile mill waste. Nonwoven fabrics are defined as fabrics (other than reinforced and laminated composites consisting of nonwovens and other products) manufactured by bonding natural and/or synthetic fibers and/or filaments by means of induced mechanical interlocking, fluid entanglement, chemical adhesion, thermal or solvent reaction, or by combination thereof other than natural hydration bonding as ocurs with natural cellulose fibers. Such means include resin bonding, web bonding, and melt bonding. Specifically includes assets used to make flocked and needle punched products other than carpets and rugs. Assets, as described above, which are used to manufacture nonwovens are elsewhere classified when located in the same plant in an integrated operation with man-made fiber producing assets. Assets used to manufacture man-made fibers and assets used in bleaching, dyeing, printing, and other similar finishing processes, are elsewhere classified.	10	7	10
23.0	**Manufacture of Apparel and Other Finished Products:** Includes assets used in the production of clothing and fabricated textile products by the cutting and sewing of woven fabrics, other textile products, and furs; but does not include assets used in the manufacture of apparel from rubber and leather.	9	5	9
24.1	**Cutting of Timber:** Includes logging machinery and equipment and roadbuilding equipment used by logging and sawmill operators and pulp manufacturers for their own account.	6	5	6
24.2	**Sawing of Dimensional Stock from Logs:** Includes machinery and equipment installed in permanent or well established sawmills.	10	7	10
24.3	**Sawing of Dimensional Stock from Logs:** Includes machinery and equipment in sawmills characterized by temporary foundations and a lack, or minimum amount, of lumberhandling, drying, and residue disposal equipment and facilities.	6	5	6
24.4	**Manufacture of Wood Products, and Furniture:** Includes assets used in the production of plywood, hardboard, flooring, veneers, furniture, and other wood products, including the treatment of poles and timber.	10	7	10
26.1	**Manufacture of Pulp and Paper:** Includes assets for pulp materials handling and storage, pulp mill processing, bleach processing, paper and paperboard manufacturing, and on-line finishing. Includes pollution control assets and all land improvements associated with the factory site or production process such as effluent ponds and canals, provided such improvements are depreciable but does not include buildings and structural components as defined in section 1.48-1(e)(1) of the regulations. Includes steam and chemical recovery boiler systems, with any rated capacity, used for the recovery and regeneration of chemicals used in manufacturing. Does not include assets used either in pulpwood logging, or in the manufacture of hardboard.	13	7	13

Publication 946 (2015)

Table B-2. **Table of Class Lives and Recovery Periods**

Asset class	Description of assets included	Class Life (in years)	Recovery Periods (in years) GDS (MACRS)	ADS
26.2	**Manufacture of Converted Paper, Paperboard, and Pulp Products:** Includes assets used for modification, or remanufacture of paper and pulp into converted products, such as paper coated off the paper machine, paper bags, paper boxes, cartons and envelopes. Does not include assets used for manufacture of nonwovens that are elsewhere classified.	10	7	10
27.0	**Printing, Publishing, and Allied Industries:** Includes assets used in printing by one or more processes, such as letter-press, lithography, gravure, or screen; the performance of services for the printing trade, such as bookbinding, typesetting, engraving, photo-engraving, and electrotyping; and the publication of newspapers, books, and periodicals.	11	7	11
28.0	**Manufacture of Chemicals and Allied Products:** Includes assets used to manufacture basic organic and inorganic chemicals; chemical products to be used in further manufacture, such as synthetic fibers and plastics materials; and finished chemical products. Includes assets used to further process man-made fibers, to manufacture plastic film, and to manufacture nonwoven fabrics, when such assets are located in the same plant in an integrated operation with chemical products producing assets. Also includes assets used to manufacture photographic supplies, such as film, photographic paper, sensitized photographic paper, and developing chemicals. Includes all land improvements associated with plant site or production processes, such as effluent ponds and canals, provided such land improvements are depreciable but does not include buildings and structural components as defined in section 1.48-1(e) of the regulations. Does not include assets used in the manufacture of finished rubber and plastic products or in the production of natural gas products, butane, propane, and by-products of natural gas production plants.	9.5	5	9.5
30.1	**Manufacture of Rubber Products:** Includes assets used for the production of products from natural, synthetic, or reclaimed rubber, gutta percha, balata, or gutta siak, such as tires, tubes, rubber footwear, mechanical rubber goods, heels and soles, flooring, and rubber sundries; and in the recapping, retreading, and rebuilding of tires.	14	7	14
30.11	**Manufacture of Rubber Products—Special Tools and Devices:** Includes assets defined as special tools, such as jigs, dies, mandrels, molds, lasts, patterns, specialty containers, pallets, shells; and tire molds, and accessory parts such as rings and insert plates used in activities as defined in class 30.1. Does not include tire building drums and accessory parts and general purpose small tools such as wrenches and drills, both power and hand-driven, and other general purpose equipment such as conveyors and transfer equipment.	4	3	4
30.2	**Manufacture of Finished Plastic Products:** Includes assets used in the manufacture of plastics products and the molding of primary plastics for the trade. Does not include assets used in the manufacture of basic plastics materials nor the manufacture of phonograph records.	11	7	11
30.21	**Manufacture of Finished Plastic Products—Special Tools:** Includes assets defined as special tools, such as jigs, dies, fixtures, molds, patterns, gauges, and specialty transfer and shipping devices, used in activities as defined in class 30.2. Special tools are specifically designed for the production or processing of particular parts and have no significant utilitarian value and cannot be adapted to further or different use after changes or improvements are made in the model design of the particular part produced by the special tools. Does not include general purpose small tools such as wrenches and drills, both hand and power-driven, and other general purpose equipment such as conveyors, transfer equipment, and materials handling devices.	3.5	3	3.5
31.0	**Manufacture of Leather and Leather Products:** Includes assets used in the tanning, currying, and finishing of hides and skins; the processing of fur pelts; and the manufacture of finished leather products, such as footwear, belting, apparel, and luggage.	11	7	11
32.1	**Manufacture of Glass Products:** Includes assets used in the production of flat, blown, or pressed products of glass, such as float and window glass, glass containers, glassware and fiberglass. Does not include assets used in the manufacture of lenses.	14	7	14
32.11	**Manufacture of Glass Products—Special Tools:** Includes assets defined as special tools such as molds, patterns, pallets, and specialty transfer and shipping devices such as steel racks to transport automotive glass, used in activities as defined in class 32.1. Special tools are specifically designed for the production or processing of particular parts and have no significant utilitarian value and cannot be adapted to further or different use after changes or improvements are made in the model design of the particular part produced by the special tools. Does not include general purpose small tools such as wrenches and drills, both hand and power-driven, and other general purpose equipment such as conveyors, transfer equipment, and materials handling devices.	2.5	3	2.5
32.2	**Manufacture of Cement:** Includes assets used in the production of cement, but does not include assets used in the manufacture of concrete and concrete products nor in any mining or extraction process.	20	15	20
32.3	**Manufacture of Other Stone and Clay Products:** Includes assets used in the manufacture of products from materials in the form of clay and stone, such as brick, tile, and pipe; pottery and related products, such as vitreous-china, plumbing fixtures, earthenware and ceramic insulating materials; and also includes assets used in manufacture of concrete and concrete products. Does not include assets used in any mining or extraction processes.	15	7	15

Publication 946 (2015)

Table B-2. **Table of Class Lives and Recovery Periods**

Asset class	Description of assets included	Class Life (in years)	Recovery Periods (in years)	
			GDS (MACRS)	ADS
33.2	**Manufacture of Primary Nonferrous Metals:** Includes assets used in the smelting, refining, and electrolysis of nonferrous metals from ore, pig, or scrap, the rolling, drawing, and alloying of nonferrous metals; the manufacture of castings, forgings, and other basic products of nonferrous metals; and the manufacture of nails, spikes, structural shapes, tubing, wire, and cable.	14	7	14
33.21	**Manufacture of Primary Nonferrous Metals—Special Tools:** Includes assets defined as special tools such as dies, jigs, molds, patterns, fixtures, gauges, and drawings concerning such special tools used in the activities as defined in class 33.2, Manufacture of Primary Nonferrous Metals. Special tools are specifically designed for the production or processing of particular products or parts and have no significant utilitarian value and cannot be adapted to further or different use after changes or improvements are made in the model design of the particular part produced by the special tools. Does not include general purpose small tools such as wrenches and drills, both hand and power-driven, and other general purpose equipment such as conveyors, transfer equipment, and materials handling devices. Rolls, mandrels and refractories are not included in class 33.21 but are included in class 33.2.	6.5	5	6.5
33.3	**Manufacture of Foundry Products:** Includes assets used in the casting of iron and steel, including related operations such as molding and coremaking. Also includes assets used in the finishing of castings and patternmaking when performed at the foundry, all special tools and related land improvements.	14	7	14
33.4	**Manufacture of Primary Steel Mill Products:** Includes assets used in the smelting, reduction, and refining of iron and steel from ore, pig, or scrap; the rolling, drawing and alloying of steel; the manufacture of nails, spikes, structural shapes, tubing, wire, and cable. Includes assets used by steel service centers, ferrous metal forges, and assets used in coke production, regardless of ownership. Also includes related land improvements and all special tools used in the above activities.	15	7	15
34.0	**Manufacture of Fabricated Metal Products:** Includes assets used in the production of metal cans, tinware, fabricated structural metal products, metal stampings, and other ferrous and nonferrous metal and wire products not elsewhere classified. Does not include assets used to manufacture non-electric heating apparatus.	12	7	12
34.01	**Manufacture of Fabricated Metal Products—Special Tools:** Includes assets defined as special tools such as dies, jigs, molds, patterns, fixtures, gauges, and returnable containers and drawings concerning such special tools used in the activities as defined in class 34.0. Special tools are specifically designed for the production or processing of particular machine components, products, or parts, and have no significant utilitarian value and cannot be adapted to further or different use after changes or improvements are made in the model design of the particular part produced by the special tools. Does not include general small tools such as wrenches and drills, both hand and power-driven, and other general purpose equipment such as conveyors, transfer equipment, and materials handling devices.	3	3	3
35.0	**Manufacture of Electrical and Non-Electrical Machinery and Other Mechanical Products:** Includes assets used to manufacture or rebuild finished machinery and equipment and replacement parts thereof such as machine tools, general industrial and special industry machinery, electrical power generation, transmission, and distribution systems, space heating, cooling, and refrigeration systems, commercial and home appliances, farm and garden machinery, construction machinery, mining and oil field machinery, internal combustion engines (except those elsewhere classified), turbines (except those that power airborne vehicles), batteries, lamps and lighting fixtures, carbon and graphite products, and electromechanical and mechanical products including business machines, instruments, watches and clocks, vending and amusement machines, photographic equipment, medical and dental equipment and appliances, and ophthalmic goods. Includes assets used by manufacturers or rebuilders of such finished machinery and equipment in activities elsewhere classified such as the manufacture of castings, forgings, rubber and plastic products, electronic subassemblies or other manufacturing activities if the interim products are used by the same manufacturer primarily in the manufacture, assembly, or rebuilding of such finished machinery and equipment. Does not include assets used in mining, assets used in the manufacture of primary ferrous and nonferrous metals, assets included in class 00.11 through 00.4 and assets elsewhere classified.	10	7	10
36.0	**Manufacture of Electronic Components, Products, and Systems:** Includes assets used in the manufacture of electronic communication, computation, instrumentation and control system, including airborne applications; also includes assets used in the manufacture of electronic products such as frequency and amplitude modulated transmitters and receivers, electronic switching stations, television cameras, video recorders, record players and tape recorders, computers and computer peripheral machines, and electronic instruments, watches, and clocks; also includes assets used in the manufacture of components, provided their primary use is products and systems defined above such as electron tubes, capacitors, coils, resistors, printed circuit substrates, switches, harness cables, lasers, fiber optic devices, and magnetic media devices. Specifically excludes assets used to manufacture electronic products and components, photocopiers, typewriters, postage meters and other electromechanical and mechanical business machines and instruments that are elsewhere classified. Does not include semiconductor manufacturing equipment included in class 36.1.	6	5	6
36.1	**Any Semiconductor Manufacturing Equipment**	5	5	5

Publication 946 (2015)

Table B-2. **Table of Class Lives and Recovery Periods**

Asset class	Description of assets included	Class Life (in years)	Recovery Periods (in years) GDS (MACRS)	ADS
37.11	**Manufacture of Motor Vehicles:** Includes assets used in the manufacture and assembly of finished automobiles, trucks, trailers, motor homes, and buses. Does not include assets used in mining, printing and publishing, production of primary metals, electricity, or steam, or the manufacture of glass, industrial chemicals, batteries, or rubber products, which are classified elsewhere. Includes assets used in manufacturing activities elsewhere classified other than those excluded above, where such activities are incidental to and an integral part of the manufacture and assembly of finished motor vehicles such as the manufacture of parts and subassemblies of fabricated metal products, electrical equipment, textiles, plastics, leather, and foundry and forging operations. Does not include any assets not classified in manufacturing activity classes, e.g., does not include any assets classified in asset guideline classes 00.11 through 00.4. Activities will be considered incidental to the manufacture and assembly of finished motor vehicles only if 75 percent or more of the value of the products produced under one roof are used for the manufacture and assembly of finished motor vehicles. Parts that are produced as a normal replacement stock complement in connection with the manufacture and assembly of finished motor vehicles are considered used for the manufacture assembly of finished motor vehicles. Does not include assets used in the manufacture of component parts if these assets are used by taxpayers not engaged in the assembly of finished motor vehicles.	12	7	12
37.12	**Manufacture of Motor Vehicles—Special Tools:** Includes assets defined as special tools, such as jigs, dies, fixtures, molds, patterns, gauges, and specialty transfer and shipping devices, owned by manufacturers of finished motor vehicles and used in qualified activities as defined in class 37.11. Special tools are specifically designed for the production or processing of particular motor vehicle components and have no significant utilitarian value, and cannot be adapted to further or different use, after changes or improvements are made in the model design of the particular part produced by the special tools. Does not include general purpose small tools such as wrenches and drills, both hand and powerdriven, and other general purpose equipment such as conveyors, transfer equipment, and materials handling devices.	3	3	3
37.2	**Manufacture of Aerospace Products:** Includes assets used in the manufacture and assembly of airborne vehicles and their component parts including hydraulic, pneumatic, electrical, and mechanical systems. Does not include assets used in the production of electronic airborne detection, guidance, control, radiation, computation, test, navigation, and communication equipment or the components thereof.	10	7	10
37.31	**Ship and Boat Building Machinery and Equipment:** Includes assets used in the manufacture and repair of ships, boats, caissons, marine drilling rigs, and special fabrications not included in asset classes 37.32 and 37.33. Specifically includes all manufacturing and repairing machinery and equipment, including machinery and equipment used in the operation of assets included in asset class 37.32. Excludes buildings and their structural components.	12	7	12
37.32	**Ship and Boat Building Dry Docks and Land Improvements:** Includes assets used in the manufacture and repair of ships, boats, caissons, marine drilling rigs, and special fabrications not included in asset classes 37.31 and 37.33. Specifically includes floating and fixed dry docks, ship basins, graving docks, shipways, piers, and all other land improvements such as water, sewer, and electric systems. Excludes buildings and their structural components.	16	10	16
37.33	**Ship and Boat Building—Special Tools:** Includes assets defined as special tools such as dies, jigs, molds, patterns, fixtures, gauges, and drawings concerning such special tools used in the activities defined in classes 37.31 and 37.32. Special tools are specifically designed for the production or processing of particular machine components, products, or parts, and have no significant utilitarian value and cannot be adapted to further or different use after changes or improvements are made in the model design of the particular part produced by the special tools. Does not include general purpose small tools such as wrenches and drills, both hand and power-driven, and other general purpose equipment such as conveyors, transfer equipment, and materials handling devices.	6.5	5	6.5
37.41	**Manufacture of Locomotives:** Includes assets used in building or rebuilding railroad locomotives (including mining and industrial locomotives). Does not include assets of railroad transportation companies or assets of companies which manufacture components of locomotives but do not manufacture finished locomotives.	11.5	7	11.5
37.42	**Manufacture of Railroad Cars:** Includes assets used in building or rebuilding railroad freight or passenger cars (including rail transit cars). Does not include assets of railroad transportation companies or assets of companies which manufacture components of railroad cars but do not manufacture finished railroad cars.	12	7	12
39.0	**Manufacture of Athletic, Jewelry, and Other Goods:** Includes assets used in the production of jewelry; musical instruments; toys and sporting goods; motion picture and television films and tapes; and pens, pencils, office and art supplies, brooms, brushes, caskets, etc. **Railroad Transportation:** Classes with the prefix 40 include the assets identified below that are used in the commercial and contract carrying of passengers and freight by rail. Assets of electrified railroads will be classified in a manner corresponding to that set forth below for railroads not independently operated as electric lines. Excludes the assets included in classes with the prefix beginning 00.1 and 00.2 above, and also excludes any non-depreciable assets included in Interstate Commerce Commission accounts enumerated for this class.	12	7	12

Publication 946 (2015)

Table B-2. **Table of Class Lives and Recovery Periods**

Asset class	Description of assets included	Class Life (in years)	Recovery Periods (in years) GDS (MACRS)	ADS
40.1	**Railroad Machinery and Equipment:** Includes assets classified in the following Interstate Commerce Commission accounts: **Roadway accounts:** (16) Station and office buildings (freight handling machinery and equipment only) (25) TOFC/COFC terminals (freight handling machinery and equipment only) (26) Communication systems (27) Signals and interlockers (37) Roadway machines (44) Shop machinery **Equipment accounts:** (52) Locomotives (53) Freight train cars (54) Passenger train cars (57) Work equipment	14	7	14
40.2	**Railroad Structures and Similar Improvements:** Includes assets classified in the following Interstate Commerce Commission road accounts: (6) Bridges, trestles, and culverts (7) Elevated structures (13) Fences, snowsheds, and signs (16) Station and office buildings (stations and other operating structures only) (17) Roadway buildings (18) Water stations (19) Fuel stations (20) Shops and enginehouses (25) TOFC/COFC terminals (operating structures only) (31) Power transmission systems (35) Miscellaneous structures (39) Public improvements construction	30	20	30
40.3	**Railroad Wharves and Docks:** Includes assets classified in the following Interstate Commission Commerce accounts: (23) Wharves and docks (24) Coal and ore wharves	20	15	20
40.4	**Railroad Track**	10	7	10
40.51	**Railroad Hydraulic Electric Generating Equipment**	50	20	50
40.52	**Railroad Nuclear Electric Generating Equipment**	20	15	20
40.53	**Railroad Steam Electric Generating Equipment**	28	20	28
40.54	**Railroad Steam, Compressed Air, and Other Power Plan Equipment**	28	20	28
41.0	**Motor Transport—Passengers:** Includes assets used in the urban and interurban commercial and contract carrying of passengers by road, except the transportation assets included in classes with the prefix 00.2.	8	5	8
42.0	**Motor Transport—Freight:** Includes assets used in the commercial and contract carrying of freight by road, except the transportation assets included in classes with the prefix 00.2.	8	5	8
44.0	**Water Transportation:** Includes assets used in the commercial and contract carrying of freight and passengers by water except the transportation assets included in classes with the prefix 00.2. Includes all related land improvements.	20	15	20
45.0	**Air Transport:** Includes assets (except helicopters) used in commercial and contract carrying of passengers and freight by air. For purposes of section 1.167(a)-11(d)(2)(iv)(a) of the regulations, expenditures for "repair, maintenance, rehabilitation, or improvement," shall consist of direct maintenance expenses (irrespective of airworthiness provisions or charges) as defined by Civil Aeronautics Board uniform accounts 5200, maintenance burden (exclusive of expenses pertaining to maintenance buildings and improvements) as defined by Civil Aeronautics Board accounts 5300, and expenditures which are not "excluded additions" as defined in section 1.167(a)-11(d)(2)(vi) of the regulations and which would be charged to property and equipment accounts in the Civil Aeronautics Board uniform system of accounts.	12	7	12
45.1	**Air Transport (restricted):** Includes each asset described in the description of class 45.0 which was held by the taxpayer on April 15, 1976, or is acquired by the taxpayer pursuant to a contract which was, on April 15, 1976, and at all times thereafter, binding on the taxpayer. This criterion of classification based on binding contract concept is to be applied in the same manner as under the general rules expressed in section 49(b)(1), (4), (5) and (8) of the Code (as in effect prior to its repeal by the Revenue Act of 1978, section 312(c)(1), (d), 1978-3 C.B. 1, 60).	6	5	6
46.0	**Pipeline Transportation:** Includes assets used in the private, commercial, and contract carrying of petroleum, gas and other products by means of pipes and conveyors. The trunk lines and related storage facilities of integrated petroleum and natural gas producers are included in this class. Excludes initial clearing and grading land improvements as specified in Rev. Rul. 72-403, 1972-2; C.B. 102, but includes all other related land improvements.	22	15	22

Publication 946 (2015)

Table B-2. **Table of Class Lives and Recovery Periods**

Asset class	Description of assets included	Class Life (in years)	Recovery Periods (in years)	
			GDS (MACRS)	ADS
48.11	**Telephone Communications:** Includes the assets classified below and that are used in the provision of commercial and contract telephonic services such as: **Telephone Central Office Buildings:** Includes assets intended to house central office equipment, as defined in Federal Communications Commission Part 31 Account No. 212 whether section 1245 or section 1250 property.	45	20	45
48.12	**Telephone Central Office Equipment:** Includes central office switching and related equipment as defined in Federal Communications Commission Part 31 Account No. 221. Does not include computer-based telephone central office switching equipment included in class 48.121. Does not include private branch exchange (PBX) equipment.	18	10	18
48.121	**Computer-based Telephone Central Office Switching Equipment:** Includes equipment whose functions are those of a computer or peripheral equipment (as defined in section 168(i)(2)(B) of the Code) used in its capacity as telephone central office equipment. Does not include private exchange (PBX) equipment.	9.5	5	9.5
48.13	**Telephone Station Equipment:** Includes such station apparatus and connections as teletypewriters, telephones, booths, private exchanges, and comparable equipment as defined in Federal Communications Commission Part 31 Account No. 231, 232, and 234.	10	7*	10*
48.14	**Telephone Distribution Plant:** Includes such assets as pole lines, cable, aerial wire, underground conduits, and comparable equipment, and related land improvements as defined in Federal Communications Commission Part 31 Account Nos. 241, 242.1, 242.2, 242.3, 242.4, 243, and 244.	24	15	24
48.2	**Radio and Television Broadcastings:** Includes assets used in radio and television broadcasting, except transmitting towers. **Telegraph, Ocean Cable, and Satellite Communications (TOCSC)** includes communications-related assets used to provide domestic and international radio-telegraph, wire-telegraph, ocean-cable, and satellite communications services; also includes related land improvements. If property described in Classes 48.31–48.45 is comparable to telephone distribution plant described in Class 48.14 and used for 2-way exchange of voice and data communication which is the equivalent of telephone communication, such property is assigned a class life of 24 years under this revenue procedure. Comparable equipment does not include cable television equipment used primarily for 1-way communication.	6	5	6
48.31	**TOCSC—Electric Power Generating and Distribution Systems:** Includes assets used in the provision of electric power by generation, modulation, rectification, channelization, control, and distribution. Does not include these assets when they are installed on customers premises.	19	10	19
48.32	**TOCSC—High Frequency Radio and Microwave Systems:** Includes assets such as transmitters and receivers, antenna supporting structures, antennas, transmission lines from equipment to antenna, transmitter cooling systems, and control and amplification equipment. Does not include cable and long-line systems.	13	7	13
48.33	**TOCSC—Cable and Long-line Systems:** Includes assets such as transmission lines, pole lines, ocean cables, buried cable and conduit, repeaters, repeater stations, and other related assets. Does not include high frequency radio or microwave systems.	26.5	20	26.5
48.34	**TOCSC—Central Office Control Equipment:** Includes assets for general control, switching, and monitoring of communications signals including electromechanical switching and channeling apparatus, multiplexing equipment patching and monitoring facilities, in-house cabling, teleprinter equipment, and associated site improvements.	16.5	10	16.5
48.35	**TOCSC—Computerized Switching, Channeling, and Associated Control Equipment:** Includes central office switching computers, interfacing computers, other associated specialized control equipment, and site improvements.	10.5	7	10.5
48.36	**TOCSC—Satellite Ground Segment Property:** Includes assets such as fixed earth station equipment, antennas, satellite communications equipment, and interface equipment used in satellite communications. Does not include general purpose equipment or equipment used in satellite space segment property.	10	7	10
48.37	**TOCSC—Satellite Space Segment Property:** Includes satellites and equipment used for telemetry, tracking, control, and monitoring when used in satellite communications.	8	5	8
48.38	**TOCSC—Equipment Installed on Customer's Premises:** Includes assets installed on customer's premises, such as computers, terminal equipment, power generation and distribution systems, private switching center, teleprinters, facsimile equipment and other associated and related equipment.	10	7	10
48.39	**TOCSC—Support and Service Equipment:** Includes assets used to support but not engage in communications. Includes store, warehouse and shop tools, and test and laboratory assets. **Cable Television (CATV):** Includes communications-related assets used to provide cable television community antenna television services. Does not include assets used to provide subscribers with two-way communications services.	13.5	7	13.5

* Property described in asset guideline class 48.13 which is qualified technological equipment as defined in section 168(i)(2) is assigned a 5-year recovery period.

Publication 946 (2015)

Table B-2. **Table of Class Lives and Recovery Periods**

Asset class	Description of assets included	Class Life (in years)	Recovery Periods (in years) GDS (MACRS)	ADS
48.41	**CATV—Headend:** Includes assets such as towers, antennas, preamplifiers, converters, modulation equipment, and program non-duplication systems. Does not include headend buildings and program origination assets.	11	7	11
48.42	**CATV—Subscriber Connection and Distribution Systems:** Includes assets such as trunk and feeder cable, connecting hardware, amplifiers, power equipment, passive devices, directional taps, pedestals, pressure taps, drop cables, matching transformers, multiple set connector equipment, and convertors.	10	7	10
48.43	**CATV—Program Origination:** Includes assets such as cameras, film chains, video tape recorders, lighting, and remote location equipment excluding vehicles. Does not include buildings and their structural components.	9	5	9
48.44	**CATV—Service and Test:** Includes assets such as oscilloscopes, field strength meters, spectrum analyzers, and cable testing equipment, but does not include vehicles.	8.5	5	8.5
48.45	**CATV—Microwave Systems:** Inlcudes assets such as towers, antennas, transmitting and receiving equipment, and broad band microwave assets is used in the provision of cable television services. Does not include assets used in the provision of common carrier services.	9.5	5	9.5
49.11	**Electric, Gas, Water and Steam, Utility Services:** Includes assets used in the production, transmission and distribution of electricity, gas, steam, or water for sale including related land improvements. **Electric Utility Hydraulic Production Plant:** Includes assets used in the hydraulic power production of electricity for sale, including related land improvements, such as dams, flumes, canals, and waterways.	50	20	50
49.12	**Electric Utility Nuclear Production Plant:** Includes assets used in the nuclear power production and electricity for sale and related land improvements. Does not include nuclear fuel assemblies.	20	15	20
49.121	**Electric Utility Nuclear Fuel Assemblies:** Includes initial core and replacement core nuclear fuel assemblies (i.e., the composite of fabricated nuclear fuel and container) when used in a boiling water, pressurized water, or high temperature gas reactor used in the production of electricity. Does not include nuclear fuel assemblies used in breader reactors.	5	5	5
49.13	**Electric Utility Steam Production Plant:** Includes assets used in the steam power production of electricity for sale, combusion turbines operated in a combined cycle with a conventional steam unit and related land improvements. Also includes package boilers, electric generators and related assets such as electricity and steam distribution systems as used by a waste reduction and resource recovery plant if the steam or electricity is normally for sale to others.	28	20	28
49.14	**Electric Utility Transmission and Distribution Plant:** Includes assets used in the transmission and distribution of electricity for sale and related land improvements. Excludes initial clearing and grading land improvements as specified in Rev. Rul. 72-403, 1972-2 C.B. 102.	30	20	30
49.15	**Electric Utility Combustion Turbine Production Plant:** Includes assets used in the production of electricity for sale by the use of such prime movers as jet engines, combustion turbines, diesel engines, gasoline engines, and other internal combustion engines, their associated power turbines and/or generators, and related land improvements. Does not include combustion turbines operated in a combined cycle with a conventional steam unit.	20	15	20
49.21	**Gas Utility Distribution Facilities:** Includes gas water heaters and gas conversion equipment installed by utility on customers' premises on a rental basis.	35	20	35
49.221	**Gas Utility Manufactured Gas Production Plants:** Includes assets used in the manufacture of gas having chemical and/or physical properties which do not permit complete interchangeability with domestic natural gas. Does not include gas-producing systems and related systems used in waste reduction and resource recovery plants which are elsewhere classified.	30	20	30
49.222	**Gas Utility Substitute Natural Gas (SNG) Production Plant (naphtha or lighter hydrocarbon feedstocks):** Includes assets used in the catalytic conversion of feedstocks or naphtha or lighter hydrocarbons to a gaseous fuel which is completely interchangeable with domestic natural gas.	14	7	14
49.223	**Substitute Natural Gas—Coal Gasification:** Includes assets used in the manufacture and production of pipeline quality gas from coal using the basic Lurgi process with advanced methanation. Includes all process plant equipment and structures used in this coal gasification process and all utility assets such as cooling systems, water supply and treatment facilities, and assets used in the production and distribution of electricity and steam for use by the taxpayer in a gasification plant and attendant coal mining site processes but not for assets used in the production and distribution of electricity and steam for sale to others. Also includes all other related land improvements. Does not include assets used in the direct mining and treatment of coal prior to the gasification process itself.	18	10	18
49.23	**Natural Gas Production Plant**	14	7	14
49.24	**Gas Utility Trunk Pipelines and Related Storage Facilities:** Excluding initial clearing and grading land improvements as specified in Rev. Rul. 72-40.	22	15	22
49.25	**Liquefied Natural Gas Plant:** Includes assets used in the liquefaction, storage, and regasification of natural gas including loading and unloading connections, instrumentation equipment and controls, pumps, vaporizers and odorizers, tanks, and related land improvements. Also includes pipeline interconnections with gas transmission lines and distribution systems and marine terminal facilities.	22	15	22

Publication 946 (2015)

Table B-2. **Table of Class Lives and Recovery Periods**

Asset class	Description of assets included	Class Life (in years)	Recovery Periods (in years) GDS (MACRS)	ADS
49.3	**Water Utilities:** Includes assets used in the gathering, treatment, and commercial distribution of water.	50	20***	50
49.4	**Central Steam Utility Production and Distribution:** Includes assets used in the production and distribution of steam for sale. Does not include assets used in waste reduction and resource recovery plants which are elsewhere classified.	28	20	28
49.5	**Waste Reduction and Resource Recovery Plants:** Includes assets used in the conversion of refuse or other solid waste or biomass to heat or to a solid, liquid, or gaseous fuel. Also includes all process plant equipment and structures at the site used to receive, handle, collect, and process refuse or other solid waste or biomass in a waterwall, combustion system, oil or gas pyrolysis system, or refuse derived fuel system to create hot water, gas, steam and electricity. Includes material recovery and support assets used in refuse or solid refuse or solid waste receiving, collecting, handling, sorting, shredding, classifying, and separation systems. Does not include any package boilers, or electric generators and related assets such as electricity, hot water, steam and manufactured gas production plants classified in classes 00.4, 49.13, 49.221, and 49.4. Does include, however, all other utilities such as water supply and treatment facilities, ash handling and other related land improvements of a waste reduction and resource recovery plant.	10	7	10
50.	**Municipal Wastewater Treatment Plant**	24	15	24
51.	**Municipal Sewer**	50	20***	50
57.0	**Distributive Trades and Services:** Includes assets used in wholesale and retail trade, and personal and professional services. Includes section 1245 assets used in marketing petroleum and petroleum products.	9	5	9*
57.1	**Distributive Trades and Services—Billboard, Service Station Buildings and Petroleum Marketing Land Improvements:** Includes section 1250 assets, including service station buildings and depreciable land improvements, whether section 1245 property or section 1250 property, used in the marketing of petroleum and petroleum products, but not including any of these facilities related to petroleum and natural gas trunk pipelines. Includes car wash buildings and related land improvements. Includes billboards, whether such assets are section 1245 property or section 1250 property. Excludes all other land improvements, buildings and structural components as defined in section 1.48-1(e) of the regulations. See *Gas station convenience stores* in chapter 3.	20	15	20
79.0	**Recreation:** Includes assets used in the provision of entertainment services on payment of a fee or admission charge, as in the operation of bowling alleys, billiard and pool establishments, theaters, concert halls, and miniature golf courses. Does not include amusement and theme parks and assets which consist primarily of specialized land improvements or structures, such as golf courses, sports stadia, race tracks, ski slopes, and buildings which house the assets used in entertainment services.	10	7	10
80.0	**Theme and Amusement Parks:** Includes assets used in the provision of rides, attractions, and amusements in activities defined as theme and amusement parks, and includes appurtenances associated with a ride, attraction, amusement or theme setting within the park such as ticket booths, facades, shop interiors, and props, special purpose structures, and buildings other than warehouses, administration buildings, hotels, and motels. Includes all land improvements for or in support of park activities (e.g., parking lots, sidewalks, waterways, bridges, fences, landscaping, etc.), and support functions (e.g., food and beverage retailing, souvenir vending and other nonlodging accommodations) if owned by the park and provided exclusively for the benefit of park patrons. Theme and amusement parks are defined as combinations of amusements, rides, and attractions which are permanently situated on park land and open to the public for the price of admission. This guideline class is a composite of all assets used in this industry except transportation equipment (general purpose trucks, cars, airplanes, etc., which are included in asset guideline classes with the prefix 00.2), assets used in the provision of administrative services (asset classes with the prefix 00.1) and warehouses, administration buildings, hotels and motels.	12.5	7	12.5
	Certain Property for Which Recovery Periods Assigned			
	A. Personal Property With No Class Life		7	12
	Section 1245 Real Property With No Class Life		7	40
	B. Qualified Technological Equipment, as defined in section 168(i)(2).	**	5	5
	C. Property Used in Connection with Research and Experimentation referred to in section 168(e)(3)(B).	**	5	class life if no class life—12
	D. Alternative energy property described in sections 48(l)(3)(A)(ix) (as in effect on the day before the date of enactment (11/5/90) of the Revenue Reconciliation Act of 1990).	**	5	class life if no class life—12
	E. Biomass property described in section 48(l)(15) (as in effect on the day before the date of enactment (11/5/90) of the Revenue Reconciliation Act of 1990) and is a qualifying small production facility within the meaning of section 3(17)(c) of the Federal Power Act (16 U.S.C. 796(17)(C)), as in effect on September 1, 1986.	**	5	class life if no class life—12
	F. Energy property described in section 48(a)(3)(A) (or would be described if "solar or wind energy" were substituted for "solar energy" in section 48(a)(3)(A)(i)).	**	5	class life if no class life—12

* Any high technology medical equipment as defined in section 168(i)(2)(C) which is described in asset guideline class 57.0 is assigned a 5-year recovery period for the alternate MACRS method.

** The class life (if any) of property described in classes B, C, D, E, or F is determined by reference to the asset guideline classes. If an item of property described in paragraphs B, C, D, E, or F is not described in any asset guideline class, such item of property has no class life.

*** Use straight line over 25 years if placed in service after June 12, 1996, unless placed in service under a binding contract in effect before June 10, 1996, and at all times until placed in service.

Publication 946 (2015)

Table A-1. **3-, 5-, 7-, 10-, 15-, and 20-Year Property Half-Year Convention**

Year	Depreciation rate for recovery period					
	3-year	5-year	7-year	10-year	15-year	20-year
1	33.33%	20.00%	14.29%	10.00%	5.00%	3.750%
2	44.45	32.00	24.49	18.00	9.50	7.219
3	14.81	19.20	17.49	14.40	8.55	6.677
4	7.41	11.52	12.49	11.52	7.70	6.177
5		11.52	8.93	9.22	6.93	5.713
6		5.76	8.92	7.37	6.23	5.285
7			8.93	6.55	5.90	4.888
8			4.46	6.55	5.90	4.522
9				6.56	5.91	4.462
10				6.55	5.90	4.461
11				3.28	5.91	4.462
12					5.90	4.461
13					5.91	4.462
14					5.90	4.461
15					5.91	4.462
16					2.95	4.461
17						4.462
18						4.461
19						4.462
20						4.461
21						2.231

Table A-2. **3-, 5-, 7-, 10-, 15-, and 20-Year Property Mid-Quarter Convention Placed in Service in First Quarter**

Year	Depreciation rate for recovery period					
	3-year	5-year	7-year	10-year	15-year	20-year
1	58.33%	35.00%	25.00%	17.50%	8.75%	6.563%
2	27.78	26.00	21.43	16.50	9.13	7.000
3	12.35	15.60	15.31	13.20	8.21	6.482
4	1.54	11.01	10.93	10.56	7.39	5.996
5		11.01	8.75	8.45	6.65	5.546
6		1.38	8.74	6.76	5.99	5.130
7			8.75	6.55	5.90	4.746
8			1.09	6.55	5.91	4.459
9				6.56	5.90	4.459
10				6.55	5.91	4.459
11				0.82	5.90	4.459
12					5.91	4.460
13					5.90	4.459
14					5.91	4.460
15					5.90	4.459
16					0.74	4.460
17						4.459
18						4.460
19						4.459
20						4.460
21						0.565

Publication 946 (2015)

Table A-3. **3-, 5-, 7-, 10-, 15-, and 20-Year Property**
Mid-Quarter Convention
Placed in Service in Second Quarter

Year	Depreciation rate for recovery period					
	3-year	5-year	7-year	10-year	15-year	20-year
1	41.67%	25.00%	17.85%	12.50%	6.25%	4.688%
2	38.89	30.00	23.47	17.50	9.38	7.148
3	14.14	18.00	16.76	14.00	8.44	6.612
4	5.30	11.37	11.97	11.20	7.59	6.116
5		11.37	8.87	8.96	6.83	5.658
6		4.26	8.87	7.17	6.15	5.233
7			8.87	6.55	5.91	4.841
8			3.34	6.55	5.90	4.478
9				6.56	5.91	4.463
10				6.55	5.90	4.463
11				2.46	5.91	4.463
12					5.90	4.463
13					5.91	4.463
14					5.90	4.463
15					5.91	4.462
16					2.21	4.463
17						4.462
18						4.463
19						4.462
20						4.463
21						1.673

Table A-4. **3-, 5-, 7-, 10-, 15-, and 20-Year Property**
Mid-Quarter Convention
Placed in Service in Third Quarter

Year	Depreciation rate for recovery period					
	3-year	5-year	7-year	10-year	15-year	20-year
1	25.00%	15.00%	10.71%	7.50%	3.75%	2.813%
2	50.00	34.00	25.51	18.50	9.63	7.289
3	16.67	20.40	18.22	14.80	8.66	6.742
4	8.33	12.24	13.02	11.84	7.80	6.237
5		11.30	9.30	9.47	7.02	5.769
6		7.06	8.85	7.58	6.31	5.336
7			8.86	6.55	5.90	4.936
8			5.53	6.55	5.90	4.566
9				6.56	5.91	4.460
10				6.55	5.90	4.460
11				4.10	5.91	4.460
12					5.90	4.460
13					5.91	4.461
14					5.90	4.460
15					5.91	4.461
16					3.69	4.460
17						4.461
18						4.460
19						4.461
20						4.460
21						2.788

Table A-5. **3-, 5-, 7-, 10-, 15-, and 20-Year Property**
Mid-Quarter Convention
Placed in Service in Fourth Quarter

Year	Depreciation rate for recovery period					
	3-year	5-year	7-year	10-year	15-year	20-year
1	8.33%	5.00%	3.57%	2.50%	1.25%	0.938%
2	61.11	38.00	27.55	19.50	9.88	7.430
3	20.37	22.80	19.68	15.60	8.89	6.872
4	10.19	13.68	14.06	12.48	8.00	6.357
5		10.94	10.04	9.98	7.20	5.880
6		9.58	8.73	7.99	6.48	5.439
7			8.73	6.55	5.90	5.031
8			7.64	6.55	5.90	4.654
9				6.56	5.90	4.458
10				6.55	5.91	4.458
11				5.74	5.90	4.458
12					5.91	4.458
13					5.90	4.458
14					5.91	4.458
15					5.90	4.458
16					5.17	4.458
17						4.458
18						4.459
19						4.458
20						4.459
21						3.901

Table A-6. **Residential Rental Property**
Mid-Month Convention
Straight Line—27.5 Years

Year	Month property placed in service											
	1	2	3	4	5	6	7	8	9	10	11	12
1	3.485%	3.182%	2.879%	2.576%	2.273%	1.970%	1.667%	1.364%	1.061%	0.758%	0.455%	0.152%
2–9	3.636	3.636	3.636	3.636	3.636	3.636	3.636	3.636	3.636	3.636	3.636	3.636
10	3.637	3.637	3.637	3.637	3.637	3.637	3.636	3.636	3.636	3.636	3.636	3.636
11	3.636	3.636	3.636	3.636	3.636	3.636	3.637	3.637	3.637	3.637	3.637	3.637
12	3.637	3.637	3.637	3.637	3.637	3.637	3.636	3.636	3.636	3.636	3.636	3.636
13	3.636	3.636	3.636	3.636	3.636	3.636	3.637	3.637	3.637	3.637	3.637	3.637
14	3.637	3.637	3.637	3.637	3.637	3.637	3.636	3.636	3.636	3.636	3.636	3.636
15	3.636	3.636	3.636	3.636	3.636	3.636	3.637	3.637	3.637	3.637	3.637	3.637
16	3.637	3.637	3.637	3.637	3.637	3.637	3.636	3.636	3.636	3.636	3.636	3.636
17	3.636	3.636	3.636	3.636	3.636	3.636	3.637	3.637	3.637	3.637	3.637	3.637
18	3.637	3.637	3.637	3.637	3.637	3.637	3.636	3.636	3.636	3.636	3.636	3.636
19	3.636	3.636	3.636	3.636	3.636	3.636	3.637	3.637	3.637	3.637	3.637	3.637
20	3.637	3.637	3.637	3.637	3.637	3.637	3.636	3.636	3.636	3.636	3.636	3.636
21	3.636	3.636	3.636	3.636	3.636	3.636	3.637	3.637	3.637	3.637	3.637	3.637
22	3.637	3.637	3.637	3.637	3.637	3.637	3.636	3.636	3.636	3.636	3.636	3.636
23	3.636	3.636	3.636	3.636	3.636	3.636	3.637	3.637	3.637	3.637	3.637	3.637
24	3.637	3.637	3.637	3.637	3.637	3.637	3.636	3.636	3.636	3.636	3.636	3.636
25	3.636	3.636	3.636	3.636	3.636	3.636	3.637	3.637	3.637	3.637	3.637	3.637
26	3.637	3.637	3.637	3.637	3.637	3.637	3.636	3.636	3.636	3.636	3.636	3.636
27	3.636	3.636	3.636	3.636	3.636	3.636	3.637	3.637	3.637	3.637	3.637	3.637
28	1.97	2.273	2.576	2.879	3.182	3.485	3.636	3.636	3.636	3.636	3.636	3.636
29							0.152	0.455	0.758	1.061	1.364	1.667

Publication 946 (2015)

Table 19-1
Estimate Annual Life Insurance Premium Rates per $1,000 of Face Value

10-Year Level Term							20-Year Level Term						
Age	**Male**			**Female**			**Age**	**Male**			**Female**		
	PREF	**NT**	**T**	**PREF**	**NT**	**T**		**PREF**	**NT**	**T**	**PREF**	**NT**	**T**
20	0.87	1.27	2.28	0.75	1.10	1.88	**20**	1.09	1.50	2.86	0.91	1.31	2.56
25	0.87	1.27	2.28	0.75	1.10	1.88	**25**	1.09	1.50	2.86	0.91	1.31	2.56
30	0.87	1.36	2.49	0.75	1.16	2.06	**30**	1.12	1.61	3.24	0.96	1.42	2.67
35	0.87	1.44	2.73	0.75	1.26	2.23	**35**	1.17	1.73	3.62	1.02	1.53	2.78
40	1.13	1.96	3.78	1.00	1.57	2.93	**40**	1.49	2.36	5.38	1.26	2.00	3.77
45	1.51	2.69	5.33	1.38	2.12	4.08	**45**	2.23	3.73	8.42	1.75	2.92	5.57
50	2.03	3.76	8.08	1.72	2.98	5.78	**50**	3.45	5.99	12.90	2.59	4.40	8.02
55	2.95	5.61	12.48	2.27	4.44	8.33	**55**	5.38	9.52	19.15	3.96	6.66	11.45
60	4.61	9.07	20.07	3.46	6.95	12.57	**60**	8.46	15.15	29.14	6.17	10.36	16.74

Whole Life							Universal Life						
Age	**Male**			**Female**			**Age**	**Male**			**Female**		
	PREF	**NT**	**T**	**PREF**	**NT**	**T**		**PREF**	**NT**	**T**	**PREF**	**NT**	**T**
20	8.39	9.02	10.55	7.55	8.12	9.95	**20**	5.25	5.78	7.17	4.53	4.65	5.97
25	9.51	10.22	12.70	8.65	9.30	11.59	**25**	6.21	6.69	8.61	5.37	5.61	7.17
30	10.86	11.68	14.77	9.82	10.56	13.48	**30**	7.41	8.13	10.29	6.45	6.81	8.73
35	12.37	13.30	16.59	10.97	11.80	14.85	**35**	9.09	9.93	12.69	7.89	8.25	10.77
40	14.42	15.50	19.31	12.54	13.48	16.69	**40**	11.25	12.33	15.69	9.69	10.17	13.41
45	17.65	18.98	24.03	15.14	16.28	20.43	**45**	14.01	15.45	19.65	12.09	12.69	16.77
50	22.45	24.14	30.65	19.09	20.53	25.39	**50**	17.61	19.17	24.45	15.09	16.05	21.33
55	28.67	30.82	39.00	24.11	25.92	30.97	**55**	22.41	24.57	31.41	18.93	20.25	26.97
60	36.06	38.77	49.39	29.75	31.99	37.25	**60**	28.77	34.53	43.65	23.97	28.29	37.53

PREF = Preferred; NT = Non-tobacco; T = Tobacco usage

Table 19-2
Premium Rates for Periods Less than One Year

Period	Percent of Annual Premium
Semiannually	51.00
Quarterly	26.00
Monthly	8.75

Table 19-3
Estimated Annual Renters Insurance Premium Rates

	$20,000 Policy Limit						$40,000 Policy Limit					
Liability	**$500 Ded.**			**$1,000 Ded.**			**$500 Ded.**			**$1,000 Ded.**		
	GOOD	OCC	BAD	GOOD	OCC	BAD	GOOD	OCC	BAD	GOOD	OCC	BAD
$300,000	141	226	253	126	203	227	195	312	349	174	280	313
$500,000	149	239	268	134	215	241	206	330	370	185	297	333
$1,000,000	169	270	303	154	246	276	233	373	418	213	339	381

GOOD = Good credit; OCC = Occasional payments past 30 days; BAD = Judgments, collection, bankruptcy

Tip 19-3
Rates for Optional Coverage and Extended Coverage Endorsements

Identity theft/fraud protection	$20/year		Jewelry, watches and furs	$0.85/$100/year
			Camera equipment	$1.35/$100/year
			Computer equipment	$0.95/$100/year
Sewer/sump pump backup protection (for property located in a basement)	$75/year		Fine art and collectibles	$1.10/$100/year
			Firearms and accessories	$1.45/$100/year
			Portable tools	$3.25/$100/year

Table 19-4
Estimated Annual Homeowner's Insurance Premium Rates per $100 of Face Value

	Frame Regular						Masonry					
Deductible	Zone 1			Zone 2			Zone 1			Zone 2		
	GOOD	OCC	BAD	GOOD	OCC	BAD	GOOD	OCC	BAD	GOOD	OCC	BAD
$1,000	0.29	0.38	0.75	0.34	0.46	0.92	0.27	0.36	0.71	0.32	0.43	0.86
$1,500	0.27	0.36	0.71	0.32	0.44	0.87	0.25	0.34	0.67	0.30	0.41	0.81

GOOD = Good credit; OCC = Occasional payments past 30 days; BAD = Judgments, collection, bankruptcy

Table 19-5
Annual Automobile Liability Insurance Premiums

	Bodily Injury & Property Damage, Including UM/UIM/Medical					
Liability Limits	Territory 1			Territory 2		
	GOOD	OCC	BAD	GOOD	OCC	BAD
50/100/50	385	600	846	354	552	778
100/300/100	425	682	961	391	627	884
250/500/250	460	750	1036	423	690	953
500/1000/500	530	843	1208	488	776	1111

GOOD = Good credit; OCC = Occasional payments past 30 days;
BAD = Judgments, collection, bankruptcy

Table 19-6

Annual Auto Insurance Premium Rates for Comprehensive and Collision

Territory 1													
		Comprehensive						Collision					
Model Class	Vehicle Age	$0 Deductible			$250 Deductible			$500 Deductible			$1,000 Deductible		
		GOOD	OCC	BAD	GOOD	OCC	BAD	GOOD	OCC	BAD	GOOD	OCC	BAD
1	0-1	584	934	1129	393	628	759	535	855	1279	471	753	1126
	2-3	520	831	1005	350	559	676	449	718	1074	396	633	946
	4-5	397	635	768	267	427	516	396	633	946	349	557	833
	6+	374	598	723	252	402	486	332	530	793	292	467	698
2	0-1	502	803	971	338	540	653	503	804	1202	443	708	1058
	2-3	447	715	864	301	481	581	417	667	998	367	587	879
	4-5	342	546	660	230	367	444	367	587	878	323	517	773
	6+	321	514	621	216	346	418	297	474	709	261	418	624
3	0-1	472	755	913	318	508	614	478	764	1142	421	672	1006
	2-3	420	672	812	283	452	546	392	627	938	345	552	826
	4-5	321	513	621	216	345	417	342	547	818	301	481	720
	6+	302	483	584	203	325	393	277	442	661	244	389	582

Territory 2													
		Comprehensive						Collision					
Model Class	Vehicle Age	$0 Deductible			$250 Deductible			$500 Deductible			$1,000 Deductible		
		GOOD	OCC	BAD	GOOD	OCC	BAD	GOOD	OCC	BAD	GOOD	OCC	BAD
1	0-1	514	822	994	346	553	668	492	787	1177	433	693	1036
	2-3	457	732	884	308	492	594	413	661	988	364	582	870
	4-5	349	559	676	235	376	454	364	582	871	321	513	767
	6+	329	526	636	221	354	427	305	488	730	269	430	642
2	0-1	442	707	854	297	475	574	463	739	1106	407	651	974
	2-3	393	629	760	265	423	511	384	614	918	338	540	808
	4-5	301	481	581	202	323	391	338	540	807	297	475	711
	6+	283	452	547	190	304	368	273	436	653	240	384	575
3	0-1	415	664	803	280	447	540	440	702	1051	387	619	925
	2-3	370	591	715	249	398	481	361	577	863	318	508	760
	4-5	283	452	546	190	304	367	315	503	752	277	443	662
	6+	266	425	514	179	286	346	255	407	608	224	358	536

GOOD = Good credit; OCC = Occasional payments past 30 days; BAD = Judgments, collection, bankruptcy

Table 19-6
Discounts and Surcharges for Automobile Insurance

Discounts			**Surcharges** *	
Good student	25%		Moving violations	$60/year/ticket
(full-time student, 16 to 24 years old,			during past 3 years	(maximum $120/year)
"B" average or 3.0 GPA or above)			At-fault accident during	$150/year/ticket
Accident free for 3 years	5%		during past 3 years	(maximum $300/year)
Multi vehicle coverage	10%		16-19 year-old driver	30%
			20-21 year-old driver	20%
			22-24 year-old driver	10%

* Surcharges are added after discounts are applied

2015 Tax Table

CAUTION

See the instructions for line 44 to see if you must use the Tax Table below to figure your tax.

Example. Mr. and Mrs. Brown are filing a joint return. Their taxable income on Form 1040, line 43, is $25,300. First, they find the $25,300-25,350 taxable income line. Next, they find the column for married filing jointly and read down the column. The amount shown where the taxable income line and filing status column meet is $2,876. This is the tax amount they should enter on Form 1040, line 44.

Sample Table

At Least	But Less Than	Single	Married filing jointly*	Married filing sepa-rately	Head of a house-hold
		Your tax is—			
25,200	**25,250**	3,323	2,861	3,323	3,126
25,250	**25,300**	3,330	2,869	3,330	3,134
25,300	**25,350**	3,338	(2,876)	3,338	3,141
25,350	**25,400**	3,345	2,884	3,345	3,149

If line 43 (taxable income) is— At least	But less than	And you are— Single	Married filing jointly *	Married filing sepa-rately	Head of a house-hold
		Your tax is—			
0	**5**	0	0	0	0
5	**15**	1	1	1	1
15	**25**	2	2	2	2
25	**50**	4	4	4	4
50	**75**	6	6	6	6
75	**100**	9	9	9	9
100	**125**	11	11	11	11
125	**150**	14	14	14	14
150	**175**	16	16	16	16
175	**200**	19	19	19	19
200	**225**	21	21	21	21
225	**250**	24	24	24	24
250	**275**	26	26	26	26
275	**300**	29	29	29	29
300	**325**	31	31	31	31
325	**350**	34	34	34	34
350	**375**	36	36	36	36
375	**400**	39	39	39	39
400	**425**	41	41	41	41
425	**450**	44	44	44	44
450	**475**	46	46	46	46
475	**500**	49	49	49	49
500	**525**	51	51	51	51
525	**550**	54	54	54	54
550	**575**	56	56	56	56
575	**600**	59	59	59	59
600	**625**	61	61	61	61
625	**650**	64	64	64	64
650	**675**	66	66	66	66
675	**700**	69	69	69	69
700	**725**	71	71	71	71
725	**750**	74	74	74	74
750	**775**	76	76	76	76
775	**800**	79	79	79	79
800	**825**	81	81	81	81
825	**850**	84	84	84	84
850	**875**	86	86	86	86
875	**900**	89	89	89	89
900	**925**	91	91	91	91
925	**950**	94	94	94	94
950	**975**	96	96	96	96
975	**1,000**	99	99	99	99

If line 43 (taxable income) is— At least	But less than	And you are— Single	Married filing jointly *	Married filing sepa-rately	Head of a house-hold
		Your tax is—			
1,000					
1,000	**1,025**	101	101	101	101
1,025	**1,050**	104	104	104	104
1,050	**1,075**	106	106	106	106
1,075	**1,100**	109	109	109	109
1,100	**1,125**	111	111	111	111
1,125	**1,150**	114	114	114	114
1,150	**1,175**	116	116	116	116
1,175	**1,200**	119	119	119	119
1,200	**1,225**	121	121	121	121
1,225	**1,250**	124	124	124	124
1,250	**1,275**	126	126	126	126
1,275	**1,300**	129	129	129	129
1,300	**1,325**	131	131	131	131
1,325	**1,350**	134	134	134	134
1,350	**1,375**	136	136	136	136
1,375	**1,400**	139	139	139	139
1,400	**1,425**	141	141	141	141
1,425	**1,450**	144	144	144	144
1,450	**1,475**	146	146	146	146
1,475	**1,500**	149	149	149	149
1,500	**1,525**	151	151	151	151
1,525	**1,550**	154	154	154	154
1,550	**1,575**	156	156	156	156
1,575	**1,600**	159	159	159	159
1,600	**1,625**	161	161	161	161
1,625	**1,650**	164	164	164	164
1,650	**1,675**	166	166	166	166
1,675	**1,700**	169	169	169	169
1,700	**1,725**	171	171	171	171
1,725	**1,750**	174	174	174	174
1,750	**1,775**	176	176	176	176
1,775	**1,800**	179	179	179	179
1,800	**1,825**	181	181	181	181
1,825	**1,850**	184	184	184	184
1,850	**1,875**	186	186	186	186
1,875	**1,900**	189	189	189	189
1,900	**1,925**	191	191	191	191
1,925	**1,950**	194	194	194	194
1,950	**1,975**	196	196	196	196
1,975	**2,000**	199	199	199	199

If line 43 (taxable income) is— At least	But less than	And you are— Single	Married filing jointly *	Married filing sepa-rately	Head of a house-hold
		Your tax is—			
2,000					
2,000	**2,025**	201	201	201	201
2,025	**2,050**	204	204	204	204
2,050	**2,075**	206	206	206	206
2,075	**2,100**	209	209	209	209
2,100	**2,125**	211	211	211	211
2,125	**2,150**	214	214	214	214
2,150	**2,175**	216	216	216	216
2,175	**2,200**	219	219	219	219
2,200	**2,225**	221	221	221	221
2,225	**2,250**	224	224	224	224
2,250	**2,275**	226	226	226	226
2,275	**2,300**	229	229	229	229
2,300	**2,325**	231	231	231	231
2,325	**2,350**	234	234	234	234
2,350	**2,375**	236	236	236	236
2,375	**2,400**	239	239	239	239
2,400	**2,425**	241	241	241	241
2,425	**2,450**	244	244	244	244
2,450	**2,475**	246	246	246	246
2,475	**2,500**	249	249	249	249
2,500	**2,525**	251	251	251	251
2,525	**2,550**	254	254	254	254
2,550	**2,575**	256	256	256	256
2,575	**2,600**	259	259	259	259
2,600	**2,625**	261	261	261	261
2,625	**2,650**	264	264	264	264
2,650	**2,675**	266	266	266	266
2,675	**2,700**	269	269	269	269
2,700	**2,725**	271	271	271	271
2,725	**2,750**	274	274	274	274
2,750	**2,775**	276	276	276	276
2,775	**2,800**	279	279	279	279
2,800	**2,825**	281	281	281	281
2,825	**2,850**	284	284	284	284
2,850	**2,875**	286	286	286	286
2,875	**2,900**	289	289	289	289
2,900	**2,925**	291	291	291	291
2,925	**2,950**	294	294	294	294
2,950	**2,975**	296	296	296	296
2,975	**3,000**	299	299	299	299

(Continued)

* This column must also be used by a qualifying widow(er).

2015 Tax Table — *Continued*

If line 43 (taxable income) is—		And you are—			
At least	But less than	Single	Married filing jointly *	Married filing separately	Head of a household
		Your tax is—			
3,000					
3,000	3,050	303	303	303	303
3,050	3,100	308	308	308	308
3,100	3,150	313	313	313	313
3,150	3,200	318	318	318	318
3,200	3,250	323	323	323	323
3,250	3,300	328	328	328	328
3,300	3,350	333	333	333	333
3,350	3,400	338	338	338	338
3,400	3,450	343	343	343	343
3,450	3,500	348	348	348	348
3,500	3,550	353	353	353	353
3,550	3,600	358	358	358	358
3,600	3,650	363	363	363	363
3,650	3,700	368	368	368	368
3,700	3,750	373	373	373	373
3,750	3,800	378	378	378	378
3,800	3,850	383	383	383	383
3,850	3,900	388	388	388	388
3,900	3,950	393	393	393	393
3,950	4,000	398	398	398	398
4,000					
4,000	4,050	403	403	403	403
4,050	4,100	408	408	408	408
4,100	4,150	413	413	413	413
4,150	4,200	418	418	418	418
4,200	4,250	423	423	423	423
4,250	4,300	428	428	428	428
4,300	4,350	433	433	433	433
4,350	4,400	438	438	438	438
4,400	4,450	443	443	443	443
4,450	4,500	448	448	448	448
4,500	4,550	453	453	453	453
4,550	4,600	458	458	458	458
4,600	4,650	463	463	463	463
4,650	4,700	468	468	468	468
4,700	4,750	473	473	473	473
4,750	4,800	478	478	478	478
4,800	4,850	483	483	483	483
4,850	4,900	488	488	488	488
4,900	4,950	493	493	493	493
4,950	5,000	498	498	498	498
5,000					
5,000	5,050	503	503	503	503
5,050	5,100	508	508	508	508
5,100	5,150	513	513	513	513
5,150	5,200	518	518	518	518
5,200	5,250	523	523	523	523
5,250	5,300	528	528	528	528
5,300	5,350	533	533	533	533
5,350	5,400	538	538	538	538
5,400	5,450	543	543	543	543
5,450	5,500	548	548	548	548
5,500	5,550	553	553	553	553
5,550	5,600	558	558	558	558
5,600	5,650	563	563	563	563
5,650	5,700	568	568	568	568
5,700	5,750	573	573	573	573
5,750	5,800	578	578	578	578
5,800	5,850	583	583	583	583
5,850	5,900	588	588	588	588
5,900	5,950	593	593	593	593
5,950	6,000	598	598	598	598
6,000					
6,000	6,050	603	603	603	603
6,050	6,100	608	608	608	608
6,100	6,150	613	613	613	613
6,150	6,200	618	618	618	618
6,200	6,250	623	623	623	623
6,250	6,300	628	628	628	628
6,300	6,350	633	633	633	633
6,350	6,400	638	638	638	638
6,400	6,450	643	643	643	643
6,450	6,500	648	648	648	648
6,500	6,550	653	653	653	653
6,550	6,600	658	658	658	658
6,600	6,650	663	663	663	663
6,650	6,700	668	668	668	668
6,700	6,750	673	673	673	673
6,750	6,800	678	678	678	678
6,800	6,850	683	683	683	683
6,850	6,900	688	688	688	688
6,900	6,950	693	693	693	693
6,950	7,000	698	698	698	698
7,000					
7,000	7,050	703	703	703	703
7,050	7,100	708	708	708	708
7,100	7,150	713	713	713	713
7,150	7,200	718	718	718	718
7,200	7,250	723	723	723	723
7,250	7,300	728	728	728	728
7,300	7,350	733	733	733	733
7,350	7,400	738	738	738	738
7,400	7,450	743	743	743	743
7,450	7,500	748	748	748	748
7,500	7,550	753	753	753	753
7,550	7,600	758	758	758	758
7,600	7,650	763	763	763	763
7,650	7,700	768	768	768	768
7,700	7,750	773	773	773	773
7,750	7,800	778	778	778	778
7,800	7,850	783	783	783	783
7,850	7,900	788	788	788	788
7,900	7,950	793	793	793	793
7,950	8,000	798	798	798	798
8,000					
8,000	8,050	803	803	803	803
8,050	8,100	808	808	808	808
8,100	8,150	813	813	813	813
8,150	8,200	818	818	818	818
8,200	8,250	823	823	823	823
8,250	8,300	828	828	828	828
8,300	8,350	833	833	833	833
8,350	8,400	838	838	838	838
8,400	8,450	843	843	843	843
8,450	8,500	848	848	848	848
8,500	8,550	853	853	853	853
8,550	8,600	858	858	858	858
8,600	8,650	863	863	863	863
8,650	8,700	868	868	868	868
8,700	8,750	873	873	873	873
8,750	8,800	878	878	878	878
8,800	8,850	883	883	883	883
8,850	8,900	888	888	888	888
8,900	8,950	893	893	893	893
8,950	9,000	898	898	898	898
9,000					
9,000	9,050	903	903	903	903
9,050	9,100	908	908	908	908
9,100	9,150	913	913	913	913
9,150	9,200	918	918	918	918
9,200	9,250	923	923	923	923
9,250	9,300	930	928	930	928
9,300	9,350	938	933	938	933
9,350	9,400	945	938	945	938
9,400	9,450	953	943	953	943
9,450	9,500	960	948	960	948
9,500	9,550	968	953	968	953
9,550	9,600	975	958	975	958
9,600	9,650	983	963	983	963
9,650	9,700	990	968	990	968
9,700	9,750	998	973	998	973
9,750	9,800	1,005	978	1,005	978
9,800	9,850	1,013	983	1,013	983
9,850	9,900	1,020	988	1,020	988
9,900	9,950	1,028	993	1,028	993
9,950	10,000	1,035	998	1,035	998
10,000					
10,000	10,050	1,043	1,003	1,043	1,003
10,050	10,100	1,050	1,008	1,050	1,008
10,100	10,150	1,058	1,013	1,058	1,013
10,150	10,200	1,065	1,018	1,065	1,018
10,200	10,250	1,073	1,023	1,073	1,023
10,250	10,300	1,080	1,028	1,080	1,028
10,300	10,350	1,088	1,033	1,088	1,033
10,350	10,400	1,095	1,038	1,095	1,038
10,400	10,450	1,103	1,043	1,103	1,043
10,450	10,500	1,110	1,048	1,110	1,048
10,500	10,550	1,118	1,053	1,118	1,053
10,550	10,600	1,125	1,058	1,125	1,058
10,600	10,650	1,133	1,063	1,133	1,063
10,650	10,700	1,140	1,068	1,140	1,068
10,700	10,750	1,148	1,073	1,148	1,073
10,750	10,800	1,155	1,078	1,155	1,078
10,800	10,850	1,163	1,083	1,163	1,083
10,850	10,900	1,170	1,088	1,170	1,088
10,900	10,950	1,178	1,093	1,178	1,093
10,950	11,000	1,185	1,098	1,185	1,098
11,000					
11,000	11,050	1,193	1,103	1,193	1,103
11,050	11,100	1,200	1,108	1,200	1,108
11,100	11,150	1,208	1,113	1,208	1,113
11,150	11,200	1,215	1,118	1,215	1,118
11,200	11,250	1,223	1,123	1,223	1,123
11,250	11,300	1,230	1,128	1,230	1,128
11,300	11,350	1,238	1,133	1,238	1,133
11,350	11,400	1,245	1,138	1,245	1,138
11,400	11,450	1,253	1,143	1,253	1,143
11,450	11,500	1,260	1,148	1,260	1,148
11,500	11,550	1,268	1,153	1,268	1,153
11,550	11,600	1,275	1,158	1,275	1,158
11,600	11,650	1,283	1,163	1,283	1,163
11,650	11,700	1,290	1,168	1,290	1,168
11,700	11,750	1,298	1,173	1,298	1,173
11,750	11,800	1,305	1,178	1,305	1,178
11,800	11,850	1,313	1,183	1,313	1,183
11,850	11,900	1,320	1,188	1,320	1,188
11,900	11,950	1,328	1,193	1,328	1,193
11,950	12,000	1,335	1,198	1,335	1,198

(Continued)

* This column must also be used by a qualifying widow(er).

2015 Tax Table — *Continued*

If line 43 (taxable income) is— At least	But less than	And you are— Single	Married filing jointly *	Married filing separately	Head of a household
		Your tax is—			
12,000					
12,000	12,050	1,343	1,203	1,343	1,203
12,050	12,100	1,350	1,208	1,350	1,208
12,100	12,150	1,358	1,213	1,358	1,213
12,150	12,200	1,365	1,218	1,365	1,218
12,200	12,250	1,373	1,223	1,373	1,223
12,250	12,300	1,380	1,228	1,380	1,228
12,300	12,350	1,388	1,233	1,388	1,233
12,350	12,400	1,395	1,238	1,395	1,238
12,400	12,450	1,403	1,243	1,403	1,243
12,450	12,500	1,410	1,248	1,410	1,248
12,500	12,550	1,418	1,253	1,418	1,253
12,550	12,600	1,425	1,258	1,425	1,258
12,600	12,650	1,433	1,263	1,433	1,263
12,650	12,700	1,440	1,268	1,440	1,268
12,700	12,750	1,448	1,273	1,448	1,273
12,750	12,800	1,455	1,278	1,455	1,278
12,800	12,850	1,463	1,283	1,463	1,283
12,850	12,900	1,470	1,288	1,470	1,288
12,900	12,950	1,478	1,293	1,478	1,293
12,950	13,000	1,485	1,298	1,485	1,298
13,000					
13,000	13,050	1,493	1,303	1,493	1,303
13,050	13,100	1,500	1,308	1,500	1,308
13,100	13,150	1,508	1,313	1,508	1,313
13,150	13,200	1,515	1,318	1,515	1,319
13,200	13,250	1,523	1,323	1,523	1,326
13,250	13,300	1,530	1,328	1,530	1,334
13,300	13,350	1,538	1,333	1,538	1,341
13,350	13,400	1,545	1,338	1,545	1,349
13,400	13,450	1,553	1,343	1,553	1,356
13,450	13,500	1,560	1,348	1,560	1,364
13,500	13,550	1,568	1,353	1,568	1,371
13,550	13,600	1,575	1,358	1,575	1,379
13,600	13,650	1,583	1,363	1,583	1,386
13,650	13,700	1,590	1,368	1,590	1,394
13,700	13,750	1,598	1,373	1,598	1,401
13,750	13,800	1,605	1,378	1,605	1,409
13,800	13,850	1,613	1,383	1,613	1,416
13,850	13,900	1,620	1,388	1,620	1,424
13,900	13,950	1,628	1,393	1,628	1,431
13,950	14,000	1,635	1,398	1,635	1,439
14,000					
14,000	14,050	1,643	1,403	1,643	1,446
14,050	14,100	1,650	1,408	1,650	1,454
14,100	14,150	1,658	1,413	1,658	1,461
14,150	14,200	1,665	1,418	1,665	1,469
14,200	14,250	1,673	1,423	1,673	1,476
14,250	14,300	1,680	1,428	1,680	1,484
14,300	14,350	1,688	1,433	1,688	1,491
14,350	14,400	1,695	1,438	1,695	1,499
14,400	14,450	1,703	1,443	1,703	1,506
14,450	14,500	1,710	1,448	1,710	1,514
14,500	14,550	1,718	1,453	1,718	1,521
14,550	14,600	1,725	1,458	1,725	1,529
14,600	14,650	1,733	1,463	1,733	1,536
14,650	14,700	1,740	1,468	1,740	1,544
14,700	14,750	1,748	1,473	1,748	1,551
14,750	14,800	1,755	1,478	1,755	1,559
14,800	14,850	1,763	1,483	1,763	1,566
14,850	14,900	1,770	1,488	1,770	1,574
14,900	14,950	1,778	1,493	1,778	1,581
14,950	15,000	1,785	1,498	1,785	1,589
15,000					
15,000	15,050	1,793	1,503	1,793	1,596
15,050	15,100	1,800	1,508	1,800	1,604
15,100	15,150	1,808	1,513	1,808	1,611
15,150	15,200	1,815	1,518	1,815	1,619
15,200	15,250	1,823	1,523	1,823	1,626
15,250	15,300	1,830	1,528	1,830	1,634
15,300	15,350	1,838	1,533	1,838	1,641
15,350	15,400	1,845	1,538	1,845	1,649
15,400	15,450	1,853	1,543	1,853	1,656
15,450	15,500	1,860	1,548	1,860	1,664
15,500	15,550	1,868	1,553	1,868	1,671
15,550	15,600	1,875	1,558	1,875	1,679
15,600	15,650	1,883	1,563	1,883	1,686
15,650	15,700	1,890	1,568	1,890	1,694
15,700	15,750	1,898	1,573	1,898	1,701
15,750	15,800	1,905	1,578	1,905	1,709
15,800	15,850	1,913	1,583	1,913	1,716
15,850	15,900	1,920	1,588	1,920	1,724
15,900	15,950	1,928	1,593	1,928	1,731
15,950	16,000	1,935	1,598	1,935	1,739
16,000					
16,000	16,050	1,943	1,603	1,943	1,746
16,050	16,100	1,950	1,608	1,950	1,754
16,100	16,150	1,958	1,613	1,958	1,761
16,150	16,200	1,965	1,618	1,965	1,769
16,200	16,250	1,973	1,623	1,973	1,776
16,250	16,300	1,980	1,628	1,980	1,784
16,300	16,350	1,988	1,633	1,988	1,791
16,350	16,400	1,995	1,638	1,995	1,799
16,400	16,450	2,003	1,643	2,003	1,806
16,450	16,500	2,010	1,648	2,010	1,814
16,500	16,550	2,018	1,653	2,018	1,821
16,550	16,600	2,025	1,658	2,025	1,829
16,600	16,650	2,033	1,663	2,033	1,836
16,650	16,700	2,040	1,668	2,040	1,844
16,700	16,750	2,048	1,673	2,048	1,851
16,750	16,800	2,055	1,678	2,055	1,859
16,800	16,850	2,063	1,683	2,063	1,866
16,850	16,900	2,070	1,688	2,070	1,874
16,900	16,950	2,078	1,693	2,078	1,881
16,950	17,000	2,085	1,698	2,085	1,889
17,000					
17,000	17,050	2,093	1,703	2,093	1,896
17,050	17,100	2,100	1,708	2,100	1,904
17,100	17,150	2,108	1,713	2,108	1,911
17,150	17,200	2,115	1,718	2,115	1,919
17,200	17,250	2,123	1,723	2,123	1,926
17,250	17,300	2,130	1,728	2,130	1,934
17,300	17,350	2,138	1,733	2,138	1,941
17,350	17,400	2,145	1,738	2,145	1,949
17,400	17,450	2,153	1,743	2,153	1,956
17,450	17,500	2,160	1,748	2,160	1,964
17,500	17,550	2,168	1,753	2,168	1,971
17,550	17,600	2,175	1,758	2,175	1,979
17,600	17,650	2,183	1,763	2,183	1,986
17,650	17,700	2,190	1,768	2,190	1,994
17,700	17,750	2,198	1,773	2,198	2,001
17,750	17,800	2,205	1,778	2,205	2,009
17,800	17,850	2,213	1,783	2,213	2,016
17,850	17,900	2,220	1,788	2,220	2,024
17,900	17,950	2,228	1,793	2,228	2,031
17,950	18,000	2,235	1,798	2,235	2,039
18,000					
18,000	18,050	2,243	1,803	2,243	2,046
18,050	18,100	2,250	1,808	2,250	2,054
18,100	18,150	2,258	1,813	2,258	2,061
18,150	18,200	2,265	1,818	2,265	2,069
18,200	18,250	2,273	1,823	2,273	2,076
18,250	18,300	2,280	1,828	2,280	2,084
18,300	18,350	2,288	1,833	2,288	2,091
18,350	18,400	2,295	1,838	2,295	2,099
18,400	18,450	2,303	1,843	2,303	2,106
18,450	18,500	2,310	1,849	2,310	2,114
18,500	18,550	2,318	1,856	2,318	2,121
18,550	18,600	2,325	1,864	2,325	2,129
18,600	18,650	2,333	1,871	2,333	2,136
18,650	18,700	2,340	1,879	2,340	2,144
18,700	18,750	2,348	1,886	2,348	2,151
18,750	18,800	2,355	1,894	2,355	2,159
18,800	18,850	2,363	1,901	2,363	2,166
18,850	18,900	2,370	1,909	2,370	2,174
18,900	18,950	2,378	1,916	2,378	2,181
18,950	19,000	2,385	1,924	2,385	2,189
19,000					
19,000	19,050	2,393	1,931	2,393	2,196
19,050	19,100	2,400	1,939	2,400	2,204
19,100	19,150	2,408	1,946	2,408	2,211
19,150	19,200	2,415	1,954	2,415	2,219
19,200	19,250	2,423	1,961	2,423	2,226
19,250	19,300	2,430	1,969	2,430	2,234
19,300	19,350	2,438	1,976	2,438	2,241
19,350	19,400	2,445	1,984	2,445	2,249
19,400	19,450	2,453	1,991	2,453	2,256
19,450	19,500	2,460	1,999	2,460	2,264
19,500	19,550	2,468	2,006	2,468	2,271
19,550	19,600	2,475	2,014	2,475	2,279
19,600	19,650	2,483	2,021	2,483	2,286
19,650	19,700	2,490	2,029	2,490	2,294
19,700	19,750	2,498	2,036	2,498	2,301
19,750	19,800	2,505	2,044	2,505	2,309
19,800	19,850	2,513	2,051	2,513	2,316
19,850	19,900	2,520	2,059	2,520	2,324
19,900	19,950	2,528	2,066	2,528	2,331
19,950	20,000	2,535	2,074	2,535	2,339
20,000					
20,000	20,050	2,543	2,081	2,543	2,346
20,050	20,100	2,550	2,089	2,550	2,354
20,100	20,150	2,558	2,096	2,558	2,361
20,150	20,200	2,565	2,104	2,565	2,369
20,200	20,250	2,573	2,111	2,573	2,376
20,250	20,300	2,580	2,119	2,580	2,384
20,300	20,350	2,588	2,126	2,588	2,391
20,350	20,400	2,595	2,134	2,595	2,399
20,400	20,450	2,603	2,141	2,603	2,406
20,450	20,500	2,610	2,149	2,610	2,414
20,500	20,550	2,618	2,156	2,618	2,421
20,550	20,600	2,625	2,164	2,625	2,429
20,600	20,650	2,633	2,171	2,633	2,436
20,650	20,700	2,640	2,179	2,640	2,444
20,700	20,750	2,648	2,186	2,648	2,451
20,750	20,800	2,655	2,194	2,655	2,459
20,800	20,850	2,663	2,201	2,663	2,466
20,850	20,900	2,670	2,209	2,670	2,474
20,900	20,950	2,678	2,216	2,678	2,481
20,950	21,000	2,685	2,224	2,685	2,489

(Continued)

* This column must also be used by a qualifying widow(er).

Table 20-1: IRS Tax Tables

2015 Tax Table — *Continued*

If line 43 (taxable income) is— At least	But less than	And you are— Single	Married filing jointly *	Married filing separately	Head of a household
		Your tax is—			
21,000					
21,000	21,050	2,693	2,231	2,693	2,496
21,050	21,100	2,700	2,239	2,700	2,504
21,100	21,150	2,708	2,246	2,708	2,511
21,150	21,200	2,715	2,254	2,715	2,519
21,200	21,250	2,723	2,261	2,723	2,526
21,250	21,300	2,730	2,269	2,730	2,534
21,300	21,350	2,738	2,276	2,738	2,541
21,350	21,400	2,745	2,284	2,745	2,549
21,400	21,450	2,753	2,291	2,753	2,556
21,450	21,500	2,760	2,299	2,760	2,564
21,500	21,550	2,768	2,306	2,768	2,571
21,550	21,600	2,775	2,314	2,775	2,579
21,600	21,650	2,783	2,321	2,783	2,586
21,650	21,700	2,790	2,329	2,790	2,594
21,700	21,750	2,798	2,336	2,798	2,601
21,750	21,800	2,805	2,344	2,805	2,609
21,800	21,850	2,813	2,351	2,813	2,616
21,850	21,900	2,820	2,359	2,820	2,624
21,900	21,950	2,828	2,366	2,828	2,631
21,950	22,000	2,835	2,374	2,835	2,639
22,000					
22,000	22,050	2,843	2,381	2,843	2,646
22,050	22,100	2,850	2,389	2,850	2,654
22,100	22,150	2,858	2,396	2,858	2,661
22,150	22,200	2,865	2,404	2,865	2,669
22,200	22,250	2,873	2,411	2,873	2,676
22,250	22,300	2,880	2,419	2,880	2,684
22,300	22,350	2,888	2,426	2,888	2,691
22,350	22,400	2,895	2,434	2,895	2,699
22,400	22,450	2,903	2,441	2,903	2,706
22,450	22,500	2,910	2,449	2,910	2,714
22,500	22,550	2,918	2,456	2,918	2,721
22,550	22,600	2,925	2,464	2,925	2,729
22,600	22,650	2,933	2,471	2,933	2,736
22,650	22,700	2,940	2,479	2,940	2,744
22,700	22,750	2,948	2,486	2,948	2,751
22,750	22,800	2,955	2,494	2,955	2,759
22,800	22,850	2,963	2,501	2,963	2,766
22,850	22,900	2,970	2,509	2,970	2,774
22,900	22,950	2,978	2,516	2,978	2,781
22,950	23,000	2,985	2,524	2,985	2,789
23,000					
23,000	23,050	2,993	2,531	2,993	2,796
23,050	23,100	3,000	2,539	3,000	2,804
23,100	23,150	3,008	2,546	3,008	2,811
23,150	23,200	3,015	2,554	3,015	2,819
23,200	23,250	3,023	2,561	3,023	2,826
23,250	23,300	3,030	2,569	3,030	2,834
23,300	23,350	3,038	2,576	3,038	2,841
23,350	23,400	3,045	2,584	3,045	2,849
23,400	23,450	3,053	2,591	3,053	2,856
23,450	23,500	3,060	2,599	3,060	2,864
23,500	23,550	3,068	2,606	3,068	2,871
23,550	23,600	3,075	2,614	3,075	2,879
23,600	23,650	3,083	2,621	3,083	2,886
23,650	23,700	3,090	2,629	3,090	2,894
23,700	23,750	3,098	2,636	3,098	2,901
23,750	23,800	3,105	2,644	3,105	2,909
23,800	23,850	3,113	2,651	3,113	2,916
23,850	23,900	3,120	2,659	3,120	2,924
23,900	23,950	3,128	2,666	3,128	2,931
23,950	24,000	3,135	2,674	3,135	2,939

If line 43 (taxable income) is— At least	But less than	And you are— Single	Married filing jointly *	Married filing separately	Head of a household
		Your tax is—			
24,000					
24,000	24,050	3,143	2,681	3,143	2,946
24,050	24,100	3,150	2,689	3,150	2,954
24,100	24,150	3,158	2,696	3,158	2,961
24,150	24,200	3,165	2,704	3,165	2,969
24,200	24,250	3,173	2,711	3,173	2,976
24,250	24,300	3,180	2,719	3,180	2,984
24,300	24,350	3,188	2,726	3,188	2,991
24,350	24,400	3,195	2,734	3,195	2,999
24,400	24,450	3,203	2,741	3,203	3,006
24,450	24,500	3,210	2,749	3,210	3,014
24,500	24,550	3,218	2,756	3,218	3,021
24,550	24,600	3,225	2,764	3,225	3,029
24,600	24,650	3,233	2,771	3,233	3,036
24,650	24,700	3,240	2,779	3,240	3,044
24,700	24,750	3,248	2,786	3,248	3,051
24,750	24,800	3,255	2,794	3,255	3,059
24,800	24,850	3,263	2,801	3,263	3,066
24,850	24,900	3,270	2,809	3,270	3,074
24,900	24,950	3,278	2,816	3,278	3,081
24,950	25,000	3,285	2,824	3,285	3,089
25,000					
25,000	25,050	3,293	2,831	3,293	3,096
25,050	25,100	3,300	2,839	3,300	3,104
25,100	25,150	3,308	2,846	3,308	3,111
25,150	25,200	3,315	2,854	3,315	3,119
25,200	25,250	3,323	2,861	3,323	3,126
25,250	25,300	3,330	2,869	3,330	3,134
25,300	25,350	3,338	2,876	3,338	3,141
25,350	25,400	3,345	2,884	3,345	3,149
25,400	25,450	3,353	2,891	3,353	3,156
25,450	25,500	3,360	2,899	3,360	3,164
25,500	25,550	3,368	2,906	3,368	3,171
25,550	25,600	3,375	2,914	3,375	3,179
25,600	25,650	3,383	2,921	3,383	3,186
25,650	25,700	3,390	2,929	3,390	3,194
25,700	25,750	3,398	2,936	3,398	3,201
25,750	25,800	3,405	2,944	3,405	3,209
25,800	25,850	3,413	2,951	3,413	3,216
25,850	25,900	3,420	2,959	3,420	3,224
25,900	25,950	3,428	2,966	3,428	3,231
25,950	26,000	3,435	2,974	3,435	3,239
26,000					
26,000	26,050	3,443	2,981	3,443	3,246
26,050	26,100	3,450	2,989	3,450	3,254
26,100	26,150	3,458	2,996	3,458	3,261
26,150	26,200	3,465	3,004	3,465	3,269
26,200	26,250	3,473	3,011	3,473	3,276
26,250	26,300	3,480	3,019	3,480	3,284
26,300	26,350	3,488	3,026	3,488	3,291
26,350	26,400	3,495	3,034	3,495	3,299
26,400	26,450	3,503	3,041	3,503	3,306
26,450	26,500	3,510	3,049	3,510	3,314
26,500	26,550	3,518	3,056	3,518	3,321
26,550	26,600	3,525	3,064	3,525	3,329
26,600	26,650	3,533	3,071	3,533	3,336
26,650	26,700	3,540	3,079	3,540	3,344
26,700	26,750	3,548	3,086	3,548	3,351
26,750	26,800	3,555	3,094	3,555	3,359
26,800	26,850	3,563	3,101	3,563	3,366
26,850	26,900	3,570	3,109	3,570	3,374
26,900	26,950	3,578	3,116	3,578	3,381
26,950	27,000	3,585	3,124	3,585	3,389

If line 43 (taxable income) is— At least	But less than	And you are— Single	Married filing jointly *	Married filing separately	Head of a household
		Your tax is—			
27,000					
27,000	27,050	3,593	3,131	3,593	3,396
27,050	27,100	3,600	3,139	3,600	3,404
27,100	27,150	3,608	3,146	3,608	3,411
27,150	27,200	3,615	3,154	3,615	3,419
27,200	27,250	3,623	3,161	3,623	3,426
27,250	27,300	3,630	3,169	3,630	3,434
27,300	27,350	3,638	3,176	3,638	3,441
27,350	27,400	3,645	3,184	3,645	3,449
27,400	27,450	3,653	3,191	3,653	3,456
27,450	27,500	3,660	3,199	3,660	3,464
27,500	27,550	3,668	3,206	3,668	3,471
27,550	27,600	3,675	3,214	3,675	3,479
27,600	27,650	3,683	3,221	3,683	3,486
27,650	27,700	3,690	3,229	3,690	3,494
27,700	27,750	3,698	3,236	3,698	3,501
27,750	27,800	3,705	3,244	3,705	3,509
27,800	27,850	3,713	3,251	3,713	3,516
27,850	27,900	3,720	3,259	3,720	3,524
27,900	27,950	3,728	3,266	3,728	3,531
27,950	28,000	3,735	3,274	3,735	3,539
28,000					
28,000	28,050	3,743	3,281	3,743	3,546
28,050	28,100	3,750	3,289	3,750	3,554
28,100	28,150	3,758	3,296	3,758	3,561
28,150	28,200	3,765	3,304	3,765	3,569
28,200	28,250	3,773	3,311	3,773	3,576
28,250	28,300	3,780	3,319	3,780	3,584
28,300	28,350	3,788	3,326	3,788	3,591
28,350	28,400	3,795	3,334	3,795	3,599
28,400	28,450	3,803	3,341	3,803	3,606
28,450	28,500	3,810	3,349	3,810	3,614
28,500	28,550	3,818	3,356	3,818	3,621
28,550	28,600	3,825	3,364	3,825	3,629
28,600	28,650	3,833	3,371	3,833	3,636
28,650	28,700	3,840	3,379	3,840	3,644
28,700	28,750	3,848	3,386	3,848	3,651
28,750	28,800	3,855	3,394	3,855	3,659
28,800	28,850	3,863	3,401	3,863	3,666
28,850	28,900	3,870	3,409	3,870	3,674
28,900	28,950	3,878	3,416	3,878	3,681
28,950	29,000	3,885	3,424	3,885	3,689
29,000					
29,000	29,050	3,893	3,431	3,893	3,696
29,050	29,100	3,900	3,439	3,900	3,704
29,100	29,150	3,908	3,446	3,908	3,711
29,150	29,200	3,915	3,454	3,915	3,719
29,200	29,250	3,923	3,461	3,923	3,726
29,250	29,300	3,930	3,469	3,930	3,734
29,300	29,350	3,938	3,476	3,938	3,741
29,350	29,400	3,945	3,484	3,945	3,749
29,400	29,450	3,953	3,491	3,953	3,756
29,450	29,500	3,960	3,499	3,960	3,764
29,500	29,550	3,968	3,506	3,968	3,771
29,550	29,600	3,975	3,514	3,975	3,779
29,600	29,650	3,983	3,521	3,983	3,786
29,650	29,700	3,990	3,529	3,990	3,794
29,700	29,750	3,998	3,536	3,998	3,801
29,750	29,800	4,005	3,544	4,005	3,809
29,800	29,850	4,013	3,551	4,013	3,816
29,850	29,900	4,020	3,559	4,020	3,824
29,900	29,950	4,028	3,566	4,028	3,831
29,950	30,000	4,035	3,574	4,035	3,839

(Continued)

* This column must also be used by a qualifying widow(er).

2015 Tax Table — *Continued*

If line 43 (taxable income) is— At least	But less than	Single	Married filing jointly *	Married filing separately	Head of a household
		Your tax is—			
30,000					
30,000	30,050	4,043	3,581	4,043	3,846
30,050	30,100	4,050	3,589	4,050	3,854
30,100	30,150	4,058	3,596	4,058	3,861
30,150	30,200	4,065	3,604	4,065	3,869
30,200	30,250	4,073	3,611	4,073	3,876
30,250	30,300	4,080	3,619	4,080	3,884
30,300	30,350	4,088	3,626	4,088	3,891
30,350	30,400	4,095	3,634	4,095	3,899
30,400	30,450	4,103	3,641	4,103	3,906
30,450	30,500	4,110	3,649	4,110	3,914
30,500	30,550	4,118	3,656	4,118	3,921
30,550	30,600	4,125	3,664	4,125	3,929
30,600	30,650	4,133	3,671	4,133	3,936
30,650	30,700	4,140	3,679	4,140	3,944
30,700	30,750	4,148	3,686	4,148	3,951
30,750	30,800	4,155	3,694	4,155	3,959
30,800	30,850	4,163	3,701	4,163	3,966
30,850	30,900	4,170	3,709	4,170	3,974
30,900	30,950	4,178	3,716	4,178	3,981
30,950	31,000	4,185	3,724	4,185	3,989
31,000					
31,000	31,050	4,193	3,731	4,193	3,996
31,050	31,100	4,200	3,739	4,200	4,004
31,100	31,150	4,208	3,746	4,208	4,011
31,150	31,200	4,215	3,754	4,215	4,019
31,200	31,250	4,223	3,761	4,223	4,026
31,250	31,300	4,230	3,769	4,230	4,034
31,300	31,350	4,238	3,776	4,238	4,041
31,350	31,400	4,245	3,784	4,245	4,049
31,400	31,450	4,253	3,791	4,253	4,056
31,450	31,500	4,260	3,799	4,260	4,064
31,500	31,550	4,268	3,806	4,268	4,071
31,550	31,600	4,275	3,814	4,275	4,079
31,600	31,650	4,283	3,821	4,283	4,086
31,650	31,700	4,290	3,829	4,290	4,094
31,700	31,750	4,298	3,836	4,298	4,101
31,750	31,800	4,305	3,844	4,305	4,109
31,800	31,850	4,313	3,851	4,313	4,116
31,850	31,900	4,320	3,859	4,320	4,124
31,900	31,950	4,328	3,866	4,328	4,131
31,950	32,000	4,335	3,874	4,335	4,139
32,000					
32,000	32,050	4,343	3,881	4,343	4,146
32,050	32,100	4,350	3,889	4,350	4,154
32,100	32,150	4,358	3,896	4,358	4,161
32,150	32,200	4,365	3,904	4,365	4,169
32,200	32,250	4,373	3,911	4,373	4,176
32,250	32,300	4,380	3,919	4,380	4,184
32,300	32,350	4,388	3,926	4,388	4,191
32,350	32,400	4,395	3,934	4,395	4,199
32,400	32,450	4,403	3,941	4,403	4,206
32,450	32,500	4,410	3,949	4,410	4,214
32,500	32,550	4,418	3,956	4,418	4,221
32,550	32,600	4,425	3,964	4,425	4,229
32,600	32,650	4,433	3,971	4,433	4,236
32,650	32,700	4,440	3,979	4,440	4,244
32,700	32,750	4,448	3,986	4,448	4,251
32,750	32,800	4,455	3,994	4,455	4,259
32,800	32,850	4,463	4,001	4,463	4,266
32,850	32,900	4,470	4,009	4,470	4,274
32,900	32,950	4,478	4,016	4,478	4,281
32,950	33,000	4,485	4,024	4,485	4,289

If line 43 (taxable income) is— At least	But less than	Single	Married filing jointly *	Married filing separately	Head of a household
		Your tax is—			
33,000					
33,000	33,050	4,493	4,031	4,493	4,296
33,050	33,100	4,500	4,039	4,500	4,304
33,100	33,150	4,508	4,046	4,508	4,311
33,150	33,200	4,515	4,054	4,515	4,319
33,200	33,250	4,523	4,061	4,523	4,326
33,250	33,300	4,530	4,069	4,530	4,334
33,300	33,350	4,538	4,076	4,538	4,341
33,350	33,400	4,545	4,084	4,545	4,349
33,400	33,450	4,553	4,091	4,553	4,356
33,450	33,500	4,560	4,099	4,560	4,364
33,500	33,550	4,568	4,106	4,568	4,371
33,550	33,600	4,575	4,114	4,575	4,379
33,600	33,650	4,583	4,121	4,583	4,386
33,650	33,700	4,590	4,129	4,590	4,394
33,700	33,750	4,598	4,136	4,598	4,401
33,750	33,800	4,605	4,144	4,605	4,409
33,800	33,850	4,613	4,151	4,613	4,416
33,850	33,900	4,620	4,159	4,620	4,424
33,900	33,950	4,628	4,166	4,628	4,431
33,950	34,000	4,635	4,174	4,635	4,439
34,000					
34,000	34,050	4,643	4,181	4,643	4,446
34,050	34,100	4,650	4,189	4,650	4,454
34,100	34,150	4,658	4,196	4,658	4,461
34,150	34,200	4,665	4,204	4,665	4,469
34,200	34,250	4,673	4,211	4,673	4,476
34,250	34,300	4,680	4,219	4,680	4,484
34,300	34,350	4,688	4,226	4,688	4,491
34,350	34,400	4,695	4,234	4,695	4,499
34,400	34,450	4,703	4,241	4,703	4,506
34,450	34,500	4,710	4,249	4,710	4,514
34,500	34,550	4,718	4,256	4,718	4,521
34,550	34,600	4,725	4,264	4,725	4,529
34,600	34,650	4,733	4,271	4,733	4,536
34,650	34,700	4,740	4,279	4,740	4,544
34,700	34,750	4,748	4,286	4,748	4,551
34,750	34,800	4,755	4,294	4,755	4,559
34,800	34,850	4,763	4,301	4,763	4,566
34,850	34,900	4,770	4,309	4,770	4,574
34,900	34,950	4,778	4,316	4,778	4,581
34,950	35,000	4,785	4,324	4,785	4,589
35,000					
35,000	35,050	4,793	4,331	4,793	4,596
35,050	35,100	4,800	4,339	4,800	4,604
35,100	35,150	4,808	4,346	4,808	4,611
35,150	35,200	4,815	4,354	4,815	4,619
35,200	35,250	4,823	4,361	4,823	4,626
35,250	35,300	4,830	4,369	4,830	4,634
35,300	35,350	4,838	4,376	4,838	4,641
35,350	35,400	4,845	4,384	4,845	4,649
35,400	35,450	4,853	4,391	4,853	4,656
35,450	35,500	4,860	4,399	4,860	4,664
35,500	35,550	4,868	4,406	4,868	4,671
35,550	35,600	4,875	4,414	4,875	4,679
35,600	35,650	4,883	4,421	4,883	4,686
35,650	35,700	4,890	4,429	4,890	4,694
35,700	35,750	4,898	4,436	4,898	4,701
35,750	35,800	4,905	4,444	4,905	4,709
35,800	35,850	4,913	4,451	4,913	4,716
35,850	35,900	4,920	4,459	4,920	4,724
35,900	35,950	4,928	4,466	4,928	4,731
35,950	36,000	4,935	4,474	4,935	4,739

If line 43 (taxable income) is— At least	But less than	Single	Married filing jointly *	Married filing separately	Head of a household
		Your tax is—			
36,000					
36,000	36,050	4,943	4,481	4,943	4,746
36,050	36,100	4,950	4,489	4,950	4,754
36,100	36,150	4,958	4,496	4,958	4,761
36,150	36,200	4,965	4,504	4,965	4,769
36,200	36,250	4,973	4,511	4,973	4,776
36,250	36,300	4,980	4,519	4,980	4,784
36,300	36,350	4,988	4,526	4,988	4,791
36,350	36,400	4,995	4,534	4,995	4,799
36,400	36,450	5,003	4,541	5,003	4,806
36,450	36,500	5,010	4,549	5,010	4,814
36,500	36,550	5,018	4,556	5,018	4,821
36,550	36,600	5,025	4,564	5,025	4,829
36,600	36,650	5,033	4,571	5,033	4,836
36,650	36,700	5,040	4,579	5,040	4,844
36,700	36,750	5,048	4,586	5,048	4,851
36,750	36,800	5,055	4,594	5,055	4,859
36,800	36,850	5,063	4,601	5,063	4,866
36,850	36,900	5,070	4,609	5,070	4,874
36,900	36,950	5,078	4,616	5,078	4,881
36,950	37,000	5,085	4,624	5,085	4,889
37,000					
37,000	37,050	5,093	4,631	5,093	4,896
37,050	37,100	5,100	4,639	5,100	4,904
37,100	37,150	5,108	4,646	5,108	4,911
37,150	37,200	5,115	4,654	5,115	4,919
37,200	37,250	5,123	4,661	5,123	4,926
37,250	37,300	5,130	4,669	5,130	4,934
37,300	37,350	5,138	4,676	5,138	4,941
37,350	37,400	5,145	4,684	5,145	4,949
37,400	37,450	5,153	4,691	5,153	4,956
37,450	37,500	5,163	4,699	5,163	4,964
37,500	37,550	5,175	4,706	5,175	4,971
37,550	37,600	5,188	4,714	5,188	4,979
37,600	37,650	5,200	4,721	5,200	4,986
37,650	37,700	5,213	4,729	5,213	4,994
37,700	37,750	5,225	4,736	5,225	5,001
37,750	37,800	5,238	4,744	5,238	5,009
37,800	37,850	5,250	4,751	5,250	5,016
37,850	37,900	5,263	4,759	5,263	5,024
37,900	37,950	5,275	4,766	5,275	5,031
37,950	38,000	5,288	4,774	5,288	5,039
38,000					
38,000	38,050	5,300	4,781	5,300	5,046
38,050	38,100	5,313	4,789	5,313	5,054
38,100	38,150	5,325	4,796	5,325	5,061
38,150	38,200	5,338	4,804	5,338	5,069
38,200	38,250	5,350	4,811	5,350	5,076
38,250	38,300	5,363	4,819	5,363	5,084
38,300	38,350	5,375	4,826	5,375	5,091
38,350	38,400	5,388	4,834	5,388	5,099
38,400	38,450	5,400	4,841	5,400	5,106
38,450	38,500	5,413	4,849	5,413	5,114
38,500	38,550	5,425	4,856	5,425	5,121
38,550	38,600	5,438	4,864	5,438	5,129
38,600	38,650	5,450	4,871	5,450	5,136
38,650	38,700	5,463	4,879	5,463	5,144
38,700	38,750	5,475	4,886	5,475	5,151
38,750	38,800	5,488	4,894	5,488	5,159
38,800	38,850	5,500	4,901	5,500	5,166
38,850	38,900	5,513	4,909	5,513	5,174
38,900	38,950	5,525	4,916	5,525	5,181
38,950	39,000	5,538	4,924	5,538	5,189

(Continued)

* This column must also be used by a qualifying widow(er).

2015 Tax Table — *Continued*

If line 43 (taxable income) is—		And you are—			
At least	But less than	Single	Married filing jointly *	Married filing sepa-rately	Head of a house-hold
		Your tax is—			
39,000					
39,000	39,050	5,550	4,931	5,550	5,196
39,050	39,100	5,563	4,939	5,563	5,204
39,100	39,150	5,575	4,946	5,575	5,211
39,150	39,200	5,588	4,954	5,588	5,219
39,200	39,250	5,600	4,961	5,600	5,226
39,250	39,300	5,613	4,969	5,613	5,234
39,300	39,350	5,625	4,976	5,625	5,241
39,350	39,400	5,638	4,984	5,638	5,249
39,400	39,450	5,650	4,991	5,650	5,256
39,450	39,500	5,663	4,999	5,663	5,264
39,500	39,550	5,675	5,006	5,675	5,271
39,550	39,600	5,688	5,014	5,688	5,279
39,600	39,650	5,700	5,021	5,700	5,286
39,650	39,700	5,713	5,029	5,713	5,294
39,700	39,750	5,725	5,036	5,725	5,301
39,750	39,800	5,738	5,044	5,738	5,309
39,800	39,850	5,750	5,051	5,750	5,316
39,850	39,900	5,763	5,059	5,763	5,324
39,900	39,950	5,775	5,066	5,775	5,331
39,950	40,000	5,788	5,074	5,788	5,339
40,000					
40,000	40,050	5,800	5,081	5,800	5,346
40,050	40,100	5,813	5,089	5,813	5,354
40,100	40,150	5,825	5,096	5,825	5,361
40,150	40,200	5,838	5,104	5,838	5,369
40,200	40,250	5,850	5,111	5,850	5,376
40,250	40,300	5,863	5,119	5,863	5,384
40,300	40,350	5,875	5,126	5,875	5,391
40,350	40,400	5,888	5,134	5,888	5,399
40,400	40,450	5,900	5,141	5,900	5,406
40,450	40,500	5,913	5,149	5,913	5,414
40,500	40,550	5,925	5,156	5,925	5,421
40,550	40,600	5,938	5,164	5,938	5,429
40,600	40,650	5,950	5,171	5,950	5,436
40,650	40,700	5,963	5,179	5,963	5,444
40,700	40,750	5,975	5,186	5,975	5,451
40,750	40,800	5,988	5,194	5,988	5,459
40,800	40,850	6,000	5,201	6,000	5,466
40,850	40,900	6,013	5,209	6,013	5,474
40,900	40,950	6,025	5,216	6,025	5,481
40,950	41,000	6,038	5,224	6,038	5,489
41,000					
41,000	41,050	6,050	5,231	6,050	5,496
41,050	41,100	6,063	5,239	6,063	5,504
41,100	41,150	6,075	5,246	6,075	5,511
41,150	41,200	6,088	5,254	6,088	5,519
41,200	41,250	6,100	5,261	6,100	5,526
41,250	41,300	6,113	5,269	6,113	5,534
41,300	41,350	6,125	5,276	6,125	5,541
41,350	41,400	6,138	5,284	6,138	5,549
41,400	41,450	6,150	5,291	6,150	5,556
41,450	41,500	6,163	5,299	6,163	5,564
41,500	41,550	6,175	5,306	6,175	5,571
41,550	41,600	6,188	5,314	6,188	5,579
41,600	41,650	6,200	5,321	6,200	5,586
41,650	41,700	6,213	5,329	6,213	5,594
41,700	41,750	6,225	5,336	6,225	5,601
41,750	41,800	6,238	5,344	6,238	5,609
41,800	41,850	6,250	5,351	6,250	5,616
41,850	41,900	6,263	5,359	6,263	5,624
41,900	41,950	6,275	5,366	6,275	5,631
41,950	42,000	6,288	5,374	6,288	5,639
42,000					
42,000	42,050	6,300	5,381	6,300	5,646
42,050	42,100	6,313	5,389	6,313	5,654
42,100	42,150	6,325	5,396	6,325	5,661
42,150	42,200	6,338	5,404	6,338	5,669
42,200	42,250	6,350	5,411	6,350	5,676
42,250	42,300	6,363	5,419	6,363	5,684
42,300	42,350	6,375	5,426	6,375	5,691
42,350	42,400	6,388	5,434	6,388	5,699
42,400	42,450	6,400	5,441	6,400	5,706
42,450	42,500	6,413	5,449	6,413	5,714
42,500	42,550	6,425	5,456	6,425	5,721
42,550	42,600	6,438	5,464	6,438	5,729
42,600	42,650	6,450	5,471	6,450	5,736
42,650	42,700	6,463	5,479	6,463	5,744
42,700	42,750	6,475	5,486	6,475	5,751
42,750	42,800	6,488	5,494	6,488	5,759
42,800	42,850	6,500	5,501	6,500	5,766
42,850	42,900	6,513	5,509	6,513	5,774
42,900	42,950	6,525	5,516	6,525	5,781
42,950	43,000	6,538	5,524	6,538	5,789
43,000					
43,000	43,050	6,550	5,531	6,550	5,796
43,050	43,100	6,563	5,539	6,563	5,804
43,100	43,150	6,575	5,546	6,575	5,811
43,150	43,200	6,588	5,554	6,588	5,819
43,200	43,250	6,600	5,561	6,600	5,826
43,250	43,300	6,613	5,569	6,613	5,834
43,300	43,350	6,625	5,576	6,625	5,841
43,350	43,400	6,638	5,584	6,638	5,849
43,400	43,450	6,650	5,591	6,650	5,856
43,450	43,500	6,663	5,599	6,663	5,864
43,500	43,550	6,675	5,606	6,675	5,871
43,550	43,600	6,688	5,614	6,688	5,879
43,600	43,650	6,700	5,621	6,700	5,886
43,650	43,700	6,713	5,629	6,713	5,894
43,700	43,750	6,725	5,636	6,725	5,901
43,750	43,800	6,738	5,644	6,738	5,909
43,800	43,850	6,750	5,651	6,750	5,916
43,850	43,900	6,763	5,659	6,763	5,924
43,900	43,950	6,775	5,666	6,775	5,931
43,950	44,000	6,788	5,674	6,788	5,939
44,000					
44,000	44,050	6,800	5,681	6,800	5,946
44,050	44,100	6,813	5,689	6,813	5,954
44,100	44,150	6,825	5,696	6,825	5,961
44,150	44,200	6,838	5,704	6,838	5,969
44,200	44,250	6,850	5,711	6,850	5,976
44,250	44,300	6,863	5,719	6,863	5,984
44,300	44,350	6,875	5,726	6,875	5,991
44,350	44,400	6,888	5,734	6,888	5,999
44,400	44,450	6,900	5,741	6,900	6,006
44,450	44,500	6,913	5,749	6,913	6,014
44,500	44,550	6,925	5,756	6,925	6,021
44,550	44,600	6,938	5,764	6,938	6,029
44,600	44,650	6,950	5,771	6,950	6,036
44,650	44,700	6,963	5,779	6,963	6,044
44,700	44,750	6,975	5,786	6,975	6,051
44,750	44,800	6,988	5,794	6,988	6,059
44,800	44,850	7,000	5,801	7,000	6,066
44,850	44,900	7,013	5,809	7,013	6,074
44,900	44,950	7,025	5,816	7,025	6,081
44,950	45,000	7,038	5,824	7,038	6,089
45,000					
45,000	45,050	7,050	5,831	7,050	6,096
45,050	45,100	7,063	5,839	7,063	6,104
45,100	45,150	7,075	5,846	7,075	6,111
45,150	45,200	7,088	5,854	7,088	6,119
45,200	45,250	7,100	5,861	7,100	6,126
45,250	45,300	7,113	5,869	7,113	6,134
45,300	45,350	7,125	5,876	7,125	6,141
45,350	45,400	7,138	5,884	7,138	6,149
45,400	45,450	7,150	5,891	7,150	6,156
45,450	45,500	7,163	5,899	7,163	6,164
45,500	45,550	7,175	5,906	7,175	6,171
45,550	45,600	7,188	5,914	7,188	6,179
45,600	45,650	7,200	5,921	7,200	6,186
45,650	45,700	7,213	5,929	7,213	6,194
45,700	45,750	7,225	5,936	7,225	6,201
45,750	45,800	7,238	5,944	7,238	6,209
45,800	45,850	7,250	5,951	7,250	6,216
45,850	45,900	7,263	5,959	7,263	6,224
45,900	45,950	7,275	5,966	7,275	6,231
45,950	46,000	7,288	5,974	7,288	6,239
46,000					
46,000	46,050	7,300	5,981	7,300	6,246
46,050	46,100	7,313	5,989	7,313	6,254
46,100	46,150	7,325	5,996	7,325	6,261
46,150	46,200	7,338	6,004	7,338	6,269
46,200	46,250	7,350	6,011	7,350	6,276
46,250	46,300	7,363	6,019	7,363	6,284
46,300	46,350	7,375	6,026	7,375	6,291
46,350	46,400	7,388	6,034	7,388	6,299
46,400	46,450	7,400	6,041	7,400	6,306
46,450	46,500	7,413	6,049	7,413	6,314
46,500	46,550	7,425	6,056	7,425	6,321
46,550	46,600	7,438	6,064	7,438	6,329
46,600	46,650	7,450	6,071	7,450	6,336
46,650	46,700	7,463	6,079	7,463	6,344
46,700	46,750	7,475	6,086	7,475	6,351
46,750	46,800	7,488	6,094	7,488	6,359
46,800	46,850	7,500	6,101	7,500	6,366
46,850	46,900	7,513	6,109	7,513	6,374
46,900	46,950	7,525	6,116	7,525	6,381
46,950	47,000	7,538	6,124	7,538	6,389
47,000					
47,000	47,050	7,550	6,131	7,550	6,396
47,050	47,100	7,563	6,139	7,563	6,404
47,100	47,150	7,575	6,146	7,575	6,411
47,150	47,200	7,588	6,154	7,588	6,419
47,200	47,250	7,600	6,161	7,600	6,426
47,250	47,300	7,613	6,169	7,613	6,434
47,300	47,350	7,625	6,176	7,625	6,441
47,350	47,400	7,638	6,184	7,638	6,449
47,400	47,450	7,650	6,191	7,650	6,456
47,450	47,500	7,663	6,199	7,663	6,464
47,500	47,550	7,675	6,206	7,675	6,471
47,550	47,600	7,688	6,214	7,688	6,479
47,600	47,650	7,700	6,221	7,700	6,486
47,650	47,700	7,713	6,229	7,713	6,494
47,700	47,750	7,725	6,236	7,725	6,501
47,750	47,800	7,738	6,244	7,738	6,509
47,800	47,850	7,750	6,251	7,750	6,516
47,850	47,900	7,763	6,259	7,763	6,524
47,900	47,950	7,775	6,266	7,775	6,531
47,950	48,000	7,788	6,274	7,788	6,539

(Continued)

2015 Tax Table — *Continued*

If line 43 (taxable income) is—		And you are—			
At least	But less than	Single	Married filing jointly *	Married filing sepa-rately	Head of a house-hold
		Your tax is—			
48,000					
48,000	48,050	7,800	6,281	7,800	6,546
48,050	48,100	7,813	6,289	7,813	6,554
48,100	48,150	7,825	6,296	7,825	6,561
48,150	48,200	7,838	6,304	7,838	6,569
48,200	48,250	7,850	6,311	7,850	6,576
48,250	48,300	7,863	6,319	7,863	6,584
48,300	48,350	7,875	6,326	7,875	6,591
48,350	48,400	7,888	6,334	7,888	6,599
48,400	48,450	7,900	6,341	7,900	6,606
48,450	48,500	7,913	6,349	7,913	6,614
48,500	48,550	7,925	6,356	7,925	6,621
48,550	48,600	7,938	6,364	7,938	6,629
48,600	48,650	7,950	6,371	7,950	6,636
48,650	48,700	7,963	6,379	7,963	6,644
48,700	48,750	7,975	6,386	7,975	6,651
48,750	48,800	7,988	6,394	7,988	6,659
48,800	48,850	8,000	6,401	8,000	6,666
48,850	48,900	8,013	6,409	8,013	6,674
48,900	48,950	8,025	6,416	8,025	6,681
48,950	49,000	8,038	6,424	8,038	6,689
49,000					
49,000	49,050	8,050	6,431	8,050	6,696
49,050	49,100	8,063	6,439	8,063	6,704
49,100	49,150	8,075	6,446	8,075	6,711
49,150	49,200	8,088	6,454	8,088	6,719
49,200	49,250	8,100	6,461	8,100	6,726
49,250	49,300	8,113	6,469	8,113	6,734
49,300	49,350	8,125	6,476	8,125	6,741
49,350	49,400	8,138	6,484	8,138	6,749
49,400	49,450	8,150	6,491	8,150	6,756
49,450	49,500	8,163	6,499	8,163	6,764
49,500	49,550	8,175	6,506	8,175	6,771
49,550	49,600	8,188	6,514	8,188	6,779
49,600	49,650	8,200	6,521	8,200	6,786
49,650	49,700	8,213	6,529	8,213	6,794
49,700	49,750	8,225	6,536	8,225	6,801
49,750	49,800	8,238	6,544	8,238	6,809
49,800	49,850	8,250	6,551	8,250	6,816
49,850	49,900	8,263	6,559	8,263	6,824
49,900	49,950	8,275	6,566	8,275	6,831
49,950	50,000	8,288	6,574	8,288	6,839
50,000					
50,000	50,050	8,300	6,581	8,300	6,846
50,050	50,100	8,313	6,589	8,313	6,854
50,100	50,150	8,325	6,596	8,325	6,861
50,150	50,200	8,338	6,604	8,338	6,869
50,200	50,250	8,350	6,611	8,350	6,879
50,250	50,300	8,363	6,619	8,363	6,891
50,300	50,350	8,375	6,626	8,375	6,904
50,350	50,400	8,388	6,634	8,388	6,916
50,400	50,450	8,400	6,641	8,400	6,929
50,450	50,500	8,413	6,649	8,413	6,941
50,500	50,550	8,425	6,656	8,425	6,954
50,550	50,600	8,438	6,664	8,438	6,966
50,600	50,650	8,450	6,671	8,450	6,979
50,650	50,700	8,463	6,679	8,463	6,991
50,700	50,750	8,475	6,686	8,475	7,004
50,750	50,800	8,488	6,694	8,488	7,016
50,800	50,850	8,500	6,701	8,500	7,029
50,850	50,900	8,513	6,709	8,513	7,041
50,900	50,950	8,525	6,716	8,525	7,054
50,950	51,000	8,538	6,724	8,538	7,066

If line 43 (taxable income) is—		And you are—			
At least	But less than	Single	Married filing jointly *	Married filing sepa-rately	Head of a house-hold
		Your tax is—			
51,000					
51,000	51,050	8,550	6,731	8,550	7,079
51,050	51,100	8,563	6,739	8,563	7,091
51,100	51,150	8,575	6,746	8,575	7,104
51,150	51,200	8,588	6,754	8,588	7,116
51,200	51,250	8,600	6,761	8,600	7,129
51,250	51,300	8,613	6,769	8,613	7,141
51,300	51,350	8,625	6,776	8,625	7,154
51,350	51,400	8,638	6,784	8,638	7,166
51,400	51,450	8,650	6,791	8,650	7,179
51,450	51,500	8,663	6,799	8,663	7,191
51,500	51,550	8,675	6,806	8,675	7,204
51,550	51,600	8,688	6,814	8,688	7,216
51,600	51,650	8,700	6,821	8,700	7,229
51,650	51,700	8,713	6,829	8,713	7,241
51,700	51,750	8,725	6,836	8,725	7,254
51,750	51,800	8,738	6,844	8,738	7,266
51,800	51,850	8,750	6,851	8,750	7,279
51,850	51,900	8,763	6,859	8,763	7,291
51,900	51,950	8,775	6,866	8,775	7,304
51,950	52,000	8,788	6,874	8,788	7,316
52,000					
52,000	52,050	8,800	6,881	8,800	7,329
52,050	52,100	8,813	6,889	8,813	7,341
52,100	52,150	8,825	6,896	8,825	7,354
52,150	52,200	8,838	6,904	8,838	7,366
52,200	52,250	8,850	6,911	8,850	7,379
52,250	52,300	8,863	6,919	8,863	7,391
52,300	52,350	8,875	6,926	8,875	7,404
52,350	52,400	8,888	6,934	8,888	7,416
52,400	52,450	8,900	6,941	8,900	7,429
52,450	52,500	8,913	6,949	8,913	7,441
52,500	52,550	8,925	6,956	8,925	7,454
52,550	52,600	8,938	6,964	8,938	7,466
52,600	52,650	8,950	6,971	8,950	7,479
52,650	52,700	8,963	6,979	8,963	7,491
52,700	52,750	8,975	6,986	8,975	7,504
52,750	52,800	8,988	6,994	8,988	7,516
52,800	52,850	9,000	7,001	9,000	7,529
52,850	52,900	9,013	7,009	9,013	7,541
52,900	52,950	9,025	7,016	9,025	7,554
52,950	53,000	9,038	7,024	9,038	7,566
53,000					
53,000	53,050	9,050	7,031	9,050	7,579
53,050	53,100	9,063	7,039	9,063	7,591
53,100	53,150	9,075	7,046	9,075	7,604
53,150	53,200	9,088	7,054	9,088	7,616
53,200	53,250	9,100	7,061	9,100	7,629
53,250	53,300	9,113	7,069	9,113	7,641
53,300	53,350	9,125	7,076	9,125	7,654
53,350	53,400	9,138	7,084	9,138	7,666
53,400	53,450	9,150	7,091	9,150	7,679
53,450	53,500	9,163	7,099	9,163	7,691
53,500	53,550	9,175	7,106	9,175	7,704
53,550	53,600	9,188	7,114	9,188	7,716
53,600	53,650	9,200	7,121	9,200	7,729
53,650	53,700	9,213	7,129	9,213	7,741
53,700	53,750	9,225	7,136	9,225	7,754
53,750	53,800	9,238	7,144	9,238	7,766
53,800	53,850	9,250	7,151	9,250	7,779
53,850	53,900	9,263	7,159	9,263	7,791
53,900	53,950	9,275	7,166	9,275	7,804
53,950	54,000	9,288	7,174	9,288	7,816

If line 43 (taxable income) is—		And you are—			
At least	But less than	Single	Married filing jointly *	Married filing sepa-rately	Head of a house-hold
		Your tax is—			
54,000					
54,000	54,050	9,300	7,181	9,300	7,829
54,050	54,100	9,313	7,189	9,313	7,841
54,100	54,150	9,325	7,196	9,325	7,854
54,150	54,200	9,338	7,204	9,338	7,866
54,200	54,250	9,350	7,211	9,350	7,879
54,250	54,300	9,363	7,219	9,363	7,891
54,300	54,350	9,375	7,226	9,375	7,904
54,350	54,400	9,388	7,234	9,388	7,916
54,400	54,450	9,400	7,241	9,400	7,929
54,450	54,500	9,413	7,249	9,413	7,941
54,500	54,550	9,425	7,256	9,425	7,954
54,550	54,600	9,438	7,264	9,438	7,966
54,600	54,650	9,450	7,271	9,450	7,979
54,650	54,700	9,463	7,279	9,463	7,991
54,700	54,750	9,475	7,286	9,475	8,004
54,750	54,800	9,488	7,294	9,488	8,016
54,800	54,850	9,500	7,301	9,500	8,029
54,850	54,900	9,513	7,309	9,513	8,041
54,900	54,950	9,525	7,316	9,525	8,054
54,950	55,000	9,538	7,324	9,538	8,066
55,000					
55,000	55,050	9,550	7,331	9,550	8,079
55,050	55,100	9,563	7,339	9,563	8,091
55,100	55,150	9,575	7,346	9,575	8,104
55,150	55,200	9,588	7,354	9,588	8,116
55,200	55,250	9,600	7,361	9,600	8,129
55,250	55,300	9,613	7,369	9,613	8,141
55,300	55,350	9,625	7,376	9,625	8,154
55,350	55,400	9,638	7,384	9,638	8,166
55,400	55,450	9,650	7,391	9,650	8,179
55,450	55,500	9,663	7,399	9,663	8,191
55,500	55,550	9,675	7,406	9,675	8,204
55,550	55,600	9,688	7,414	9,688	8,216
55,600	55,650	9,700	7,421	9,700	8,229
55,650	55,700	9,713	7,429	9,713	8,241
55,700	55,750	9,725	7,436	9,725	8,254
55,750	55,800	9,738	7,444	9,738	8,266
55,800	55,850	9,750	7,451	9,750	8,279
55,850	55,900	9,763	7,459	9,763	8,291
55,900	55,950	9,775	7,466	9,775	8,304
55,950	56,000	9,788	7,474	9,788	8,316
56,000					
56,000	56,050	9,800	7,481	9,800	8,329
56,050	56,100	9,813	7,489	9,813	8,341
56,100	56,150	9,825	7,496	9,825	8,354
56,150	56,200	9,838	7,504	9,838	8,366
56,200	56,250	9,850	7,511	9,850	8,379
56,250	56,300	9,863	7,519	9,863	8,391
56,300	56,350	9,875	7,526	9,875	8,404
56,350	56,400	9,888	7,534	9,888	8,416
56,400	56,450	9,900	7,541	9,900	8,429
56,450	56,500	9,913	7,549	9,913	8,441
56,500	56,550	9,925	7,556	9,925	8,454
56,550	56,600	9,938	7,564	9,938	8,466
56,600	56,650	9,950	7,571	9,950	8,479
56,650	56,700	9,963	7,579	9,963	8,491
56,700	56,750	9,975	7,586	9,975	8,504
56,750	56,800	9,988	7,594	9,988	8,516
56,800	56,850	10,000	7,601	10,000	8,529
56,850	56,900	10,013	7,609	10,013	8,541
56,900	56,950	10,025	7,616	10,025	8,554
56,950	57,000	10,038	7,624	10,038	8,566

(Continued)

* This column must also be used by a qualifying widow(er).

2015 Tax Table — *Continued*

If line 43 (taxable income) is—		And you are—			
At least	But less than	Single	Married filing jointly *	Married filing separately	Head of a household
		Your tax is—			
57,000					
57,000	57,050	10,050	7,631	10,050	8,579
57,050	57,100	10,063	7,639	10,063	8,591
57,100	57,150	10,075	7,646	10,075	8,604
57,150	57,200	10,088	7,654	10,088	8,616
57,200	57,250	10,100	7,661	10,100	8,629
57,250	57,300	10,113	7,669	10,113	8,641
57,300	57,350	10,125	7,676	10,125	8,654
57,350	57,400	10,138	7,684	10,138	8,666
57,400	57,450	10,150	7,691	10,150	8,679
57,450	57,500	10,163	7,699	10,163	8,691
57,500	57,550	10,175	7,706	10,175	8,704
57,550	57,600	10,188	7,714	10,188	8,716
57,600	57,650	10,200	7,721	10,200	8,729
57,650	57,700	10,213	7,729	10,213	8,741
57,700	57,750	10,225	7,736	10,225	8,754
57,750	57,800	10,238	7,744	10,238	8,766
57,800	57,850	10,250	7,751	10,250	8,779
57,850	57,900	10,263	7,759	10,263	8,791
57,900	57,950	10,275	7,766	10,275	8,804
57,950	58,000	10,288	7,774	10,288	8,816
58,000					
58,000	58,050	10,300	7,781	10,300	8,829
58,050	58,100	10,313	7,789	10,313	8,841
58,100	58,150	10,325	7,796	10,325	8,854
58,150	58,200	10,338	7,804	10,338	8,866
58,200	58,250	10,350	7,811	10,350	8,879
58,250	58,300	10,363	7,819	10,363	8,891
58,300	58,350	10,375	7,826	10,375	8,904
58,350	58,400	10,388	7,834	10,388	8,916
58,400	58,450	10,400	7,841	10,400	8,929
58,450	58,500	10,413	7,849	10,413	8,941
58,500	58,550	10,425	7,856	10,425	8,954
58,550	58,600	10,438	7,864	10,438	8,966
58,600	58,650	10,450	7,871	10,450	8,979
58,650	58,700	10,463	7,879	10,463	8,991
58,700	58,750	10,475	7,886	10,475	9,004
58,750	58,800	10,488	7,894	10,488	9,016
58,800	58,850	10,500	7,901	10,500	9,029
58,850	58,900	10,513	7,909	10,513	9,041
58,900	58,950	10,525	7,916	10,525	9,054
58,950	59,000	10,538	7,924	10,538	9,066
59,000					
59,000	59,050	10,550	7,931	10,550	9,079
59,050	59,100	10,563	7,939	10,563	9,091
59,100	59,150	10,575	7,946	10,575	9,104
59,150	59,200	10,588	7,954	10,588	9,116
59,200	59,250	10,600	7,961	10,600	9,129
59,250	59,300	10,613	7,969	10,613	9,141
59,300	59,350	10,625	7,976	10,625	9,154
59,350	59,400	10,638	7,984	10,638	9,166
59,400	59,450	10,650	7,991	10,650	9,179
59,450	59,500	10,663	7,999	10,663	9,191
59,500	59,550	10,675	8,006	10,675	9,204
59,550	59,600	10,688	8,014	10,688	9,216
59,600	59,650	10,700	8,021	10,700	9,229
59,650	59,700	10,713	8,029	10,713	9,241
59,700	59,750	10,725	8,036	10,725	9,254
59,750	59,800	10,738	8,044	10,738	9,266
59,800	59,850	10,750	8,051	10,750	9,279
59,850	59,900	10,763	8,059	10,763	9,291
59,900	59,950	10,775	8,066	10,775	9,304
59,950	60,000	10,788	8,074	10,788	9,316
60,000					
60,000	60,050	10,800	8,081	10,800	9,329
60,050	60,100	10,813	8,089	10,813	9,341
60,100	60,150	10,825	8,096	10,825	9,354
60,150	60,200	10,838	8,104	10,838	9,366
60,200	60,250	10,850	8,111	10,850	9,379
60,250	60,300	10,863	8,119	10,863	9,391
60,300	60,350	10,875	8,126	10,875	9,404
60,350	60,400	10,888	8,134	10,888	9,416
60,400	60,450	10,900	8,141	10,900	9,429
60,450	60,500	10,913	8,149	10,913	9,441
60,500	60,550	10,925	8,156	10,925	9,454
60,550	60,600	10,938	8,164	10,938	9,466
60,600	60,650	10,950	8,171	10,950	9,479
60,650	60,700	10,963	8,179	10,963	9,491
60,700	60,750	10,975	8,186	10,975	9,504
60,750	60,800	10,988	8,194	10,988	9,516
60,800	60,850	11,000	8,201	11,000	9,529
60,850	60,900	11,013	8,209	11,013	9,541
60,900	60,950	11,025	8,216	11,025	9,554
60,950	61,000	11,038	8,224	11,038	9,566
61,000					
61,000	61,050	11,050	8,231	11,050	9,579
61,050	61,100	11,063	8,239	11,063	9,591
61,100	61,150	11,075	8,246	11,075	9,604
61,150	61,200	11,088	8,254	11,088	9,616
61,200	61,250	11,100	8,261	11,100	9,629
61,250	61,300	11,113	8,269	11,113	9,641
61,300	61,350	11,125	8,276	11,125	9,654
61,350	61,400	11,138	8,284	11,138	9,666
61,400	61,450	11,150	8,291	11,150	9,679
61,450	61,500	11,163	8,299	11,163	9,691
61,500	61,550	11,175	8,306	11,175	9,704
61,550	61,600	11,188	8,314	11,188	9,716
61,600	61,650	11,200	8,321	11,200	9,729
61,650	61,700	11,213	8,329	11,213	9,741
61,700	61,750	11,225	8,336	11,225	9,754
61,750	61,800	11,238	8,344	11,238	9,766
61,800	61,850	11,250	8,351	11,250	9,779
61,850	61,900	11,263	8,359	11,263	9,791
61,900	61,950	11,275	8,366	11,275	9,804
61,950	62,000	11,288	8,374	11,288	9,816
62,000					
62,000	62,050	11,300	8,381	11,300	9,829
62,050	62,100	11,313	8,389	11,313	9,841
62,100	62,150	11,325	8,396	11,325	9,854
62,150	62,200	11,338	8,404	11,338	9,866
62,200	62,250	11,350	8,411	11,350	9,879
62,250	62,300	11,363	8,419	11,363	9,891
62,300	62,350	11,375	8,426	11,375	9,904
62,350	62,400	11,388	8,434	11,388	9,916
62,400	62,450	11,400	8,441	11,400	9,929
62,450	62,500	11,413	8,449	11,413	9,941
62,500	62,550	11,425	8,456	11,425	9,954
62,550	62,600	11,438	8,464	11,438	9,966
62,600	62,650	11,450	8,471	11,450	9,979
62,650	62,700	11,463	8,479	11,463	9,991
62,700	62,750	11,475	8,486	11,475	10,004
62,750	62,800	11,488	8,494	11,488	10,016
62,800	62,850	11,500	8,501	11,500	10,029
62,850	62,900	11,513	8,509	11,513	10,041
62,900	62,950	11,525	8,516	11,525	10,054
62,950	63,000	11,538	8,524	11,538	10,066
63,000					
63,000	63,050	11,550	8,531	11,550	10,079
63,050	63,100	11,563	8,539	11,563	10,091
63,100	63,150	11,575	8,546	11,575	10,104
63,150	63,200	11,588	8,554	11,588	10,116
63,200	63,250	11,600	8,561	11,600	10,129
63,250	63,300	11,613	8,569	11,613	10,141
63,300	63,350	11,625	8,576	11,625	10,154
63,350	63,400	11,638	8,584	11,638	10,166
63,400	63,450	11,650	8,591	11,650	10,179
63,450	63,500	11,663	8,599	11,663	10,191
63,500	63,550	11,675	8,606	11,675	10,204
63,550	63,600	11,688	8,614	11,688	10,216
63,600	63,650	11,700	8,621	11,700	10,229
63,650	63,700	11,713	8,629	11,713	10,241
63,700	63,750	11,725	8,636	11,725	10,254
63,750	63,800	11,738	8,644	11,738	10,266
63,800	63,850	11,750	8,651	11,750	10,279
63,850	63,900	11,763	8,659	11,763	10,291
63,900	63,950	11,775	8,666	11,775	10,304
63,950	64,000	11,788	8,674	11,788	10,316
64,000					
64,000	64,050	11,800	8,681	11,800	10,329
64,050	64,100	11,813	8,689	11,813	10,341
64,100	64,150	11,825	8,696	11,825	10,354
64,150	64,200	11,838	8,704	11,838	10,366
64,200	64,250	11,850	8,711	11,850	10,379
64,250	64,300	11,863	8,719	11,863	10,391
64,300	64,350	11,875	8,726	11,875	10,404
64,350	64,400	11,888	8,734	11,888	10,416
64,400	64,450	11,900	8,741	11,900	10,429
64,450	64,500	11,913	8,749	11,913	10,441
64,500	64,550	11,925	8,756	11,925	10,454
64,550	64,600	11,938	8,764	11,938	10,466
64,600	64,650	11,950	8,771	11,950	10,479
64,650	64,700	11,963	8,779	11,963	10,491
64,700	64,750	11,975	8,786	11,975	10,504
64,750	64,800	11,988	8,794	11,988	10,516
64,800	64,850	12,000	8,801	12,000	10,529
64,850	64,900	12,013	8,809	12,013	10,541
64,900	64,950	12,025	8,816	12,025	10,554
64,950	65,000	12,038	8,824	12,038	10,566
65,000					
65,000	65,050	12,050	8,831	12,050	10,579
65,050	65,100	12,063	8,839	12,063	10,591
65,100	65,150	12,075	8,846	12,075	10,604
65,150	65,200	12,088	8,854	12,088	10,616
65,200	65,250	12,100	8,861	12,100	10,629
65,250	65,300	12,113	8,869	12,113	10,641
65,300	65,350	12,125	8,876	12,125	10,654
65,350	65,400	12,138	8,884	12,138	10,666
65,400	65,450	12,150	8,891	12,150	10,679
65,450	65,500	12,163	8,899	12,163	10,691
65,500	65,550	12,175	8,906	12,175	10,704
65,550	65,600	12,188	8,914	12,188	10,716
65,600	65,650	12,200	8,921	12,200	10,729
65,650	65,700	12,213	8,929	12,213	10,741
65,700	65,750	12,225	8,936	12,225	10,754
65,750	65,800	12,238	8,944	12,238	10,766
65,800	65,850	12,250	8,951	12,250	10,779
65,850	65,900	12,263	8,959	12,263	10,791
65,900	65,950	12,275	8,966	12,275	10,804
65,950	66,000	12,288	8,974	12,288	10,816

(Continued)

* This column must also be used by a qualifying widow(er).

2015 Tax Table — *Continued*

If line 43 (taxable income) is—		And you are—			
At least	But less than	Single	Married filing jointly *	Married filing sepa-rately	Head of a house-hold
		Your tax is—			
66,000					
66,000	66,050	12,300	8,981	12,300	10,829
66,050	66,100	12,313	8,989	12,313	10,841
66,100	66,150	12,325	8,996	12,325	10,854
66,150	66,200	12,338	9,004	12,338	10,866
66,200	66,250	12,350	9,011	12,350	10,879
66,250	66,300	12,363	9,019	12,363	10,891
66,300	66,350	12,375	9,026	12,375	10,904
66,350	66,400	12,388	9,034	12,388	10,916
66,400	66,450	12,400	9,041	12,400	10,929
66,450	66,500	12,413	9,049	12,413	10,941
66,500	66,550	12,425	9,056	12,425	10,954
66,550	66,600	12,438	9,064	12,438	10,966
66,600	66,650	12,450	9,071	12,450	10,979
66,650	66,700	12,463	9,079	12,463	10,991
66,700	66,750	12,475	9,086	12,475	11,004
66,750	66,800	12,488	9,094	12,488	11,016
66,800	66,850	12,500	9,101	12,500	11,029
66,850	66,900	12,513	9,109	12,513	11,041
66,900	66,950	12,525	9,116	12,525	11,054
66,950	67,000	12,538	9,124	12,538	11,066
67,000					
67,000	67,050	12,550	9,131	12,550	11,079
67,050	67,100	12,563	9,139	12,563	11,091
67,100	67,150	12,575	9,146	12,575	11,104
67,150	67,200	12,588	9,154	12,588	11,116
67,200	67,250	12,600	9,161	12,600	11,129
67,250	67,300	12,613	9,169	12,613	11,141
67,300	67,350	12,625	9,176	12,625	11,154
67,350	67,400	12,638	9,184	12,638	11,166
67,400	67,450	12,650	9,191	12,650	11,179
67,450	67,500	12,663	9,199	12,663	11,191
67,500	67,550	12,675	9,206	12,675	11,204
67,550	67,600	12,688	9,214	12,688	11,216
67,600	67,650	12,700	9,221	12,700	11,229
67,650	67,700	12,713	9,229	12,713	11,241
67,700	67,750	12,725	9,236	12,725	11,254
67,750	67,800	12,738	9,244	12,738	11,266
67,800	67,850	12,750	9,251	12,750	11,279
67,850	67,900	12,763	9,259	12,763	11,291
67,900	67,950	12,775	9,266	12,775	11,304
67,950	68,000	12,788	9,274	12,788	11,316
68,000					
68,000	68,050	12,800	9,281	12,800	11,329
68,050	68,100	12,813	9,289	12,813	11,341
68,100	68,150	12,825	9,296	12,825	11,354
68,150	68,200	12,838	9,304	12,838	11,366
68,200	68,250	12,850	9,311	12,850	11,379
68,250	68,300	12,863	9,319	12,863	11,391
68,300	68,350	12,875	9,326	12,875	11,404
68,350	68,400	12,888	9,334	12,888	11,416
68,400	68,450	12,900	9,341	12,900	11,429
68,450	68,500	12,913	9,349	12,913	11,441
68,500	68,550	12,925	9,356	12,925	11,454
68,550	68,600	12,938	9,364	12,938	11,466
68,600	68,650	12,950	9,371	12,950	11,479
68,650	68,700	12,963	9,379	12,963	11,491
68,700	68,750	12,975	9,386	12,975	11,504
68,750	68,800	12,988	9,394	12,988	11,516
68,800	68,850	13,000	9,401	13,000	11,529
68,850	68,900	13,013	9,409	13,013	11,541
68,900	68,950	13,025	9,416	13,025	11,554
68,950	69,000	13,038	9,424	13,038	11,566

If line 43 (taxable income) is—		And you are—			
At least	But less than	Single	Married filing jointly *	Married filing sepa-rately	Head of a house-hold
		Your tax is—			
69,000					
69,000	69,050	13,050	9,431	13,050	11,579
69,050	69,100	13,063	9,439	13,063	11,591
69,100	69,150	13,075	9,446	13,075	11,604
69,150	69,200	13,088	9,454	13,088	11,616
69,200	69,250	13,100	9,461	13,100	11,629
69,250	69,300	13,113	9,469	13,113	11,641
69,300	69,350	13,125	9,476	13,125	11,654
69,350	69,400	13,138	9,484	13,138	11,666
69,400	69,450	13,150	9,491	13,150	11,679
69,450	69,500	13,163	9,499	13,163	11,691
69,500	69,550	13,175	9,506	13,175	11,704
69,550	69,600	13,188	9,514	13,188	11,716
69,600	69,650	13,200	9,521	13,200	11,729
69,650	69,700	13,213	9,529	13,213	11,741
69,700	69,750	13,225	9,536	13,225	11,754
69,750	69,800	13,238	9,544	13,238	11,766
69,800	69,850	13,250	9,551	13,250	11,779
69,850	69,900	13,263	9,559	13,263	11,791
69,900	69,950	13,275	9,566	13,275	11,804
69,950	70,000	13,288	9,574	13,288	11,816
70,000					
70,000	70,050	13,300	9,581	13,300	11,829
70,050	70,100	13,313	9,589	13,313	11,841
70,100	70,150	13,325	9,596	13,325	11,854
70,150	70,200	13,338	9,604	13,338	11,866
70,200	70,250	13,350	9,611	13,350	11,879
70,250	70,300	13,363	9,619	13,363	11,891
70,300	70,350	13,375	9,626	13,375	11,904
70,350	70,400	13,388	9,634	13,388	11,916
70,400	70,450	13,400	9,641	13,400	11,929
70,450	70,500	13,413	9,649	13,413	11,941
70,500	70,550	13,425	9,656	13,425	11,954
70,550	70,600	13,438	9,664	13,438	11,966
70,600	70,650	13,450	9,671	13,450	11,979
70,650	70,700	13,463	9,679	13,463	11,991
70,700	70,750	13,475	9,686	13,475	12,004
70,750	70,800	13,488	9,694	13,488	12,016
70,800	70,850	13,500	9,701	13,500	12,029
70,850	70,900	13,513	9,709	13,513	12,041
70,900	70,950	13,525	9,716	13,525	12,054
70,950	71,000	13,538	9,724	13,538	12,066
71,000					
71,000	71,050	13,550	9,731	13,550	12,079
71,050	71,100	13,563	9,739	13,563	12,091
71,100	71,150	13,575	9,746	13,575	12,104
71,150	71,200	13,588	9,754	13,588	12,116
71,200	71,250	13,600	9,761	13,600	12,129
71,250	71,300	13,613	9,769	13,613	12,141
71,300	71,350	13,625	9,776	13,625	12,154
71,350	71,400	13,638	9,784	13,638	12,166
71,400	71,450	13,650	9,791	13,650	12,179
71,450	71,500	13,663	9,799	13,663	12,191
71,500	71,550	13,675	9,806	13,675	12,204
71,550	71,600	13,688	9,814	13,688	12,216
71,600	71,650	13,700	9,821	13,700	12,229
71,650	71,700	13,713	9,829	13,713	12,241
71,700	71,750	13,725	9,836	13,725	12,254
71,750	71,800	13,738	9,844	13,738	12,266
71,800	71,850	13,750	9,851	13,750	12,279
71,850	71,900	13,763	9,859	13,763	12,291
71,900	71,950	13,775	9,866	13,775	12,304
71,950	72,000	13,788	9,874	13,788	12,316

If line 43 (taxable income) is—		And you are—			
At least	But less than	Single	Married filing jointly *	Married filing sepa-rately	Head of a house-hold
		Your tax is—			
72,000					
72,000	72,050	13,800	9,881	13,800	12,329
72,050	72,100	13,813	9,889	13,813	12,341
72,100	72,150	13,825	9,896	13,825	12,354
72,150	72,200	13,838	9,904	13,838	12,366
72,200	72,250	13,850	9,911	13,850	12,379
72,250	72,300	13,863	9,919	13,863	12,391
72,300	72,350	13,875	9,926	13,875	12,404
72,350	72,400	13,888	9,934	13,888	12,416
72,400	72,450	13,900	9,941	13,900	12,429
72,450	72,500	13,913	9,949	13,913	12,441
72,500	72,550	13,925	9,956	13,925	12,454
72,550	72,600	13,938	9,964	13,938	12,466
72,600	72,650	13,950	9,971	13,950	12,479
72,650	72,700	13,963	9,979	13,963	12,491
72,700	72,750	13,975	9,986	13,975	12,504
72,750	72,800	13,988	9,994	13,988	12,516
72,800	72,850	14,000	10,001	14,000	12,529
72,850	72,900	14,013	10,009	14,013	12,541
72,900	72,950	14,025	10,016	14,025	12,554
72,950	73,000	14,038	10,024	14,038	12,566
73,000					
73,000	73,050	14,050	10,031	14,050	12,579
73,050	73,100	14,063	10,039	14,063	12,591
73,100	73,150	14,075	10,046	14,075	12,604
73,150	73,200	14,088	10,054	14,088	12,616
73,200	73,250	14,100	10,061	14,100	12,629
73,250	73,300	14,113	10,069	14,113	12,641
73,300	73,350	14,125	10,076	14,125	12,654
73,350	73,400	14,138	10,084	14,138	12,666
73,400	73,450	14,150	10,091	14,150	12,679
73,450	73,500	14,163	10,099	14,163	12,691
73,500	73,550	14,175	10,106	14,175	12,704
73,550	73,600	14,188	10,114	14,188	12,716
73,600	73,650	14,200	10,121	14,200	12,729
73,650	73,700	14,213	10,129	14,213	12,741
73,700	73,750	14,225	10,136	14,225	12,754
73,750	73,800	14,238	10,144	14,238	12,766
73,800	73,850	14,250	10,151	14,250	12,779
73,850	73,900	14,263	10,159	14,263	12,791
73,900	73,950	14,275	10,166	14,275	12,804
73,950	74,000	14,288	10,174	14,288	12,816
74,000					
74,000	74,050	14,300	10,181	14,300	12,829
74,050	74,100	14,313	10,189	14,313	12,841
74,100	74,150	14,325	10,196	14,325	12,854
74,150	74,200	14,338	10,204	14,338	12,866
74,200	74,250	14,350	10,211	14,350	12,879
74,250	74,300	14,363	10,219	14,363	12,891
74,300	74,350	14,375	10,226	14,375	12,904
74,350	74,400	14,388	10,234	14,388	12,916
74,400	74,450	14,400	10,241	14,400	12,929
74,450	74,500	14,413	10,249	14,413	12,941
74,500	74,550	14,425	10,256	14,425	12,954
74,550	74,600	14,438	10,264	14,438	12,966
74,600	74,650	14,450	10,271	14,450	12,979
74,650	74,700	14,463	10,279	14,463	12,991
74,700	74,750	14,475	10,286	14,475	13,004
74,750	74,800	14,488	10,294	14,488	13,016
74,800	74,850	14,500	10,301	14,500	13,029
74,850	74,900	14,513	10,309	14,513	13,041
74,900	74,950	14,525	10,319	14,525	13,054
74,950	75,000	14,538	10,331	14,538	13,066

(Continued)

* This column must also be used by a qualifying widow(er).

2015 Tax Table — *Continued*

If line 43 (taxable income) is— / And you are— / Your tax is—

75,000

At least	But less than	Single	Married filing jointly *	Married filing separately	Head of a household
75,000	75,050	14,550	10,344	14,550	13,079
75,050	75,100	14,563	10,356	14,563	13,091
75,100	75,150	14,575	10,369	14,575	13,104
75,150	75,200	14,588	10,381	14,588	13,116
75,200	75,250	14,600	10,394	14,600	13,129
75,250	75,300	14,613	10,406	14,613	13,141
75,300	75,350	14,625	10,419	14,625	13,154
75,350	75,400	14,638	10,431	14,638	13,166
75,400	75,450	14,650	10,444	14,650	13,179
75,450	75,500	14,663	10,456	14,663	13,191
75,500	75,550	14,675	10,469	14,675	13,204
75,550	75,600	14,688	10,481	14,688	13,216
75,600	75,650	14,700	10,494	14,701	13,229
75,650	75,700	14,713	10,506	14,715	13,241
75,700	75,750	14,725	10,519	14,729	13,254
75,750	75,800	14,738	10,531	14,743	13,266
75,800	75,850	14,750	10,544	14,757	13,279
75,850	75,900	14,763	10,556	14,771	13,291
75,900	75,950	14,775	10,569	14,785	13,304
75,950	76,000	14,788	10,581	14,799	13,316

76,000

At least	But less than	Single	Married filing jointly *	Married filing separately	Head of a household
76,000	76,050	14,800	10,594	14,813	13,329
76,050	76,100	14,813	10,606	14,827	13,341
76,100	76,150	14,825	10,619	14,841	13,354
76,150	76,200	14,838	10,631	14,855	13,366
76,200	76,250	14,850	10,644	14,869	13,379
76,250	76,300	14,863	10,656	14,883	13,391
76,300	76,350	14,875	10,669	14,897	13,404
76,350	76,400	14,888	10,681	14,911	13,416
76,400	76,450	14,900	10,694	14,925	13,429
76,450	76,500	14,913	10,706	14,939	13,441
76,500	76,550	14,925	10,719	14,953	13,454
76,550	76,600	14,938	10,731	14,967	13,466
76,600	76,650	14,950	10,744	14,981	13,479
76,650	76,700	14,963	10,756	14,995	13,491
76,700	76,750	14,975	10,769	15,009	13,504
76,750	76,800	14,988	10,781	15,023	13,516
76,800	76,850	15,000	10,794	15,037	13,529
76,850	76,900	15,013	10,806	15,051	13,541
76,900	76,950	15,025	10,819	15,065	13,554
76,950	77,000	15,038	10,831	15,079	13,566

77,000

At least	But less than	Single	Married filing jointly *	Married filing separately	Head of a household
77,000	77,050	15,050	10,844	15,093	13,579
77,050	77,100	15,063	10,856	15,107	13,591
77,100	77,150	15,075	10,869	15,121	13,604
77,150	77,200	15,088	10,881	15,135	13,616
77,200	77,250	15,100	10,894	15,149	13,629
77,250	77,300	15,113	10,906	15,163	13,641
77,300	77,350	15,125	10,919	15,177	13,654
77,350	77,400	15,138	10,931	15,191	13,666
77,400	77,450	15,150	10,944	15,205	13,679
77,450	77,500	15,163	10,956	15,219	13,691
77,500	77,550	15,175	10,969	15,233	13,704
77,550	77,600	15,188	10,981	15,247	13,716
77,600	77,650	15,200	10,994	15,261	13,729
77,650	77,700	15,213	11,006	15,275	13,741
77,700	77,750	15,225	11,019	15,289	13,754
77,750	77,800	15,238	11,031	15,303	13,766
77,800	77,850	15,250	11,044	15,317	13,779
77,850	77,900	15,263	11,056	15,331	13,791
77,900	77,950	15,275	11,069	15,345	13,804
77,950	78,000	15,288	11,081	15,359	13,816

78,000

At least	But less than	Single	Married filing jointly *	Married filing separately	Head of a household
78,000	78,050	15,300	11,094	15,373	13,829
78,050	78,100	15,313	11,106	15,387	13,841
78,100	78,150	15,325	11,119	15,401	13,854
78,150	78,200	15,338	11,131	15,415	13,866
78,200	78,250	15,350	11,144	15,429	13,879
78,250	78,300	15,363	11,156	15,443	13,891
78,300	78,350	15,375	11,169	15,457	13,904
78,350	78,400	15,388	11,181	15,471	13,916
78,400	78,450	15,400	11,194	15,485	13,929
78,450	78,500	15,413	11,206	15,499	13,941
78,500	78,550	15,425	11,219	15,513	13,954
78,550	78,600	15,438	11,231	15,527	13,966
78,600	78,650	15,450	11,244	15,541	13,979
78,650	78,700	15,463	11,256	15,555	13,991
78,700	78,750	15,475	11,269	15,569	14,004
78,750	78,800	15,488	11,281	15,583	14,016
78,800	78,850	15,500	11,294	15,597	14,029
78,850	78,900	15,513	11,306	15,611	14,041
78,900	78,950	15,525	11,319	15,625	14,054
78,950	79,000	15,538	11,331	15,639	14,066

79,000

At least	But less than	Single	Married filing jointly *	Married filing separately	Head of a household
79,000	79,050	15,550	11,344	15,653	14,079
79,050	79,100	15,563	11,356	15,667	14,091
79,100	79,150	15,575	11,369	15,681	14,104
79,150	79,200	15,588	11,381	15,695	14,116
79,200	79,250	15,600	11,394	15,709	14,129
79,250	79,300	15,613	11,406	15,723	14,141
79,300	79,350	15,625	11,419	15,737	14,154
79,350	79,400	15,638	11,431	15,751	14,166
79,400	79,450	15,650	11,444	15,765	14,179
79,450	79,500	15,663	11,456	15,779	14,191
79,500	79,550	15,675	11,469	15,793	14,204
79,550	79,600	15,688	11,481	15,807	14,216
79,600	79,650	15,700	11,494	15,821	14,229
79,650	79,700	15,713	11,506	15,835	14,241
79,700	79,750	15,725	11,519	15,849	14,254
79,750	79,800	15,738	11,531	15,863	14,266
79,800	79,850	15,750	11,544	15,877	14,279
79,850	79,900	15,763	11,556	15,891	14,291
79,900	79,950	15,775	11,569	15,905	14,304
79,950	80,000	15,788	11,581	15,919	14,316

80,000

At least	But less than	Single	Married filing jointly *	Married filing separately	Head of a household
80,000	80,050	15,800	11,594	15,933	14,329
80,050	80,100	15,813	11,606	15,947	14,341
80,100	80,150	15,825	11,619	15,961	14,354
80,150	80,200	15,838	11,631	15,975	14,366
80,200	80,250	15,850	11,644	15,989	14,379
80,250	80,300	15,863	11,656	16,003	14,391
80,300	80,350	15,875	11,669	16,017	14,404
80,350	80,400	15,888	11,681	16,031	14,416
80,400	80,450	15,900	11,694	16,045	14,429
80,450	80,500	15,913	11,706	16,059	14,441
80,500	80,550	15,925	11,719	16,073	14,454
80,550	80,600	15,938	11,731	16,087	14,466
80,600	80,650	15,950	11,744	16,101	14,479
80,650	80,700	15,963	11,756	16,115	14,491
80,700	80,750	15,975	11,769	16,129	14,504
80,750	80,800	15,988	11,781	16,143	14,516
80,800	80,850	16,000	11,794	16,157	14,529
80,850	80,900	16,013	11,806	16,171	14,541
80,900	80,950	16,025	11,819	16,185	14,554
80,950	81,000	16,038	11,831	16,199	14,566

81,000

At least	But less than	Single	Married filing jointly *	Married filing separately	Head of a household
81,000	81,050	16,050	11,844	16,213	14,579
81,050	81,100	16,063	11,856	16,227	14,591
81,100	81,150	16,075	11,869	16,241	14,604
81,150	81,200	16,088	11,881	16,255	14,616
81,200	81,250	16,100	11,894	16,269	14,629
81,250	81,300	16,113	11,906	16,283	14,641
81,300	81,350	16,125	11,919	16,297	14,654
81,350	81,400	16,138	11,931	16,311	14,666
81,400	81,450	16,150	11,944	16,325	14,679
81,450	81,500	16,163	11,956	16,339	14,691
81,500	81,550	16,175	11,969	16,353	14,704
81,550	81,600	16,188	11,981	16,367	14,716
81,600	81,650	16,200	11,994	16,381	14,729
81,650	81,700	16,213	12,006	16,395	14,741
81,700	81,750	16,225	12,019	16,409	14,754
81,750	81,800	16,238	12,031	16,423	14,766
81,800	81,850	16,250	12,044	16,437	14,779
81,850	81,900	16,263	12,056	16,451	14,791
81,900	81,950	16,275	12,069	16,465	14,804
81,950	82,000	16,288	12,081	16,479	14,816

82,000

At least	But less than	Single	Married filing jointly *	Married filing separately	Head of a household
82,000	82,050	16,300	12,094	16,493	14,829
82,050	82,100	16,313	12,106	16,507	14,841
82,100	82,150	16,325	12,119	16,521	14,854
82,150	82,200	16,338	12,131	16,535	14,866
82,200	82,250	16,350	12,144	16,549	14,879
82,250	82,300	16,363	12,156	16,563	14,891
82,300	82,350	16,375	12,169	16,577	14,904
82,350	82,400	16,388	12,181	16,591	14,916
82,400	82,450	16,400	12,194	16,605	14,929
82,450	82,500	16,413	12,206	16,619	14,941
82,500	82,550	16,425	12,219	16,633	14,954
82,550	82,600	16,438	12,231	16,647	14,966
82,600	82,650	16,450	12,244	16,661	14,979
82,650	82,700	16,463	12,256	16,675	14,991
82,700	82,750	16,475	12,269	16,689	15,004
82,750	82,800	16,488	12,281	16,703	15,016
82,800	82,850	16,500	12,294	16,717	15,029
82,850	82,900	16,513	12,306	16,731	15,041
82,900	82,950	16,525	12,319	16,745	15,054
82,950	83,000	16,538	12,331	16,759	15,066

83,000

At least	But less than	Single	Married filing jointly *	Married filing separately	Head of a household
83,000	83,050	16,550	12,344	16,773	15,079
83,050	83,100	16,563	12,356	16,787	15,091
83,100	83,150	16,575	12,369	16,801	15,104
83,150	83,200	16,588	12,381	16,815	15,116
83,200	83,250	16,600	12,394	16,829	15,129
83,250	83,300	16,613	12,406	16,843	15,141
83,300	83,350	16,625	12,419	16,857	15,154
83,350	83,400	16,638	12,431	16,871	15,166
83,400	83,450	16,650	12,444	16,885	15,179
83,450	83,500	16,663	12,456	16,899	15,191
83,500	83,550	16,675	12,469	16,913	15,204
83,550	83,600	16,688	12,481	16,927	15,216
83,600	83,650	16,700	12,494	16,941	15,229
83,650	83,700	16,713	12,506	16,955	15,241
83,700	83,750	16,725	12,519	16,969	15,254
83,750	83,800	16,738	12,531	16,983	15,266
83,800	83,850	16,750	12,544	16,997	15,279
83,850	83,900	16,763	12,556	17,011	15,291
83,900	83,950	16,775	12,569	17,025	15,304
83,950	84,000	16,788	12,581	17,039	15,316

(Continued)

* This column must also be used by a qualifying widow(er).

2015 Tax Table — *Continued*

If line 43 (taxable income) is— At least	But less than	And you are— Single	Married filing jointly *	Married filing sepa-rately	Head of a house-hold
		Your tax is—			
84,000					
84,000	84,050	16,800	12,594	17,053	15,329
84,050	84,100	16,813	12,606	17,067	15,341
84,100	84,150	16,825	12,619	17,081	15,354
84,150	84,200	16,838	12,631	17,095	15,366
84,200	84,250	16,850	12,644	17,109	15,379
84,250	84,300	16,863	12,656	17,123	15,391
84,300	84,350	16,875	12,669	17,137	15,404
84,350	84,400	16,888	12,681	17,151	15,416
84,400	84,450	16,900	12,694	17,165	15,429
84,450	84,500	16,913	12,706	17,179	15,441
84,500	84,550	16,925	12,719	17,193	15,454
84,550	84,600	16,938	12,731	17,207	15,466
84,600	84,650	16,950	12,744	17,221	15,479
84,650	84,700	16,963	12,756	17,235	15,491
84,700	84,750	16,975	12,769	17,249	15,504
84,750	84,800	16,988	12,781	17,263	15,516
84,800	84,850	17,000	12,794	17,277	15,529
84,850	84,900	17,013	12,806	17,291	15,541
84,900	84,950	17,025	12,819	17,305	15,554
84,950	85,000	17,038	12,831	17,319	15,566
85,000					
85,000	85,050	17,050	12,844	17,333	15,579
85,050	85,100	17,063	12,856	17,347	15,591
85,100	85,150	17,075	12,869	17,361	15,604
85,150	85,200	17,088	12,881	17,375	15,616
85,200	85,250	17,100	12,894	17,389	15,629
85,250	85,300	17,113	12,906	17,403	15,641
85,300	85,350	17,125	12,919	17,417	15,654
85,350	85,400	17,138	12,931	17,431	15,666
85,400	85,450	17,150	12,944	17,445	15,679
85,450	85,500	17,163	12,956	17,459	15,691
85,500	85,550	17,175	12,969	17,473	15,704
85,550	85,600	17,188	12,981	17,487	15,716
85,600	85,650	17,200	12,994	17,501	15,729
85,650	85,700	17,213	13,006	17,515	15,741
85,700	85,750	17,225	13,019	17,529	15,754
85,750	85,800	17,238	13,031	17,543	15,766
85,800	85,850	17,250	13,044	17,557	15,779
85,850	85,900	17,263	13,056	17,571	15,791
85,900	85,950	17,275	13,069	17,585	15,804
85,950	86,000	17,288	13,081	17,599	15,816
86,000					
86,000	86,050	17,300	13,094	17,613	15,829
86,050	86,100	17,313	13,106	17,627	15,841
86,100	86,150	17,325	13,119	17,641	15,854
86,150	86,200	17,338	13,131	17,655	15,866
86,200	86,250	17,350	13,144	17,669	15,879
86,250	86,300	17,363	13,156	17,683	15,891
86,300	86,350	17,375	13,169	17,697	15,904
86,350	86,400	17,388	13,181	17,711	15,916
86,400	86,450	17,400	13,194	17,725	15,929
86,450	86,500	17,413	13,206	17,739	15,941
86,500	86,550	17,425	13,219	17,753	15,954
86,550	86,600	17,438	13,231	17,767	15,966
86,600	86,650	17,450	13,244	17,781	15,979
86,650	86,700	17,463	13,256	17,795	15,991
86,700	86,750	17,475	13,269	17,809	16,004
86,750	86,800	17,488	13,281	17,823	16,016
86,800	86,850	17,500	13,294	17,837	16,029
86,850	86,900	17,513	13,306	17,851	16,041
86,900	86,950	17,525	13,319	17,865	16,054
86,950	87,000	17,538	13,331	17,879	16,066

If line 43 (taxable income) is— At least	But less than	And you are— Single	Married filing jointly *	Married filing sepa-rately	Head of a house-hold
		Your tax is—			
87,000					
87,000	87,050	17,550	13,344	17,893	16,079
87,050	87,100	17,563	13,356	17,907	16,091
87,100	87,150	17,575	13,369	17,921	16,104
87,150	87,200	17,588	13,381	17,935	16,116
87,200	87,250	17,600	13,394	17,949	16,129
87,250	87,300	17,613	13,406	17,963	16,141
87,300	87,350	17,625	13,419	17,977	16,154
87,350	87,400	17,638	13,431	17,991	16,166
87,400	87,450	17,650	13,444	18,005	16,179
87,450	87,500	17,663	13,456	18,019	16,191
87,500	87,550	17,675	13,469	18,033	16,204
87,550	87,600	17,688	13,481	18,047	16,216
87,600	87,650	17,700	13,494	18,061	16,229
87,650	87,700	17,713	13,506	18,075	16,241
87,700	87,750	17,725	13,519	18,089	16,254
87,750	87,800	17,738	13,531	18,103	16,266
87,800	87,850	17,750	13,544	18,117	16,279
87,850	87,900	17,763	13,556	18,131	16,291
87,900	87,950	17,775	13,569	18,145	16,304
87,950	88,000	17,788	13,581	18,159	16,316
88,000					
88,000	88,050	17,800	13,594	18,173	16,329
88,050	88,100	17,813	13,606	18,187	16,341
88,100	88,150	17,825	13,619	18,201	16,354
88,150	88,200	17,838	13,631	18,215	16,366
88,200	88,250	17,850	13,644	18,229	16,379
88,250	88,300	17,863	13,656	18,243	16,391
88,300	88,350	17,875	13,669	18,257	16,404
88,350	88,400	17,888	13,681	18,271	16,416
88,400	88,450	17,900	13,694	18,285	16,429
88,450	88,500	17,913	13,706	18,299	16,441
88,500	88,550	17,925	13,719	18,313	16,454
88,550	88,600	17,938	13,731	18,327	16,466
88,600	88,650	17,950	13,744	18,341	16,479
88,650	88,700	17,963	13,756	18,355	16,491
88,700	88,750	17,975	13,769	18,369	16,504
88,750	88,800	17,988	13,781	18,383	16,516
88,800	88,850	18,000	13,794	18,397	16,529
88,850	88,900	18,013	13,806	18,411	16,541
88,900	88,950	18,025	13,819	18,425	16,554
88,950	89,000	18,038	13,831	18,439	16,566
89,000					
89,000	89,050	18,050	13,844	18,453	16,579
89,050	89,100	18,063	13,856	18,467	16,591
89,100	89,150	18,075	13,869	18,481	16,604
89,150	89,200	18,088	13,881	18,495	16,616
89,200	89,250	18,100	13,894	18,509	16,629
89,250	89,300	18,113	13,906	18,523	16,641
89,300	89,350	18,125	13,919	18,537	16,654
89,350	89,400	18,138	13,931	18,551	16,666
89,400	89,450	18,150	13,944	18,565	16,679
89,450	89,500	18,163	13,956	18,579	16,691
89,500	89,550	18,175	13,969	18,593	16,704
89,550	89,600	18,188	13,981	18,607	16,716
89,600	89,650	18,200	13,994	18,621	16,729
89,650	89,700	18,213	14,006	18,635	16,741
89,700	89,750	18,225	14,019	18,649	16,754
89,750	89,800	18,238	14,031	18,663	16,766
89,800	89,850	18,250	14,044	18,677	16,779
89,850	89,900	18,263	14,056	18,691	16,791
89,900	89,950	18,275	14,069	18,705	16,804
89,950	90,000	18,288	14,081	18,719	16,816

If line 43 (taxable income) is— At least	But less than	And you are— Single	Married filing jointly *	Married filing sepa-rately	Head of a house-hold
		Your tax is—			
90,000					
90,000	90,050	18,300	14,094	18,733	16,829
90,050	90,100	18,313	14,106	18,747	16,841
90,100	90,150	18,325	14,119	18,761	16,854
90,150	90,200	18,338	14,131	18,775	16,866
90,200	90,250	18,350	14,144	18,789	16,879
90,250	90,300	18,363	14,156	18,803	16,891
90,300	90,350	18,375	14,169	18,817	16,904
90,350	90,400	18,388	14,181	18,831	16,916
90,400	90,450	18,400	14,194	18,845	16,929
90,450	90,500	18,413	14,206	18,859	16,941
90,500	90,550	18,425	14,219	18,873	16,954
90,550	90,600	18,438	14,231	18,887	16,966
90,600	90,650	18,450	14,244	18,901	16,979
90,650	90,700	18,463	14,256	18,915	16,991
90,700	90,750	18,475	14,269	18,929	17,004
90,750	90,800	18,488	14,281	18,943	17,016
90,800	90,850	18,502	14,294	18,957	17,029
90,850	90,900	18,516	14,306	18,971	17,041
90,900	90,950	18,530	14,319	18,985	17,054
90,950	91,000	18,544	14,331	18,999	17,066
91,000					
91,000	91,050	18,558	14,344	19,013	17,079
91,050	91,100	18,572	14,356	19,027	17,091
91,100	91,150	18,586	14,369	19,041	17,104
91,150	91,200	18,600	14,381	19,055	17,116
91,200	91,250	18,614	14,394	19,069	17,129
91,250	91,300	18,628	14,406	19,083	17,141
91,300	91,350	18,642	14,419	19,097	17,154
91,350	91,400	18,656	14,431	19,111	17,166
91,400	91,450	18,670	14,444	19,125	17,179
91,450	91,500	18,684	14,456	19,139	17,191
91,500	91,550	18,698	14,469	19,153	17,204
91,550	91,600	18,712	14,481	19,167	17,216
91,600	91,650	18,726	14,494	19,181	17,229
91,650	91,700	18,740	14,506	19,195	17,241
91,700	91,750	18,754	14,519	19,209	17,254
91,750	91,800	18,768	14,531	19,223	17,266
91,800	91,850	18,782	14,544	19,237	17,279
91,850	91,900	18,796	14,556	19,251	17,291
91,900	91,950	18,810	14,569	19,265	17,304
91,950	92,000	18,824	14,581	19,279	17,316
92,000					
92,000	92,050	18,838	14,594	19,293	17,329
92,050	92,100	18,852	14,606	19,307	17,341
92,100	92,150	18,866	14,619	19,321	17,354
92,150	92,200	18,880	14,631	19,335	17,366
92,200	92,250	18,894	14,644	19,349	17,379
92,250	92,300	18,908	14,656	19,363	17,391
92,300	92,350	18,922	14,669	19,377	17,404
92,350	92,400	18,936	14,681	19,391	17,416
92,400	92,450	18,950	14,694	19,405	17,429
92,450	92,500	18,964	14,706	19,419	17,441
92,500	92,550	18,978	14,719	19,433	17,454
92,550	92,600	18,992	14,731	19,447	17,466
92,600	92,650	19,006	14,744	19,461	17,479
92,650	92,700	19,020	14,756	19,475	17,491
92,700	92,750	19,034	14,769	19,489	17,504
92,750	92,800	19,048	14,781	19,503	17,516
92,800	92,850	19,062	14,794	19,517	17,529
92,850	92,900	19,076	14,806	19,531	17,541
92,900	92,950	19,090	14,819	19,545	17,554
92,950	93,000	19,104	14,831	19,559	17,566

* This column must also be used by a qualifying widow(er).

(Continued)

2015 Tax Table — *Continued*

If line 43 (taxable income) is— At least	But less than	And you are— Single	Married filing jointly *	Married filing separately	Head of a household
		Your tax is—			
93,000					
93,000	93,050	19,118	14,844	19,573	17,579
93,050	93,100	19,132	14,856	19,587	17,591
93,100	93,150	19,146	14,869	19,601	17,604
93,150	93,200	19,160	14,881	19,615	17,616
93,200	93,250	19,174	14,894	19,629	17,629
93,250	93,300	19,188	14,906	19,643	17,641
93,300	93,350	19,202	14,919	19,657	17,654
93,350	93,400	19,216	14,931	19,671	17,666
93,400	93,450	19,230	14,944	19,685	17,679
93,450	93,500	19,244	14,956	19,699	17,691
93,500	93,550	19,258	14,969	19,713	17,704
93,550	93,600	19,272	14,981	19,727	17,716
93,600	93,650	19,286	14,994	19,741	17,729
93,650	93,700	19,300	15,006	19,755	17,741
93,700	93,750	19,314	15,019	19,769	17,754
93,750	93,800	19,328	15,031	19,783	17,766
93,800	93,850	19,342	15,044	19,797	17,779
93,850	93,900	19,356	15,056	19,811	17,791
93,900	93,950	19,370	15,069	19,825	17,804
93,950	94,000	19,384	15,081	19,839	17,816
94,000					
94,000	94,050	19,398	15,094	19,853	17,829
94,050	94,100	19,412	15,106	19,867	17,841
94,100	94,150	19,426	15,119	19,881	17,854
94,150	94,200	19,440	15,131	19,895	17,866
94,200	94,250	19,454	15,144	19,909	17,879
94,250	94,300	19,468	15,156	19,923	17,891
94,300	94,350	19,482	15,169	19,937	17,904
94,350	94,400	19,496	15,181	19,951	17,916
94,400	94,450	19,510	15,194	19,965	17,929
94,450	94,500	19,524	15,206	19,979	17,941
94,500	94,550	19,538	15,219	19,993	17,954
94,550	94,600	19,552	15,231	20,007	17,966
94,600	94,650	19,566	15,244	20,021	17,979
94,650	94,700	19,580	15,256	20,035	17,991
94,700	94,750	19,594	15,269	20,049	18,004
94,750	94,800	19,608	15,281	20,063	18,016
94,800	94,850	19,622	15,294	20,077	18,029
94,850	94,900	19,636	15,306	20,091	18,041
94,900	94,950	19,650	15,319	20,105	18,054
94,950	95,000	19,664	15,331	20,119	18,066
95,000					
95,000	95,050	19,678	15,344	20,133	18,079
95,050	95,100	19,692	15,356	20,147	18,091
95,100	95,150	19,706	15,369	20,161	18,104
95,150	95,200	19,720	15,381	20,175	18,116
95,200	95,250	19,734	15,394	20,189	18,129
95,250	95,300	19,748	15,406	20,203	18,141
95,300	95,350	19,762	15,419	20,217	18,154
95,350	95,400	19,776	15,431	20,231	18,166
95,400	95,450	19,790	15,444	20,245	18,179
95,450	95,500	19,804	15,456	20,259	18,191
95,500	95,550	19,818	15,469	20,273	18,204
95,550	95,600	19,832	15,481	20,287	18,216
95,600	95,650	19,846	15,494	20,301	18,229
95,650	95,700	19,860	15,506	20,315	18,241
95,700	95,750	19,874	15,519	20,329	18,254
95,750	95,800	19,888	15,531	20,343	18,266
95,800	95,850	19,902	15,544	20,357	18,279
95,850	95,900	19,916	15,556	20,371	18,291
95,900	95,950	19,930	15,569	20,385	18,304
95,950	96,000	19,944	15,581	20,399	18,316
96,000					
96,000	96,050	19,958	15,594	20,413	18,329
96,050	96,100	19,972	15,606	20,427	18,341
96,100	96,150	19,986	15,619	20,441	18,354
96,150	96,200	20,000	15,631	20,455	18,366
96,200	96,250	20,014	15,644	20,469	18,379
96,250	96,300	20,028	15,656	20,483	18,391
96,300	96,350	20,042	15,669	20,497	18,404
96,350	96,400	20,056	15,681	20,511	18,416
96,400	96,450	20,070	15,694	20,525	18,429
96,450	96,500	20,084	15,706	20,539	18,441
96,500	96,550	20,098	15,719	20,553	18,454
96,550	96,600	20,112	15,731	20,567	18,466
96,600	96,650	20,126	15,744	20,581	18,479
96,650	96,700	20,140	15,756	20,595	18,491
96,700	96,750	20,154	15,769	20,609	18,504
96,750	96,800	20,168	15,781	20,623	18,516
96,800	96,850	20,182	15,794	20,637	18,529
96,850	96,900	20,196	15,806	20,651	18,541
96,900	96,950	20,210	15,819	20,665	18,554
96,950	97,000	20,224	15,831	20,679	18,566
97,000					
97,000	97,050	20,238	15,844	20,693	18,579
97,050	97,100	20,252	15,856	20,707	18,591
97,100	97,150	20,266	15,869	20,721	18,604
97,150	97,200	20,280	15,881	20,735	18,616
97,200	97,250	20,294	15,894	20,749	18,629
97,250	97,300	20,308	15,906	20,763	18,641
97,300	97,350	20,322	15,919	20,777	18,654
97,350	97,400	20,336	15,931	20,791	18,666
97,400	97,450	20,350	15,944	20,805	18,679
97,450	97,500	20,364	15,956	20,819	18,691
97,500	97,550	20,378	15,969	20,833	18,704
97,550	97,600	20,392	15,981	20,847	18,716
97,600	97,650	20,406	15,994	20,861	18,729
97,650	97,700	20,420	16,006	20,875	18,741
97,700	97,750	20,434	16,019	20,889	18,754
97,750	97,800	20,448	16,031	20,903	18,766
97,800	97,850	20,462	16,044	20,917	18,779
97,850	97,900	20,476	16,056	20,931	18,791
97,900	97,950	20,490	16,069	20,945	18,804
97,950	98,000	20,504	16,081	20,959	18,816
98,000					
98,000	98,050	20,518	16,094	20,973	18,829
98,050	98,100	20,532	16,106	20,987	18,841
98,100	98,150	20,546	16,119	21,001	18,854
98,150	98,200	20,560	16,131	21,015	18,866
98,200	98,250	20,574	16,144	21,029	18,879
98,250	98,300	20,588	16,156	21,043	18,891
98,300	98,350	20,602	16,169	21,057	18,904
98,350	98,400	20,616	16,181	21,071	18,916
98,400	98,450	20,630	16,194	21,085	18,929
98,450	98,500	20,644	16,206	21,099	18,941
98,500	98,550	20,658	16,219	21,113	18,954
98,550	98,600	20,672	16,231	21,127	18,966
98,600	98,650	20,686	16,244	21,141	18,979
98,650	98,700	20,700	16,256	21,155	18,991
98,700	98,750	20,714	16,269	21,169	19,004
98,750	98,800	20,728	16,281	21,183	19,016
98,800	98,850	20,742	16,294	21,197	19,029
98,850	98,900	20,756	16,306	21,211	19,041
98,900	98,950	20,770	16,319	21,225	19,054
98,950	99,000	20,784	16,331	21,239	19,066
99,000					
99,000	99,050	20,798	16,344	21,253	19,079
99,050	99,100	20,812	16,356	21,267	19,091
99,100	99,150	20,826	16,369	21,281	19,104
99,150	99,200	20,840	16,381	21,295	19,116
99,200	99,250	20,854	16,394	21,309	19,129
99,250	99,300	20,868	16,406	21,323	19,141
99,300	99,350	20,882	16,419	21,337	19,154
99,350	99,400	20,896	16,431	21,351	19,166
99,400	99,450	20,910	16,444	21,365	19,179
99,450	99,500	20,924	16,456	21,379	19,191
99,500	99,550	20,938	16,469	21,393	19,204
99,550	99,600	20,952	16,481	21,407	19,216
99,600	99,650	20,966	16,494	21,421	19,229
99,650	99,700	20,980	16,506	21,435	19,241
99,700	99,750	20,994	16,519	21,449	19,254
99,750	99,800	21,008	16,531	21,463	19,266
99,800	99,850	21,022	16,544	21,477	19,279
99,850	99,900	21,036	16,556	21,491	19,291
99,900	99,950	21,050	16,569	21,505	19,304
99,950	100,000	21,064	16,581	21,519	19,316

$100,000 or over use the Tax Computation Worksheet

* This column must also be used by a qualifying widow(er).

2015 Tax Computation Worksheet—Line 44

CAUTION *See the instructions for line 44 to see if you must use the worksheet below to figure your tax.*

Note. If you are required to use this worksheet to figure the tax on an amount from another form or worksheet, such as the Qualified Dividends and Capital Gain Tax Worksheet, the Schedule D Tax Worksheet, Schedule J, Form 8615, or the Foreign Earned Income Tax Worksheet, enter the amount from that form or worksheet in column (a) of the row that applies to the amount you are looking up. Enter the result on the appropriate line of the form or worksheet that you are completing.

Section A—Use if your filing status is **Single.** Complete the row below that applies to you.

Taxable income. If line 43 is—	**(a)** Enter the amount from line 43	**(b)** Multiplication amount	**(c)** Multiply (a) by (b)	**(d)** Subtraction amount	**Tax.** Subtract (d) from (c). Enter the result here and on Form 1040, line 44
At least $100,000 but not over $189,300	$	× 28% (0.28)	$	$ 6,928.75	$
Over $189,300 but not over $411,500	$	× 33% (0.33)	$	$ 16,393.75	$
Over $411,500 but not over $413,200	$	× 35% (0.35)	$	$ 24,623.75	$
Over $413,200	$	× 39.6% (0.396)	$	$ 43,630.95	$

Section B—Use if your filing status is **Married filing jointly** or **Qualifying widow(er).** Complete the row below that applies to you.

Taxable income. If line 43 is—	**(a)** Enter the amount from line 43	**(b)** Multiplication amount	**(c)** Multiply (a) by (b)	**(d)** Subtraction amount	**Tax.** Subtract (d) from (c). Enter the result here and on Form 1040, line 44
At least $100,000 but not over $151,200	$	× 25% (0.25)	$	$ 8,412.50	$
Over $151,200 but not over $230,450	$	× 28% (0.28)	$	$ 12,948.50	$
Over $230,450 but not over $411,500	$	× 33% (0.33)	$	$ 24,471.00	$
Over $411,500 but not over $464,850	$	× 35% (0.35)	$	$ 32,701.00	$
Over $464,850	$	× 39.6% (0.396)	$	$ 54,084.10	$

Section C—Use if your filing status is **Married filing separately.** Complete the row below that applies to you.

Taxable income. If line 43 is—	**(a)** Enter the amount from line 43	**(b)** Multiplication amount	**(c)** Multiply (a) by (b)	**(d)** Subtraction amount	**Tax.** Subtract (d) from (c). Enter the result here and on Form 1040, line 44
At least $100,000 but not over $115,225	$	× 28% (0.28)	$	$ 6,474.25	$
Over $115,225 but not over $205,750	$	× 33% (0.33)	$	$ 12,235.50	$
Over $205,750 but not over $232,425	$	× 35% (0.35)	$	$ 16,350.50	$
Over $232,425	$	× 39.6% (0.396)	$	$ 27,042.05	$

Section D—Use if your filing status is **Head of household.** Complete the row below that applies to you.

Taxable income. If line 43 is—	**(a)** Enter the amount from line 43	**(b)** Multiplication amount	**(c)** Multiply (a) by (b)	**(d)** Subtraction amount	**Tax.** Subtract (d) from (c). Enter the result here and on Form 1040, line 44
At least $100,000 but not over $129,600	$	× 25% (0.25)	$	$ 5,677.50	$
Over $129,600 but not over $209,850	$	× 28% (0.28)	$	$ 9,565.50	$
Over $209,850 but not over $411,500	$	× 33% (0.33)	$	$ 20,058.00	$
Over $411,500 but not over $439,000	$	× 35% (0.35)	$	$ 28,288.00	$
Over $439,000	$	× 39.6% (0.396)	$	$ 48,482.00	$

Table 20-2: IRS Tax Computation Worksheet and Rate Schedules

Schedule X—If your filing status is **Single**

If your taxable income is: Over—	But not over—	The tax is:	of the amount over—
$0	$9,225	.... 10%	$0
9,225	37,450	$922.50 + 15%	9,225
37,450	90,750	5,156.25 + 25%	37,450
90,750	189,300	18,481.25 + 28%	90,750
189,300	411,500	46,075.25 + 33%	189,300
411,500	413,200	119,401.25 + 35%	411,500
413,200	....	119,996.25 + 39.6%	413,200

Schedule Y-1—If your filing status is **Married filing jointly** or **Qualifying widow(er)**

If your taxable income is: Over—	But not over—	The tax is:	of the amount over—
$0	$18,450	.... 10%	$0
18,450	74,900	$1,845.00 + 15%	18,450
74,900	151,200	10,312.50 + 25%	74,900
151,200	230,450	29,387.50 + 28%	151,200
230,450	411,500	51,577.50 + 33%	230,450
411,500	464,850	111,324.00 + 35%	411,500
464,850	....	129,996.50 + 39.6%	464,850

Schedule Y-2—If your filing status is **Married filing separately**

If your taxable income is: Over—	But not over—	The tax is:	of the amount over—
$0	$9,225	.... 10%	$0
9,225	37,450	$922.50 + 15%	9,225
37,450	75,600	5,156.25 + 25%	37,450
75,600	115,225	14,693.75 + 28%	75,600
115,225	205,750	25,788.75 + 33%	115,225
205,750	232,425	55,662.00 + 35%	205,750
232,425	....	64,998.25 + 39.6%	232,425

Schedule Z—If your filing status is **Head of household**

If your taxable income is: Over—	But not over—	The tax is:	of the amount over—
$0	$13,150	.... 10%	$0
13,150	50,200	$1,315.00 + 15%	13,150
50,200	129,600	6,872.50 + 25%	50,200
129,600	209,850	26,722.50 + 28%	129,600
209,850	411,500	49,192.50 + 33%	209,850
411,500	439,000	115,737.00 + 35%	411,500
439,000	....	125,362.00 + 39.6%	439,000